IRON ADMIRALS

Recent Titles in
Contributions in Military Studies

IRON ADMIRALS

Naval Leadership in the Twentieth Century

Ronald Andidora

Contributions in Military Studies, Number 194

GREENWOOD PRESS
Westport, Connecticut • London

Library of Congress Cataloging-in-Publication Data

Andidora, Ronald, 1953–
    Iron admirals : naval leadership in the twentieth century / Ronald Andidora.
      p. cm.—(Contributions in military studies, ISSN 0883–6884 ; no. 194)
    Includes bibliographical references and index.
    ISBN 0–313–31266–4 (alk. paper)
    1. History, Naval—20th century. 2. Admirals—Biography. I. Title. II. Series.
D436.A63 2000
   359′.009′04—dc21   99–049147

British Library Cataloguing in Publication Data is available.

Library of Congress Catalog Card Number: 99–049147
ISBN: 0–313–31266–4
ISSN: 0883–6884

First published in 2000

Greenwood Press, 88 Post Road West, Westport, CT 06881
An imprint of Greenwood Publishing Group, Inc.
www.greenwood.com

Printed in the United States of America

The paper used in this book complies with the
Permanent Paper Standard issued by the National
Information Standards Organization (Z39.48–1984).

10 9 8 7 6 5 4 3 2 1

To my Mother and Father
for always putting me first.

Contents

Photo essay follows page 90.

Maps

Preface

The antecedents of this book trace back to a pictorial history of the U.S. Navy in World War II, which my father gave me before I was able to properly care for it. My historical curiosity survives in a far more healthy condition than that of the hallowed tome. Next stop is the Carbondale Public Library that served as a young boy's island refuge in a sea of anti-intellectualism. There, I discovered more ancient texts that revealed details about exotic wonders such as frigates, dreadnoughts, and battlecruisers. Finally, comes the University of Scranton where a legion of professors placed individual events in their historical context and inculcated the Jesuit tradition of analytical thinking.

This book itself is not a comprehensive history of modern naval warfare. Instead, it focuses on the four men who successfully commanded battle fleets in the twentieth century. As such, it is part biographical sketch, part narrative, and part analysis of command decisions. The last aspect will undoubtedly raise some issues as to just how "successful" these subjects were in their endeavors, especially in the cases of John Jellicoe and William Halsey. To those readers who disagree with my conclusions, I thank you for engaging in the informed debate that is the path to historical truth.

Acknowledgments

The maps and diagrams that support this text are attributable to the graphic talents of Dawn Smith. I thank her for her time and patience.

The photographs of the *Iron Duke*, *Mikasa*, and Admiral Spruance were acquired from the Naval Historical Center in Washington, D.C. All other photographs came from the U.S. Naval Institute in Annapolis, Maryland.

Finally, a word of thanks to my wife, Judy, for her moral support, computer skills, and editorial comments.

1

Nelson's Legacy

I

Napoleon Bonaparte once said, with a mixture of envy and frustration, "Wherever you find a fathom of water, there you will find the British."[1] He spoke from firsthand knowledge because the Royal Navy played the role of nemesis throughout the epoch that bears his name. At sea, the British navy surpassed the record of Napoleon's *Grand Armée* on land, winning every fleet battle and prevailing in the vast majority of encounters between individual ships. England's wooden walls shielded her from invasion and fostered her trade and industry, allowing the emperor's implacable foe to provide political leadership and financial backing for the various coalitions that finally brought him down. The British Fleet was also a sword that severed the lines of French maritime commerce and thrust the Duke of Wellington's troops onto the Iberian Peninsula and into Belgium. Wellington himself, normally parsimonious with his praise, gave the following testament, "I never found naval men at a loss. Tell them to do anything that is not impossible, and depend upon it, they will do it."[2] It was entirely fitting that after his final defeat at Waterloo in 1815, Napoleon's last view of France came from the deck of HMS *Bellerophon*, a seventy-four-gun ship-of-the-line that had served in the King's navy for the entire twenty-two-year struggle against revolutionary and imperial France.

The embodiment of the British naval achievement during that period was Vice-Admiral Lord Horatio Nelson, arguably the most inspirational figure in the annuals of his service. Nelson's place in history is rooted in a series of decisive victories that had significant strategic consequences. In 1798, he destroyed Admiral François Paul Brueys' fleet in Aboukir Bay at the mouth of the Nile, thereby thwarting Napoleon's attempt to conquer Egypt and restoring British naval predominance in the Mediterranean. Three years later, Nelson braved Copenhagen's shoals and shore batteries to batter the Danish Fleet into submission and guarantee the security of England's Baltic trade routes. Finally, on October 21, 1805, he annihilated Admiral Pierre Charles Villeneuve's combined French and Spanish force off Cape Trafalgar, reducing Napoleon's planned invasion of England to a pipe dream. The heroic quality of Nelson's victories was amplified by their overwhelming nature and the fact that they were won against superior numbers. Although he was outgunned at the Nile, Nelson captured or destroyed 11 of the 13 ships-of-the-line that faced him, with two frigates thrown in for good measure. At Trafalgar, his battle line was outnumbered thirty-three to twenty-seven but managed to take or destroy eighteen of its opponents. No British vessel was lost in either engagement.[3]

But success alone does not bring immortality. Style is also required and Nelson possessed the traits necessary to make him an enduring personage as well as a victorious commander. He was courageous, with a propensity for seeking danger that earned him a multitude of wounds and cost him an arm and an eye. Nelson's streak of insubordination also added to his mystique. While serving under Admiral Sir John Jervis at the Battle of Cape St. Vincent, he foiled the Spanish Fleet's escape by taking his ship out of line on his own initiative, ignoring British fighting instructions, which made the maintenance of the battle line inviolable. Other ships followed his example, resulting in the capture of four enemy vessels, two of which surrendered to Nelson's own ship, *Captain*, after he himself led the boarding parties. At Copenhagen, he ignored his commander in chief's signal to break off action, putting his telescope to his blind eye and continuing the pounding match until the Danes capitulated. Finally, Nelson sealed his image as the perfect romantic hero by dying at the moment of his greatest triumph. At Trafalgar, he fell to a sharpshooter's bullet while directing the action from the deck of his flagship, HMS *Victory*.

Nelson left posterity with a body of dicta on naval operations that presents an unequivocal testament to the virtues of audacity. But Nelson's own audacious behavior was based on solid foundations that distinguished it from recklessness. He knew that the instrument that he wielded in battle was far superior to that which was held by his opponents. England's naval officers had been professionalized long before Nelson received his commission and they possessed a remarkable ability to mold their polyglot crews into able seamen and fierce fighters. In contrast, France had lost about three quarters of her fleet officers due to the excesses of the Revolution.[4] Many had died on the guillotine while others fled the country out of fear for their lives or disgust over the sweeping egalitarianism that eroded their navy's discipline and efficiency. Napoleon employed his battle squadrons as a "fleet-in-being," preserving them as a threat but seldom letting them sail to carry out the threat. The British admiralty, on the other hand, had a centuries-old tradition of taking the offensive and continued to believe that a ship belonged on the ocean. Thus, England's already confident officers and men were further emboldened by their months at sea, usually in close blockade of adversaries whose morale sank as they lay huddled in port. Perhaps Jervis best summed up the attitude of those within his service by rendering the following verdict on the prospects for a French invasion, "I do not say, my Lords, that the French will not come. I only say they will not come by sea."[5]

Nelson improved on this advantage by taking his captains into his confidence, informing them of his plans in detail and discussing the possible consequences. This practice established strong mental and emotion bonds between Nelson and his "band of brothers," turning the latter into devoted and like-minded subordinates who could be allowed a great deal of discretion while carrying out their commander's wishes. During the approach of the fleets at Trafalgar, Nelson sent off a series of signals culminating with his now famous, "England expects that every man will do his duty." As he watched the flags being hoisted up to the *Victory's* mastheads, Vice-Admiral Sir Cuthbert Collingwood, the British second in command said, "I wish Nelson would stop signaling. We all know well enough what to do."[6]

Although Nelson's special relationship with his officers has become legendary, he did not neglect the men of the lower decks either. Nelson made every effort to ensure the physical well-being of his sailors by providing them with decent food, proper ventilation, regular exercise, and periodic entertainment. After the Nile, he cajoled the admiralty into providing an additional 60,000 pounds in prize money for the French ships that had been destroyed by fire in order to increase the shares of his sailors and inferior officers. Nelson also nurtured the spiritual welfare of his charges by distributing bibles, conducting public services, and even composing an occasional prayer of inspiration. None of this should be taken to imply that Nelson was a lax disciplinarian. Flogging did occur on ships under this direct command and he gave his subordinate captains wide latitude in their own use of the punishment. Furthermore, when the fleet was racked by mutinies in 1797, Nelson made it clear to his men and his superiors that he approved of the harsh punishments, including hangings, dealt out to the mutineers. However, it is illustrative of the affection felt for Nelson by the ranks that his own command never faced any such breakdowns in morale.

Nelson's methods of making war were innovative but not entirely novel. His victory at Copenhagen was basically a slugging match against a fleet at anchor supported by shore batteries. The engagement at Aboukir Bay was also fought against an anchored fleet but included two distinct aspects of the "Nelson Touch." First, he completely surprised Admiral Brueys by attacking at dusk and forcing a night battle to decide the issue. Second, he assaulted the French Fleet from both the seaward and landward sides of the bay, the latter maneuver hazarding the shoals between the enemy ships and the shore. In exchange for one ship run aground, Nelson's risk allowed the British to concentrate overwhelming fire power on the head of the French column and then repeat the onslaught against each new target as they moved down the line.

At Trafalgar, Nelson attacked in two divisions, cutting Villeneuve's line in two places and overwhelming his center and rear before his van could turn back and participate in the melee. Such tactics were, of course, contrary to the British fighting instructions, which required sea battles to be fought in single line ahead on a course parallel to the enemy's and forbid departure from the battle line until the enemy was disabled or on the run.[7] On first glance, Nelson's method seems to reinforce his image as an iconoclast but in fact neither his tactics nor his attitude was revolutionary. The Royal Navy did not reach its apex during the Napoleonic wars under the stewardship of stodgy traditionalists. Admiral George Rodney had broken the French line at the Battle of the Saints in 1782 and Admiral Sir Richard Howe repeated the maneuver twelve years later on the Glorious First of June. At Camperdown in 1797, Admiral Adam Duncan attacked the Dutch in two lines, a more rigid precursor of Nelson's formation at Trafalgar. British naval leadership was open to new ideas and was far more concerned with results than formalities. At Cape St. Vincent, Jervis ordered additional ships to follow Nelson's lead and afterward commended him lavishly to his face as well as in dispatches to the admiralty. When reminded by his chief of staff that Nelson's conduct was a breach of the fighting instructions, Jervis replied, "It certainly was so, and if ever you commit such a breach, I will forgive you also."[8]

Nelson raised his navy's performance to yet a higher level at Trafalgar, partially due to the flexible command arrangement made possible by his rapport with his captains. (New signal codes, recently introduced into the fleet, also helped by providing a faster means of communication between ships.) But the heart of the "Nelson Touch" was his overriding ambition to destroy the enemy rather than just defeat him, a sentiment clearly conveyed by his affinity for the word, "annihilate." Prior to Trafalgar, he explained his plan verbally to his officers and then sent them a written summation that concluded:

Something must be left to chance; nothing is sure in a sea fight. Shot will carry away the masts and yards of friends as well as foes; but I look with confidence to a victory before the van of the enemy can succor their rear, and then that most of the British fleet would be ready to receive them, or to pursue them should they endeavor to make off. Captains are to look to their particular line as their rallying point. But, in case signals can neither be seen or perfectly understood, no captain can do very wrong if he places his ship alongside that of an enemy.[9]

Thus, the British ships charged into the battle helter-skelter, in a loose formation more appropriate for a general chase than the early stages of an engagement against superior numbers. Such tactics had their limits, for the British would undoubtedly have been roughly handled if they so casually exposed their bows to a more skilled opponent. But Nelson was well aware of the relative abilities of the contending fleets. His final signal, "Engage the enemy more closely," went to the *Victory's* mastheads before a single English cannon had been fired in anger. This was not a premature command in a fleet whose universally held belief was that it had nothing to fear from an enemy except his escape.

When distilled to its essence, Nelson's success as a commander can be traced to the same elements as those comprising the formula of other great military and naval leaders. He possessed the organizational ability to forge existing assets and trends into a viable doctrine, the personal charisma to have it accepted religiously by those under his command, and the sound judgment to employ it triumphantly in battle. But Nelson's historical impact went far beyond that which can be provided by analysis. He achieved that rare cosmic conjunction of style, substance, and circumstance that is the stuff of legends. After his death, Nelson's accumulated dicta became dogma within the Royal Navy, inculcating its members with a prime directive to seek out enemy fleets and annihilate them, regardless of the risks involved. By imbibing the froth of their icon's triumphs, British naval personnel acquired an almost mystical belief in their own invincibility. The mystique spread worldwide, as other navies came to view Nelson as the epitome of sea-borne leadership and tacitly assumed that his heirs possessed the same qualities as their patron. In summary, Nelson's legacy to the Royal Navy was a moral superiority that was maintained for more than a century, even through periods when the fleet's material assets and fighting skills did not justify it.

II

Napoleonic naval battles were fought by sail-powered wooden vessels that represented the ultimate refinement of designs that had existed for more than 150 years. For the first three decades after Waterloo, the British admiralty showed little inclination to advance its technology, despite the fact that England's merchant marine paced the world in steam propulsion. This resistance to change was partially based on the faulty premise that you can foil progress by not participating in it. England was predominant in the existing naval designs, thus her admirals did not wish to contribute toward their obsolescence. However, there were also some sound reasons for the policy. A steam-driven fleet would require an extensive network of coaling stations to make it a viable protector of Britain's global empire. Furthermore, steamships were driven by side-mounted paddle wheels that made vulnerable targets and reduced the number of guns in a ship's broadside by as much as one third. So, although the Royal Navy possessed more than one hundred steamships by 1845, most were auxiliaries and not one of them belonged to the battle fleet.[10]

The advent of the screw propeller eliminated the admiralty's technical reservations, but the conversion to steam did not proceed apace until political events pushed it along. When the French navy went heavily into steam propulsion in the late 1840s, the Royal Navy was forced to follow suit. Throughout the rest of the century, France would attempt to make end-runs around England's naval supremacy by employing new technologies. Fortunately for Great Britain, a superior industrial base and maritime infrastructure allowed her to respond to French innovations by improving on them and then rapidly producing them for her own fleet. That scenario applied to the introduction of rifled artillery, which sounded the death knell of the wooden warship, as well as to the coming of the armored vessels that answered the new weapon's destructive power.

During the summer of 1860, France commissioned *La Gloire*, the world's first sea-going ironclad warship. However, she was superseded the following autumn when HMS *Warrior* emerged from its shipyard on the Thames to join Queen Victoria's battle fleet. The British counterpoint was superior to France's initial offering in every way except their identical 4½-inch wrought iron armor plates. While *La Gloire* carried thirty-six 50-pound guns and could make just over 13 knots, *Warrior* could move its mixture of thirty-eight 68 pounders and 110 pounders at a top speed of 14½ knots.[11] Furthermore, the French "ironclad" was just that, a timber hulled vessel with iron plates bolted on it. *Warrior* and her sister *Black Prince* were truly the new breed, the first warships of all iron construction.

No survey of this period can be complete without at least mentioning the first clash of ironclads that took place at Hampton Roads on March 9, 1862, when the Union's *Monitor* jousted inconclusively with the Confederacy's *Virginia*. However, it should be remembered that neither of the American ships were sea-going vessels and neither one of them could have survived an encounter with the *Warrior* or *La Gloire*. The encounter off Virginia's coast did portend an important development in future ship design. Both *La Gloire* and *Warrior* were known as "belt and battery" vessels because their guns were arranged along the ship's sides and fired through gun ports cut into the hull. This was a layout identical to that of the wooden sailing ships of the previous several hundred years. But John Ericsson's *Monitor* utilized a revolving turret to house its two guns, an innovation first suggested by the inventor to Napoleon III in 1854 and actually patented by the Royal Navy's Captain Cowper Coles in 1859.[12] The rapidity with which the United States finally deployed the turret at sea also shows how the exigencies of war can overcome bureaucratic inertia.

For the next thirty years, the world's navies groped their way through evolving ship designs, most of which included both sails and steam, and some of which looked like creations of Jules Verne. Gradually, the new form took shape as sailing masts disappeared and muzzle-loaders, broadside batteries, and iron gave way to breech-loaders, turrets, and steel. This evolution was not merely a question of technological innovations but also the mental and emotional capacity to recognize and accept their true significance. For instance, Great Britain produced what should have been the prototypical "modern" battleship when HMS *Devastation* went to sea in 1873 sporting two twin centerline turrets and no sailing masts. But the British admiralty did not view *Devastation* as the new model on which to preserve its naval supremacy but rather as a "special," suitable only for operations in home waters where short cruising distances justified its lack of sails. Three years later, England's shipyards sent HMS *Inflexible* to sea fully rigged to supplement its steam propulsion and armed with two turrets placed diagonally amidships! Historically, *Inflexible* was a magnificent representation of an age in the midst of technological flux, but in terms of naval design, she was a definite retrogression.

The underlying dynamic of the naval design process was a competition between guns and armor, the parameters of which were framed by the limitations of existing propulsion systems. In the years of iron and gunpowder, the penetrating power of a ship's armament generally lagged behind the designers' ability to provide it with protection. Advances in metallurgy initially supported the status quo as new nickel and chromium steel alloys allowed shipbuilders to sheath their creations in armor that was both stronger and lighter than that of their predecessors. But these same metallurgical techniques coupled with a revolution in propellants then threatened to turn the situation upside down. First slow-burning powders and later the so-called "smokeless powders" such as cordite served to increase a shell's velocity by producing gases that accelerated the projectile throughout its entire trip up the gun barrel, a dramatic improvement over the single thrust forward afforded by the ignition of simple gunpowder. Soon, long-barreled, breech-loading steel artillery was employing the new propellants to hurl lethal chromium steel shells at ever-increasing velocities. Enhanced velocity also allowed the hardened projectiles to reach any given range at a flatter trajectory, a great boon to accuracy in an age devoid of sophisticated range finders.

As the contest between guns and armor accelerated, a third contender appeared in the form of the torpedo. Early torpedoes were little more than floating mines, but the weapon acquired a new lethality when English engineer Robert Whitehead fitted one with a compressed air engine and a propeller. Whitehead's early models were not particularly accurate and could travel only 300 yards at 12 knots or 1,200 yards at 9 knots.[13] Despite these limitations, French naval strategists saw yet another panacea and began to build flotillas of small fast torpedo boats that would be elusive targets for the powerful but slow-firing guns of England's battle fleet. Their counterparts across the channel were so impressed that they imposed a three-year moratorium on big ship construction while counter measures were developed. Britain's answers were soon forthcoming. Galvanized wire nets were devised to protect ships at anchor and light, quick-firing guns were produced to swat the gnats before they could deliver their sting. Additionally, a new type of warship, originally called a "torpedo boat destroyer" but soon referred to without its prefix, was designed to provide a screening escort for the battle line.

By the 1890s, the amorphous state of naval design had crystallized into relatively uniform ship types. Battleships ranged from 11,000 to 15,000 tons in displacement, were protected by a thick belt of armor and could steam at speeds of up to 18 knots. Their main armament, usually four 12-inch guns, was carried in twin turrets fore and aft, with secondary armament placed in casements along the length of the ship in between. Because the big guns had ranges far exceeding their accuracy, it was assumed that any clash between battle fleets would take place within the range of the secondary batteries, allowing them to be employed against the unprotected parts of enemy battleships. Smaller guns in open mounts were arranged topside to deal with hostile torpedo craft.

Next in the hierarchy came armored cruisers, usually displacing less than 10,000 tons but including a few that matched the size of a small battleship. These vessels were three or four knots faster than a battleship, carried smaller guns in their main batteries and were protected by a thinner belt of armor. They were considered capital ships that could fight in the battle line but their speed also made them ideal for use against commerce raiders or other independent missions.

Remaining warships larger than destroyers were collectively grouped under the heading of protected cruisers. These ships were a mishmash of designs and capabilities, displacing 2,000 to 7,000 tons and possessing no armored belt. The lowest class of protected cruiser had almost no armor whatsoever and was suitable only for scouting or operating with torpedo flotillas. They eventually became known as light cruisers, although this nomenclature was not universally adopted until the second decade of the twentieth century.

Meanwhile, destroyers were becoming more formidable, exceeding 300 tons in displacement and capable of speeds in excess of 30 knots. Although they had been conceived as an antidote to torpedo boats, destroyers carried their own torpedo tubes in addition to their quick-firing artillery pieces. Therefore, it soon became apparent that the fleet's protector provided a speedier and more stable platform to deliver the weapons it had been designed to thwart. Destroyers were then expected to supplement torpedo boats in the attack role while still maintaining their status as guardians of their own big ships.

In 1898, the U.S. Navy gave the world a blurred glimpse of the new system in action when it obliterated Spanish squadrons at Manila Bay and off Santiago, Cuba. But the small size of these engagements and the disproportionate material advantage enjoyed by the Americans in each of them rendered their instructional value almost nil. At Manila Bay, Commodore George Dewey's four cruisers and two gunboats planted the American flag in Asia by vanquishing seven old Spanish warships, one of which was wooden. In the decisive clash off Santiago, America's four battleships and two armored cruisers massacred the four Spanish armored cruisers that sailed against them. The Spanish-American War was not a true test of existing naval technology but merely a predictable victory of a modern fleet over a transitory one.

The world's newfound stability in warship design lasted into the new century but would not long withstand the tide of scientific advancements engulfing every aspect of the human condition. Ideas for the next generation of battleships were already germinating in the minds of admirals and engineers while experimental submarines hinted at the revolutionary changes in naval warfare that loomed over the horizon. But in 1904, the existing system would get what turned out to be its only real test in combat. Surprisingly, the contest was not held in European waters. Instead, it occurred half-way around the globe in a clash between a moldering Eurasian Empire and a rising Asian nation that had only recently shed the bonds of feudal backwardness.

2

Samurai in Nelson's Shadow

I

On the morning of July 8, 1853, Commodore Matthew Calbraith Perry led four U.S. Navy ships into Japan's Edo Bay. The nation that he approached was insular by virtue of its worldview as well as its geography. Japan was a feudal society whose daimyo overlords ruled private fiefdoms and commanded personal armies made up of hereditary warriors called samurai. Although the emperor reigned in his splendid palace at Kyoto, true executive power emanated from the shogun's fortress at Edo. The shogun was a military dictator who embodied the all-pervasive authority of the samurai caste. His office was created in 1192 when Japan's most powerful warrior decided to rule in his own right rather than pay homage to existing imperial institutions. The shogunate gradually reduced the emperor to a figurehead and then saw its own power diluted by the rise of the daimyo. However, in the early seventeenth Century, Ieyasu Tokugawa reestablished the shogun's ascendancy over the local warlords. His descendants remained in charge for more than 250 years.

Japan's first contact with Western civilization dated from the arrival of a Portuguese ship in 1542. Her rulers came to view the resulting intercourse with Europe as a dubious blessing. The foul smelling, hairy barbarians brought cholera and venereal disease along with the benefits of foreign trade. Their most virulent strain of infection was Christianity. Jesuits, Franciscans, and Dominicans vied for Japanese souls with a great degree of success. Ieyasu Tokugawa understood that Europe's monarchs used spiritual conversion as an avenue for temporal conquest. He was partially guided to this conclusion by the counsels of Will Adams, a stranded English pilot who had no love for Catholics. In 1614, Tokugawa expelled the foreign missionaries and decreed that their converts must renounce their new faith. His successors issued similar edicts pertaining to matters of commerce. Foreign ships were virtually banned from Japan's ports and domestic vessels were restricted to tiny dimensions that made them unsafe for ocean travel. Thus, the Japanese slipped into an isolationist slumber that held sway over them until the arrival of Perry's squadron.

Perry brought a letter from President Millard Fillmore requesting the establishment of trade relations, proper treatment for shipwrecked U.S. sailors, and the use of Japanese port facilities by U.S. ships. After delivering the note, Perry sailed away, leaving the shogun and his advisors to their deliberations. He returned the following February with a larger force and remained until his case was won. The Treaty of Kanagawa guaranteed fair treatment for U.S. sailors, allowed for the provisioning of U.S. ships, and opened two small ports to U.S. trade.[1] Similar agreements quickly followed with Russia, Great Britain, Holland, and France.

Japan's acquiescence to Western contamination was attributable to military impotence. The shogun and his advisors knew that the samurai could not stand against the foreigners' modern weaponry. However, a strong nationalist faction favored resistance at any cost. These firebrands precipitated numerous incidents that were often answered by bombardments from Western naval flotillas. The warships' impunity convinced the more enlightened nationalists that effective opposition required modernization. This group of young samurai regarded the shogun as a symbol of the old order and the major roadblock to progress. In 1867, they forced the great warlord to relinquish his office and pass full executive power to the young Emperor Mutsuhito. When the shogun's armies contested the change, the arbiters of sword and musket ruled against them. The next summer, the emperor took residence in Edo, which became known as Tokyo or "Eastern Capitol."

The transfer of power that brought Mutsuhito to Tokyo is often called the "Imperial Restoration." This is only partially accurate since the mikado had never lost his position or status, but merely his ability to govern. By any nomenclature, the reassertion of imperial authority was a boon to Japan's modernization. The emperor and most of his close associates were young men. Their zeal and energy accelerated the pace of westernization until feudal society was completely swept away. The daimyos were bought out and replaced by a centralized prefectural system. State-imposed ignorance gave way to compulsory education. Trade barriers fell, small industries sprang up and banks were formed. Changes were so rapid and profound that Japanese historians have dubbed Mutsuhito the Emperor Meiji, or "emperor of enlightened government."

Japan's government placed a heavy emphasis on military "enlightenment." Her army initially chose to imitate the French system but switched to the Prussian model after the latter's resounding victory in the Franco-Prussian War. The introduction of universal conscription in 1873 provided the foundation for a modern fighting force and officially ended the samurai's monopoly on military power. Japan's embryonic navy turned to England for its model. One characteristic that distinguished Japan's militarization from those of other developing countries was her devotion to training personnel as well as acquiring materiel. Thus, the new regime not only contracted for modern ships and guns, but also arranged to send her most capable young men abroad for instruction in the weapons' manufacture and employment. On returning, the officers served as a cadre to teach their countrymen the fine points of warfare in the industrial age.

By 1894, the Japanese were ready to test their prowess in battle. China served as the opponent. The Middle Kingdom was already reeling under European exploitation and proved no more successful in warding off the advances of its neighbor. Japan enjoyed overwhelming success on both land and sea. In May 1895, her triumph was cemented in the Treaty of Shimonoseki. By its terms, Japan acquired the island of Formosa and Manchuria's Liaotung Peninsula, as well as an indemnity that far exceeded the cost of the war. China also renounced any claim on Korea, which served as a tacit signal that Japan was free to pursue her own ambitions in the Hermit Kingdom.[2] The Liaotung, with its ice-free harbor at Port Arthur, was an acquisition of great strategic significance. It gave the Japanese a firm foothold on the Asian mainland that could be used as a base of operations against either Korea or China.

Europe did not look kindly on competition from the Asian upstart. France, Russia, and Germany intervened and forced Japan to relinquish its claim on the Liaotung in exchange for an increased indemnity. Russia soon began to stake some claims of her own. In 1896, the czar's government secured a right of way through Manchuria in order to provide a smoother path for the Trans-Siberian Railroad. One year later, Russia installed herself on the Liaotung Peninsula, acquiring in Port Arthur a much coveted warm water port. The Russians then extorted a thirty-six-year lease on Port Arthur and its environs. By employing intrigue, bribery, and intimidation, Russia proceeded to expand her presence in Manchuria to the point of virtual annexation.

Japan watched these developments with growing alarm but could only bristle while spending the Chinese indemnity to expand the army and pur-

chase modern battleships. Other nations also viewed Russia's encroach-
ment with a jaundiced eye. The United States, in a series of diplomatic
notes, expressed its support of an "open door policy" that guaranteed China's territorial integrity as well as equal access to her markets.[3] Great Britain went even further. In 1902, she abandoned her policy of "splendid
isolation" and forced a defensive alliance with Japan. The Anglo-Japanese
Treaty of Alliance provided that one signatory would aid the other only in
an Asian war between a signatory and more than one other power.[4] Thus, Japan could count on England to serve as a bulwark against the intervention of
other powers in the inevitable future conflict with Russia.

When war finally came, Korea was the tinderbox. In 1903, the czar gave
his blessing to the development of timber resources along the Yalu River.
Japan's leaders were well aware that commerce had replaced Christianity as
the precursor of European political control. They could not accept a Russian
presence along the watery boundary between Korea and Manchuria. Korea's
geographic position made it a potential base for operations against Japan's
maritime trade and a springboard for an invasion of her home islands. After
fruitless negotiations, during which Japan even offered Russia a free hand
in Manchuria in exchange for Japanese predominance in Korea, the Meiji
government became convinced that war was the only viable alternative.

Japanese military leaders were ardent believers in the offensive and
planned to swiftly take the war to the Russian Army in Manchuria. Their
strategy was heavily dependent on the success of the navy. As an island, Japan needed to establish and maintain sea control in order to project her land
forces onto the mainland. The Combined Fleet's modern warships and
skilled personnel were up to the task, but their commander was not. Admiral
Sonojo Hidaka suffered from a digestive ailment that limited his ability to
face the rigors of the coming campaign. Therefore, on October 17, 1903,
Hidaka was relieved and Japan's naval fortunes were entrusted to Admiral
Heihachiro Togo.

II

Japan's future naval hero was born on January 27, 1848, in Satsuma
province on the island of Kyushu. He carried the surname Nakagoro until
age thirteen, at which time he underwent the ritual induction into the ranks
of the samurai and became Heihachiro, meaning "peaceful son." (Once assumed, a samurai's majority name is also applied retroactively in descrip-
tions of his early life.) Togo's temperament did not reflect his moniker. He
was a stubborn and aggressive child, a determined but ungifted student, and
a master at sword play. The latter trait is often illustrated by a story, not nec-

essarily apocryphal, which has the young Heihachiro disappear from a family picnic only to be rediscovered practicing his swordsmanship by decapitating some carp in a nearby pond.[5]

A tale of more reliable origin is perhaps better illustrative of Togo's character. While traveling with his family, Heihachiro quarreled with his eldest brother, Sokuro, and understandably got the worst of it. However, when Sokuro later sent his young sibling to fetch him a glass of water, he was given a drink laced with pepper. The resulting shrieks of pain and anger attracted the attention of the boys' father who ordered his youngest son to seek forgiveness from his eldest. Surprisingly, Heihachiro refused and was banished from his family for ten days. After serving his punishment, which could best be described as a version of house arrest, Heihachiro dutifully returned to the family circle with no complaint and no apology.[6] Togo's violent temper and stubborn determination would always remain with him. Fortunately for his country, samurai discipline would eventually control the former and properly direct the latter.

Togo found a worthy outlet for his aggression at age fifteen when he manned a cannon in opposition to the British bombardment of Kagoshima. He joined Satsuma's navy in 1866 and saw his first action on the water when he fought for the emperor in the conflict that followed the Restoration. His reward was an appointment to the position of apprentice officer in the new Imperial Navy. The young Japanese midshipmen adopted Lord Nelson as their role model and measured their performances against his legacy. In 1871, twelve of their number got the opportunity to view that legacy firsthand while learning the fine points of naval science in England. Togo was among the chosen. After a crash course in English, he and his companions set out on what would be a seven-year quest for knowledge in their idol's motherland.

Japan had hoped to enroll her young officers in the Royal Naval College, the British equivalent of the U.S. Naval Academy. This request was never seriously considered and the twelve acolytes were instead given billets at the Thames Nautical Training Center whose "classroom" was the training ship *Worcester*. Prior to reporting to the *Worcester*, each Japanese officer spent time at a boardinghouse, both to polish their skills in the English language and to observe all they could about the English people. While soaking in the local color, Togo made numerous pilgrimages to Nelson's hallowed flag ship, HMS *Victory*, where he undoubtedly contemplated his own future glories.

Soon after his formal training began, Togo was dubbed "Johnny Chinaman" by his English classmates, a designation he took with bad grace and often disputed with fisticuffs. Togo's pugilistic prowess soon earned him a grudging respect, despite his diminutive size of 5′3″ and 130 pounds. But the locals could never understand why an Asiatic would get so upset about being misidentified, as if they would complacently accept being called a Frenchman or a Spaniard!

Togo studied for two years at the Thames Nautical Training Center and then circled the globe on an eight-month training cruise. His naval instructor remembered him as an apt pupil, although "not what one would call smart, but diligent and painstaking."[7] This verdict was somewhat similar to that of his Japanese teacher's on his performance as a boy: "Intelligent. Not brilliant. Wishes to make progress in his work and applies himself with determination."[8] After finishing his personal shakedown cruise, Togo faced even more daunting academic challenges while studying mathematics and navigation at Cambridge. His final duty was to serve as "inspector" for the *Fuso*, one of three Japanese warships then under construction in Great Britain. True to form, he haunted the shipyard and irritated the workers with his polite, but incessant questions about their craft.

While Togo was in England, a revolt on Kyushu pitted his family against the central government. Had he been in Japan, Heihachiro would have felt great pressure to support his family and might have fallen in battle beside his eldest brother Sokuro. When word of the uprising reached the Japanese midshipmen, many expected Togo to return home. But Togo remained at his post and made it crystal clear that his duty lay in service to the emperor. This was the first act in the formation of a deep bond between the two men. Togo's subsequent career was underscored by a devotion to his sovereign that bordered on worship. Mutsuhito, in turn, appreciated his officer's loyalty and looked favorably on him for the remainder of his life.

After returning to Japan, Togo received rapid promotion, by applying the same stubborn dedication to duty and detail that had carried him through his training. In early 1881, he felt secure enough to take a wife and purchase a house in Tokyo. But Togo's stubbornness could still be misdirected. In February 1883, while serving as first officer of the *Amagi*, Lieutenant Commander Togo found himself temporarily in charge due to the captain's absence. His first command decision was to determine the proper salute for a visiting British warship. Unfortunately, he calculated and fired an inadequate number of guns, and was immediately informed of such by the British captain. Togo responded by firing off a still smaller number of guns and told the Englishman, "If you will be good enough to add the two salutes together, you will find the number correct."[9]

Her majesty's captain reported this affront directly to the Japanese admiralty, which then directed Togo to re-fire the proper number of guns all together. Incredibly, the *Amagi*'s executive officer refused holding firmly to his view that regulations did not require a salute to be given in one salvo. It was as if Togo had been transported back in time to the day so many years before when he defied his father by refusing to apologize to his oldest brother for putting pepper in his water. Even more incredibly, this time he paid no penalty for his stubbornness. When summoned to naval headquarters several days alter, the incident was not even mentioned and Togo instead merely received the emperor's compliments for his prior service in Korea. A few days after returning to the *Amagi*, Togo was informed that he had been given his first outright command of a ship in the Imperial Navy. It now became apparent just how much the Meiji had appreciated Togo's decision to forego family loyalties and cast his lot with the regime. Togo's acceleration through the stratosphere continued until he made captain in 1886. He then abruptly fell back to earth, spending most of the next four years on sick leave due to the ravages of rheumatic fever. It appeared to many within the naval establishment that a brilliant career had ended. Togo never assumed this, however, and made good use of his time on the shelf by reading every volume he could find on international law. He returned to sea as captain of the cruiser *Naniwa* and promptly put his newly acquired knowledge to use. While in Hawaii, Togo refused to return an escaped Japanese criminal to the local authorities. The *Naniwa*'s captain cited the lack of an extradition treaty and the extra-territoriality of warships that made them tantamount to parcels of their native land. When his government finally ordered the prisoner's return, he chose to turn the man over to the Japanese counsel rather than the police, telling him, "Do as you please with him, only do it where I cannot see."[10]

Captain Togo's next brush with international law was considerably more serious. In the opening stages of the war with China, the *Naniwa* came on the *Kowshing*, a British merchant ship carrying Chinese troops. Togo intended to bring the *Kowshing* to the Japanese naval base at Sasebo for internment. But when the ship's captain attempted to comply, he was restrained by his armed passengers. The *Naniwa* then sank the *Kowshing* and rescued a good number of her crew. However, the Japanese cruiser either ignored the drowning soldiers or shot them as they floundered. The "civilized" world would prove to be much more concerned with the sinking of a neutral vessel than the massacre of some Chinese infantrymen. Great Britain initially reacted with outrage, but was calmed by her own international lawyers who pointed out that the sunken ship carried war contraband and the Japanese commander had issued proper warnings before sinking her.[11] Togo thus became a world figure and a national hero. He had put his years of convalescence to good use.

The *Naniwa* and her captain participated in every major action of the Sino-Japanese War, the most notable being the drubbing inflicted on the Chinese fleet at the Battle of the Yalu on September 17, 1894. Togo emerged from the Chinese War as a rear admiral and went ashore for four years, first to head the Advanced Naval War College and then to command the naval complex at Sasebo. In 1900, he returned to sea as a vice admiral in order to deal with the spasm of Chinese nationalism known as the Boxer Rebellion. The Boxers rose up in opposition to China's exploitation and were struck down by expeditionary forces that included contingents from Japan, the United States, and the European powers. Togo's service with the accompanying international naval force gave him the opportunity to size up the vessels of his fellow imperialists. He paid particular attention to the Russians and found them unimpressive, noting their lax discipline and inadequate training. After the Boxers were crushed, Admiral Togo returned to dry land. He was overseeing the completion of the naval base at Maizuru when he received his summons to lead the Combined Fleet against Russia.

III

The Japanese intended to enter Manchuria by landing their First Army in Korea and driving north across the Yalu River. Once the Yalu River crossing was made, additional armies would be landed directly on the Liaotung Peninsula. Japan's success on land was contingent on moving swiftly. The Yalu River had to be crossed and the passes into Manchuria secured before the Russians could mass sufficient strength to block them. Therefore, The army chose to land at Chemulpo (Inchon) on Korea's western coast. But this plan would be entirely dependent on the establishment and maintenance of command of the sea by the Japanese Fleet. Chemulpo was less than 250 miles from Port Arthur and the proposed landing sites on the Liaotung Peninsula were much closer than that. Failure at sea would force Japanese armies to land at Fusan (Pusan) on Korea's southeastern coast. A drive from Fusan would require the Japanese divisions to march nearly the entire length of the Korean Peninsula. This would give the Russians additional time to block the approaches to Manchuria as well as to redress their local inferiority by redeploying troops from Europe. Of course, failure to maintain sea control would also jeopardize the communications and supply of any Japanese forces which were deployed onto the Asian mainland. Thus, the responsibility for success or failure in the coming struggle rested heavily on Togo and his combined fleet.

When he assumed the burden of his nation's fortunes, Togo was already a legend within the Japanese navy. His service record was impeccable and he seemed the embodiment of the martial virtues of discipline, courage and

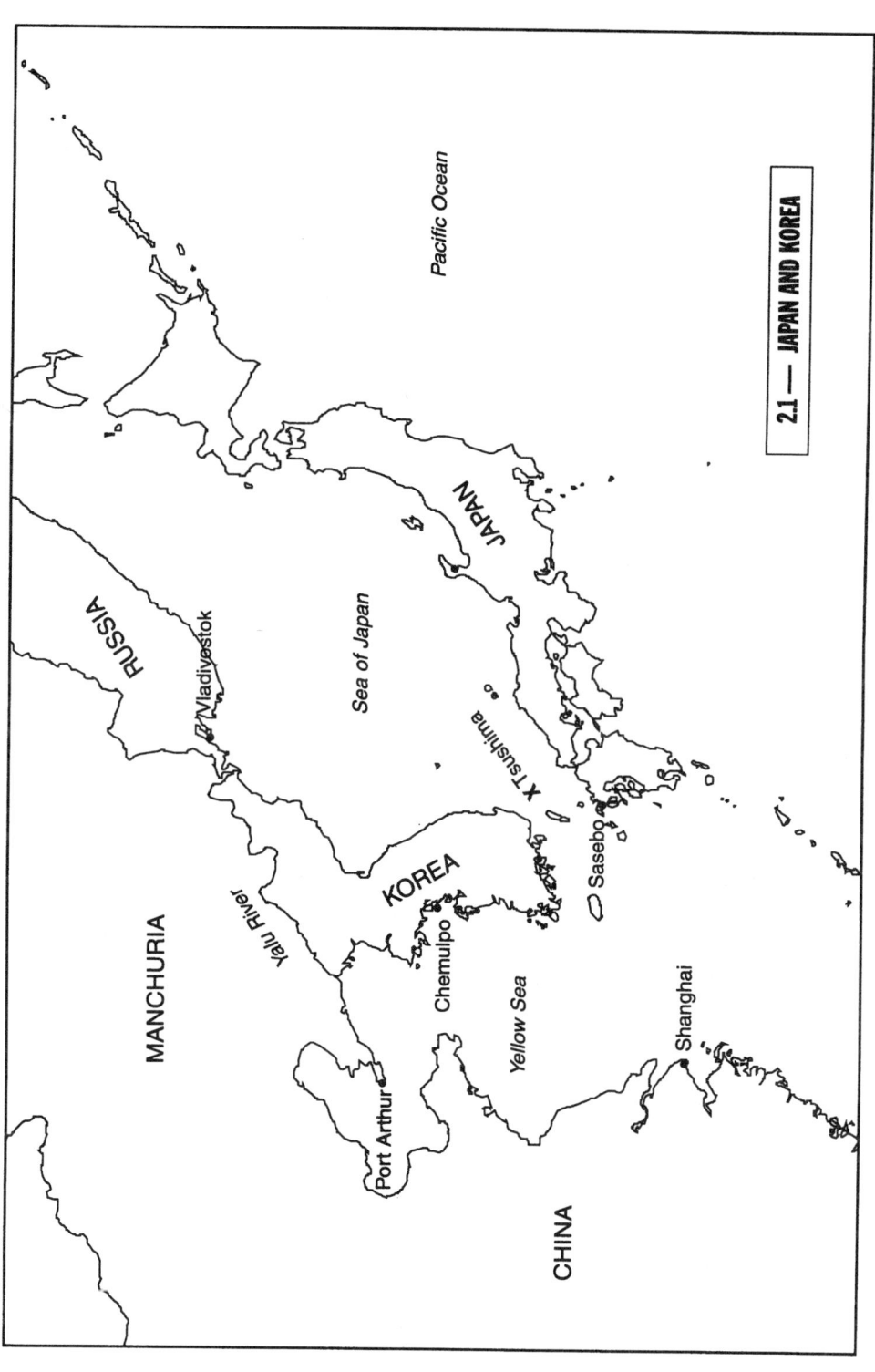

2.1 — JAPAN AND KOREA

dedication to duty. However, it would be misplaced romanticism to cast Togo as a universally loved figure in the mold of Nelson. His reputation as both a "great and terrible" leader is well illustrated by the diary entry of a young officer made on the eve of hostilities with Russia: "The entire fleet is under the orders of Admiral Togo and we must rejoice that it is so. However, I am glad to be commanding a torpedo boat, which keeps me at some distance from him."[12]

The Japanese commander went to sea on February 6, 1904, at the head of a formidable array of warships. His First Division contained six of the most modern battleships in the world, each equipped with four 12-inch guns in their main batteries, as well as numerous 6-inch and 12-pound quick-firing guns in their secondary batteries. Togo exercised direct control of this group from his own *Mikasa*, the most powerful battleship then afloat. Vice-Admiral Hikonojo Kamimura's Second Division was composed of six large armored cruisers, each possessing a main battery of four rapid-firing 8-inch guns plus a lavish allotment of secondary armament. These twelve ships constituted the Japanese battleline. They were supplemented by sixteen protected cruisers organized into four divisions of four ships each. These vessels had minimal armor and varied greatly in their speed and weaponry. Finally, the Combined Fleet's torpedo arm included nineteen destroyers and eighty-five torpedo boats.[13]

The apparent strength of the czar's Pacific Squadron was also impressive. Vice-Admiral Oscar Victorovitch Stark possessed a battle line of seven battleships and four armored cruisers, supported by seven protected cruisers and twenty-five destroyers.[14] But closer scrutiny reveals grave Russian weaknesses that diluted their materiel potency. Russian battleships were smaller and slower than their Japanese counterparts and had been built under haphazard programs that did not provide the uniform specifications necessary to operate together effectively. In contrast, Japan's capital ships had been built to operate as a homogeneous force and even her wide variety of protected cruisers were fairly similar within each division. Stark's battleships also possessed inferior artillery that fired lighter shells at shorter ranges than Japanese guns of the same caliber.[15] All of the Russian vessels were handicapped by shoddy propulsion systems that never produced their advertised speeds even when working properly.[16] Also, the squadron's three largest armored cruisers and its most modern protected cruiser were based at Vladovostok, miles from Port Arthur and ice bound when hostilities commenced.

Japan's advantageous position was further enhanced by the superior training and morale of her naval personnel. The emperor's ships were manned by well-trained, confident crews and commanded by officers whose devotion to their profession bordered on fanaticism. This was in stark contrast to the czar's vessels where sullen men were led by officers who owed their positions to family connections and had little inclination to learn the skills of their profession. According to England's F.T. Jane, the men of the Russian Fleet believed they existed to be shot at rather than to shoot at others.[17] Logistically, Togo had access to modern bases at Yokosuka, Sasebo, Maizuru, and Kure, whereas Stark could only turn to more limited facilities at Port Arthur and Vladovostok. All of this was topped off by an excellent Japanese intelligence network whose sources ranged from corrupt Russian officials in St. Petersburg to disguised Japanese officers in Manchuria. Russian security was abysmal, partially due to the Russians' inability to racially distinguish between the Japanese agents and the Chinese or Korean laborers with whom they mingled. The Meiji government and its military leaders were kept well informed of Russia's internal divisions at home, her tactical dispositions in Manchuria, and the shortcomings of her men and equipment everywhere.

The generally positive state of Japan's naval affairs contained one troubling aspect. Togo's advantage in firepower, other than that which was attributable to the proficiency of his highly trained gunners, was based primarily on his superior secondary armament and the quick-firing 8–inch batteries of the armored cruisers. This translated into more guns, which could fire faster but at a shorter range. His material meshed nicely with Nelson's doctrine of "hail of fire," to which the Japanese adhered in their tactical thinking. Its stated objective was for one to close with the enemy and overwhelm him by a superior volume of gunfire.[18] But, acceptance of this doctrine magnified Togo's strategic dilemma. In closing on the enemy, he would expose his battle fleet, Japan's *only* battle fleet, to extensive damage before the bulk of his own armament could be effectively employed. Togo was aggressive by nature and his inclinations undoubtedly favored destroying the enemy fleet in a head-on confrontation. But if he suffered great losses in the process, Japan could still lose the war when Russia's Baltic Fleet was re-deployed to the Pacific. The Japanese had only a few relics in reserve and had no indigenous capacity to build ships larger than destroyers. Except for two recently purchased armored cruisers then in transit, Togo would have to fight the whole war with only those assets currently on hand. In order to further reduce the odds against him, the Japanese commander decided to resort to some new technology and some unchivalrous behavior.

IV

On the evening of February 8, Togo sent ten of his destroyers to attack the Russian warships at Port Arthur. Although the Japanese government had already severed diplomatic relations with St. Petersburg, it had yet to issue any formal declaration of war. Togo had no qualms about striking while technically at peace. This was old hat to him. In 1894, he engaged Chinese warships and sank the *Kowshing* before war was legally declared. His philosophy of war was ruthlessly pragmatic and would have found agreement with the hustler's adage, "never give a sucker an even break." While planning the coming naval campaign against Russia, Togo had actually asked his government to ensure complete surprise by allowing him to strike before negotiations were broken off. But Tokyo's reply made it crystal clear that the Combined Fleet was not to set sail until diplomatic relations had been severed. When this occurred, Togo summoned his fleet commanders and ships captains to the *Mikasa* and read them the emperor's war communique. The news was received with mixed emotions as the relief of pent-up anticipation mingled with anxiety for success. Togo sensed this, and told the assemblage, "The thoughts of victory or defeat belong, properly, to the time before the fighting takes place. Once you cross fire with the enemy, you should never think of victory or defeat. Those who are desirous of not being defeated shall undoubtedly be defeated."[19]

Togo's sucker punch would be provided by a recent development in naval science, the self-propelled Whitehead torpedo. The weapon had been much improved since its initial design and was now capable of traveling 1,000 yards at 33 knots or about 4,500 yards at 19 knots.[20] But, these specifications were technical rather than tactical. Naval drills had repeatedly shown that torpedoes were neither accurat nor reliable at their long-range settings. They could be thrown off course by the current or might malfunction and simply sink to the bottom. Thus, the torpedo was still less than ideal for employment against moving targets at sea. However, it was more than adequate for the unprepared, stationary vessels that the Japanese destroyers found anchored in the roadstead outside of Port Arthur.

Admiral Stark had not been completely negligent in his dispositions. He established destroyer patrols, instructed the cruisers *Pallada* and *Askold* to conduct sweeps with their searchlights and ordered the fleet to put out its torpedo nets. But many captains ignored the latter directive and neither the patrolling destroyers nor the duty cruisers could penetrate the snowy darkness sufficiently to spot the approaching danger. Just before midnight, Japan's 300-ton greyhounds glided to within 600 yards of their prey and launched eighteen torpedoes, three of which found their marks. The cruiser *Pallada* and battleships *Retvizan* and *Tsarevitch* all had enormous holes blown into their sides and had to be grounded to avoid sinking. Despite fusillades of fire from the startled Russian ships, all ten destroyers withdrew unscathed.

By crippling the three Russian warships, Togo's torpedo flotillas not only further tipped the material balance in Japan's favor, but also produced a paralytic psychosis among the czar's Pacific Squadron. When Togo led his battle fleet to Port Arthur the next day, he found the enemy fleet still in the roadstead, huddled beneath their forts. Despite their obvious confusion and inactivity, the Japanese commander chose not to press his attack, but settled for a long-range exchange of gunnery. Rear Admiral Shigeto Dewa's Third Division of protected cruisers joined the battleships and armored cruisers in this endeavor. The Russian ships replied, joined by fire from the forts, and gave out as much punishment as they received. Numerous Japanese ships were hit, including the battleships *Mikasa, Shikishima, Fuji,* and *Hatsuse,* but none suffered seriously enough to necessitate their leaving the fight. After about one hour, Togo broke off action and withdrew, correctly assuming that the Russians would retire to the safety of their inner harbor. Not all of Togo's officers approved of his tactics. Admiral Kamimura strongly suggested another attack early next morning, but his commander demurred.

A Japanese destroyer captain went even further, writing that Togo's caution robbed the nation of a "glorious victory" and musing that Nelson would not have remained similarly inactive in such a situation.[21] This unflattering comparison is unduly harsh but not completely inappropriate. Although the preemptive attack on Port Arthur does conjure up images of Nelson's daring sortie into the harbor at Copenhagen, the images fade rapidly under closer scrutiny. Whereas Nelson brought his battle line under the guns of the Danish forts, Togo risked only his destroyers at Port Arthur. Nevertheless, Togo would have been irresponsible to seek "glory" by risking his country's only battle fleet at this stage of the war. Russian gunnery had been surprisingly good on February 9 and there was always the threat of mines with which to contend. Japan's main business lay more than two hundred miles to the east and the fleet had to be preserved while it was being transacted.

All of the sound and fury at Port Arthur was intended to provide a screen for the seizure of a foothold in Korea. That task was assigned to a 3,000 man advance guard carried on three transports and escorted by Vice-Admiral Sotokichi Uryu's Fourth Division. Uryu's four protected cruisers were stiffened by the armored cruiser *Asama* and then further reinforced by the small cruiser *Chiyoda,* which had been on station at Chemulpo since the previous April. The Japanese expedition arrived at the Korean port on the evening of February 8 and proceeded to disembark its passengers. This activity went unreported because Chemulpo's telegraph cable had been cut the day before. It concluded successfully despite the presence of the protected cruiser *Varyag* and the gunboat *Koreetz,* which were overawed into quiescence by the superior force that covered the landings. When the Russian ships attempted to escape, they were pummeled by Uryu's cruisers and driven back into the harbor. Both captains then scuttled their vessels.

Back at Port Arthur, the Russian Pacific Squadron lay inactive in a dazed stupor, limiting its operations to mine laying. Even this activity ceased when it produced a minor disaster with comic-opera overtones. On February 11, the mine-layer *Yeneisei* floundered in heavy seas, hit one of its own mines, and sank with the loss of most of its crew. When the small cruiser *Boyarin* was dispatched to investigate the *Yeneisei*'s disappearance, it too struck a "friendly" mine and went to the bottom.

Togo was pleased that the Russian ships remained in their sanctuary and attempted to turn their safe haven against them by sealing them inside it. On the night of February 24, the Japanese made the first of an eventual three attempts to bottle up the Russians by sinking merchant ships in the harbor's channel. Just before dawn, lookouts on the stranded *Retvizan* spied the five old cargo ships steaming into the channel's entrance. Her guns combined with those of the surrounding forts to blow the intruders to pieces. During the next day's follow-up bombardment by the Japanese battle fleet, Russian cruisers were able to retire into the harbor, illustrating the limited success of the previous night's venture. But although the Russian Fleet could get out, it showed no inclination to do so. Admiral Stark instituted a "no risk" policy that preserved his ships but surrendered the sea lanes by default. With its passageway secured, the First Army's Twelfth Division streamed through Chemulpo and headed for the Yalu River.

The atmosphere at Port Arthur changed abruptly with the arrival of a new commander on March 7. Admiral Stephen Ossipovitch Makarov was an individual who possessed a rare combination of energy, intelligence, and courage. A decorated hero of the Turkish War of 1877–78, he had also designed the world's first ice breaker and authored a book on naval tactics, which Togo had ordered to be translated into Japanese during his tenure at the Naval War College. Makarov's presence immediately revitalized the czar's Pacific Squadron. His no-nonsense leadership and the arrival of trained workmen from Russia accelerated the repair of the ships that had been damaged on the war's opening night. The *Retvizan* and the *Tsarevitch* were soon refloated and moved into the harbor. Further repairs, however, would be seriously hindered by the lack of any dry dock large enough to hold a cruiser or battleship. An apocryphal story was circulating in Port Arthur that St. Petersburg had refused to fund such "luxuries" as dry docks because damaged battleships could be repaired in the extensive facilities of Japan![22] Makarov also stepped up the pace of fleet operations. He ordered the destroyers to undertake active patrolling against their Japanese counterparts and he made a concerted effort to improve the ability of the battle fleet to navigate through the narrow and shallow entrance to the harbor. Where once it had taken twenty-four hours for the entire fleet to enter or leave the harbor, Makarov's incessant practice reduced the time to two-and-a-half hours.

Meanwhile, Togo's fleet was constantly at sea, guaranteeing the unhindered flow of men and supplies to Korea. It was represented at Port Arthur primarily by the ever present destroyers that aggressively searched for targets of opportunity and anxiously watched for any signs of Russian Fleet activity. Elements of the Japanese battle fleet also bombarded Port Arthur on two occasions during this period. During the first, Togo's battleships shelled the town and the harbor for a nerve-shattering four hours. This ordeal was especially galling to the Russians because they had been unable to respond in any fashion. The guns of the forts could not reach the Japanese assailants and the fleet could not sortie in the low tide. Afterward, Makarov instituted a system of indirect fire whereby the heavy guns on the ships within the harbor could be directed from the surrounding hills. When the Japanese battleships returned ten days later, indirect fire held them to a range that rendered their bombardment ineffective. The increasingly nimble Russian fleet then sortied and inflicted serious damage on the battleship *Fuji*, which was forced to retire to Japan for repairs. Clearly, Makarov's courage and energy had become infectious throughout his command.

The significance of the improved Russian performance was not lost on Togo. His realization that the Russian navy was now both able and willing to fight prompted the second attempt to block the channel with merchantmen. This effort proved no more successful than the first. However, Togo was well acquainted with Makarov's methods and periodically refreshed his memory from a translation of the Russian admiral's book that he kept on the nightstand in his cabin. He realized that the fact that the Russians were now more inclined to leave their sanctuary presented opportunities as well as problems. By mining Makarov's passageway, Togo hoped to extract a fee for the boldness of his adversary. During the night of April 11, under the cover of snow squalls, the Japanese sowed a field of mines around the harbor's entrance. This labor would soon bear sweet fruit.

In the next morning's early light, a Russian destroyer returning from patrol came under fire from Japanese cruisers and destroyers. Four Russian cruisers raced to her aid followed by Makarov in the battleship *Petropavlovsk*, and the remaining four undamaged battleships. Too late to save the destroyer, the Russians hotly engaged the cruisers until Makarov realized that he was being drawn into the clutches of the Japanese First and Second Divisions. The recent arrival of the new armored cruisers *Nisshin* and *Kasuga* had swollen the ranks of the Combined Fleet to fourteen capital ships. Dewa's Third Division, reinforced by the armored cruisers *Asama* and *Tokiwa*, served as bait while Togo's six battleships and Kaminura's six armored cruisers lurked over the horizon. Makarov was a lion, but his courage was ruled by reason. When he realized that he had been tricked into confronting a vastly superior force, the Russian commander promptly turned his fleet in an all-out dash for the harbor. As it neared the harbor's entrance, the *Petropavlovsk* struck a mine and went down in a brilliant flash, her propellers still turning. With her went Makarov, the soul of the czar's Pacific Squadron. When the Japanese bombarded the town on the following day, not a ship sortied to meet them. Gloom and inactivity had returned as the Russian watchwords at Port Arthur.

When Makarov's demise had been confirmed, some of Togo's officers came to him and suggested that he send a personal message of condolence to the Russians. The *Bushido*, a code of warrior behavior based on traditional ideals, required the modern samurai to be a courteous as well as competent killer. It seemed appropriate to the Japanese officers that some gesture be made on the passing of an adversary as worthy as Makarov. But Togo would not participate in what he viewed as archaic romanticism. Makarov was the greatest obstacle in the path of Togo's mission and he had been removed from the scene by a deliberate tactical decision. No message was sent to the Russians.

Meanwhile, the land war had progressed to a point that necessitated the landing of the Japanese Second Army on the Liaotung Peninsula, some 60 miles from Port Arthur. Togo could not guarantee security for this operation as long as the harbor remained open. Therefore, the third blocking attempt was undertaken on May 2, this time with twelve ships. The final attempt at corking the bottle was only partially successful, narrowing but not closing the channel. Nevertheless, Togo reported that the channel was closed and the landings went ahead as planned. Despite Russian inactivity, Togo was cognizant of the danger involved in amphibious operations in such close proximity to the enemy fleet. He had to back up his rash pronouncement with an active blockade that kept some of his capital ships close to the harbor. In doing so, he gave Russia its only naval victory of the war. On May 16, the battleships *Hatsuse* and *Yashima* struck mines and sank with heavy loss of life. This disaster occurred in the midst of what turned out to be a bad week for Japanese ships. Two days before, the *Kasuga* collided with the protected cruiser *Yoshino* while steaming through a thick fog, sinking her with the loss of more than three hundred men. The *Kasuga* itself was damaged sufficiently to require a month in the dockyard. Several smaller ships, including the destroyer *Akatsuki* were also lost during this period.

The *Hatsuse* went down in full view of Port Arthur, but the loss of the *Yashima* was concealed until after the war. Nevertheless, the loss of two battleships dangerously reduced Japan's margin of superiority and gave the Russians a glimmer of hope for naval resurgence. The Vladovostok Squadron was playing its part by cruising the Sea of Japan and sinking merchantmen, including the *Hitachi Maru*, which carried eighteen 11-inch Krupp siege guns earmarked for employment against Port Arthur. Makarov would have exploited the situation to make Togo's life miserable. But his successor, Rear Admiral Vilgelon Karolvitch Vitgeft, was not so inclined. The new Russian commander eschewed all maritime operations. On June 6, the same day that Togo was promoted to full admiral, General Maresuke Nogi's Third Army landed at Dalny, a mere 40 miles north of his objective: Port Arthur. The developing siege of Port Arthur by the Japanese Army provided sufficient motivation for Vitgeft to attempt an escape to Vladovostok on June 23. But when confronted by Togo's battle fleet, the Russian admiral lost his nerve and returned to port. Togo, smarting over the loss of his two battleships and mindful of the tasks still facing him, did not undertake an active pursuit.

After his aborted sortie, Vitgeft was content to let his fleet languish in the harbor, yielding more and more of its men and guns for the landward defense of the forts. It finally took a directive from the czar himself to move him to make another attempt to escape before the squadron was lost to the siege. On August 10, Vitgeft placed his flag on the *Tsarevitch* and led five other battleships, four cruisers, and a handful of destroyers out of the harbor.[23] Only the armored cruiser *Bayan*, still immobilized from striking a mine and the smaller torpedo craft were left behind. Vitgeft had no illusions about the fate of his rag-tag squadron, as he dismissed all words of encouragement with a wave of his hand and a promise to meet the speaker "in the next world."[24]

Togo had maintained his fleet in close proximity to Port Arthur for many weeks in anticipation of the departure of the Russian Fleet. His available strength had declined substantially since its apex at the time of Makarov's demise. On August 10, the Japanese battle line consisted of the battleships *Mikasa, Asahi, Fuji, Shikishima*, and the armored cruisers *Kasuga* and *Nisshin*. In close support were the armored cruisers *Yagumo* and *Asama*, two divisions of protected cruisers, and the usual legion of destroyers and torpedo boats.[25] (The other armored cruisers had been assigned to Vice-Admiral Kamimura, who was in the Sea of Japan attempting to neutralize the troublesome Vladovostosk squadron.) Togo's eight capital ships carried a broadside of sixteen 12-inch, one 10-inch, fourteen 8-inch, and fifty-three 6-inch guns with a total weight of 25,000 pounds against Vitgeft's six battleships that ostensibly possessed sixteen 12-inch, eight 10-inch, and thirty-six 6-inch guns capable of hauling 19,000 pounds of metal.[26] How-

ever, the actual Russian totals were slightly short of their assigned armament because some of their smaller guns had not been retrieved from the
forts and one of the *Sevastopol's* damaged 12-inchers had been replaced by
a wooden facsimile.[27] The Japanese approached the Battle of the Yellow
Sea with a clear superiority in every ship type except battleships. However,
their myriad of torpedo craft would be only a minor factor during the daylight hours and their inferiority in heavy guns would be a great handicap to
the long-range, low-risk tactics that Togo planned to employ.

At approximately 11:30 a.m., the morning mists lifted and the opposing
fleets sighted each other. Togo was disappointed at the size of the fleet that
confronted him. He had hoped that more of the larger Russian ships would
be too damaged to leave port. The Russian Fleet was too strong to engage at
decisive range, but too numerous to risk escape by dispersal. Togo chose to
engage the Russian Fleet at a discrete distance and attempt to turn it back to
Port Arthur where it would eventually succumb to the siege. For several
hours, the two fleets maneuvered and engaged each other at ranges of between 8,000 and 11,000 yards. Surprisingly, the Russian squadron matched
the Japanese in both sailing and shooting. Finally, Togo drew his ships out
of range in order to rest his crews and to give Vitgeft the opportunity to return to Port Arthur. Although his men took good advantage of the respite to
refresh themselves, Togo's adversary remained unhesitatingly on course for
Vladovostok.

At about 4 p.m., the Japanese closed to within 5 miles of the Russian
Fleet and the battle began anew. For more than two hours, the antagonists
fought a running engagement at a range in excess of 7,000 yards. The *Mikasa* suffered heavily during this long range duel, sustaining numerous hits,
one of which knocked out her after turret. Casualties piled up on the flagship, almost overwhelming its first aid teams and creating a near panic on
her bridge. But the Japanese commander remained visibly unperturbed and
calmly reminded his men of their duty by reciting the latest Imperial edict to
"break the enemy though you crush your own body's bones."[28] A Russian
shell fragment then inflicted a flesh wound on Togo himself, who, display-
ing his usual indifference to danger, refused to leave the bridge. Hits on the
battleships *Asahi* and *Shikishima* further reduced the already outnumbered
Japanese main batteries to eleven working guns. Although the Russian
ships also sustained damage, they maintained their course toward their chosen sanctuary. Whether buoyed by the czar's directive or driven by the imperative of survival, the once vacillating Vitgeft had turned resolute in his
determination to get his fleet to Vladovostok.

Then at 6:37 p.m., with the Russians only thirty minutes away from the
safety of darkness, Japanese guns found the range of the *Tsarevitch*. Two

12-inch shells slammed into the flagship, killing or wounding every man on the bridge and conning towner. Admiral Vitgeft was literally blown to pieces, leaving only a piece of one leg behind. Other dead bodies jammed the ship's steering wheel and caused the *Tsarevitch* to circle back through its own battle line. Chaos immediately ensued among the other Russian ships. Rear Admiral Prince Ukhtomski, on the battleship *Peresvyet*, tried to restore order by signalling "follow me." But the loss of his ship's masts required the signal to be hoisted on the bridge rails where it went unnoticed for some time. Togo took advantage of the confusion by closing the range and forming his ships into an arc around the muddled Russian formation. Most of his firepower was directed at the *Retvizan*, which was the only Russian battleship still fighting. The *Retvizan* was battered by hits from guns of all calibers as it was now within the effective range of the Japanese secondary armament as well as their main batteries. However, the cruisers *Askold*, *Diana*, and *Pallada* came to her assistance and drew off enough fire to allow her to lead the now reforming Russian Fleet back toward Port Arthur. Unwilling to expose his precious ships to torpedo attack in the gathering darkness, Togo declined to seek his Trafalger and instead turned the pursuit over to his own torpedo craft. By the time these ships were able to join the battle, darkness had completely fallen. The Japanese destroyers and torpedo boats proved ineffective in their night attacks, inflicting only minor damage on the battleship *Poltava*.

Of all the Russian ships which entered the Yellow Sea on August 10, 1904, only the cruiser *Novik* was sunk. The gallant little cruiser remained at large for three weeks, trying to reach Vladovostok. She was finally cornered by two more powerful Japanese cruisers, the *Tsushima* and *Chitose*, and was scuttled after giving a good account of herself in the unequal struggle. Five battleships, one cruiser, and three destroyers made it back to the temporary safety of Port Arthur. The battleship *Tsarevitch*, cruisers *Askold* and *Diana*, and the remaining destroyers found their way to neutral ports where they were interned for the war's duration.[29] But the life of the Russian Pacific Squadron ended at the Battle of the Yellow Sea. Togo had effectively destroyed his nemesis by forcing it back to a base whose capture was now just a matter of time. More importantly, the Japanese Fleet remained intact. Four days hence, Kamimura would finally engage the Vladovostok squadron, sinking one of the big Russian cruisers and crippling the other two. Neither those ships nor the ones back at Port Arthur would again venture forth to challenge Japanese naval supremacy.

As the siege ring tightened around Port Arthur, the ships in the harbor suffered increasingly at the hands of Japanese artillery fire. The fall of 203 Metre Hill on December 5 gave the Japanese a position capable of direct observation of the harbor and its denizens. Only the battleship *Sevastopol* survived the rain of fire that followed. After moving to an anchorage in the outer harbor, *Sevastopol* fought off torpedo attacks for nearly three weeks. On January 2, 1905, the day after Port Arthur surrendered, the heavily damaged warship was towed out to sea and scuttled.

When Togo hiked to the top of 203 Metre Hill to assess the situation, the battered hulks that now inhabited the harbor convinced him that he could finally retire his fleet to Japan. Although he was characteristically stoic, it is not hard to image that the moment's joy and relief was somewhat mitigated by the fact that it was the guns of the army, rather than his battleships, that administered the coup-de-grace to the czar's Pacific Squadron. But this was the culmination of the strategy that Togo had pursued from the start. His opening move robbed the Russians of their equilibrium and his subsequent pace of operations established the Japanese Fleet as a debilitating omnipresence in the Russian psyche. Throughout the campaign, Togo never lost the initiative and always dictated the terms of engagement. He controlled the sea lanes, supported the army and destroyed Russian sea power while preserving his emperor's fleet for future operations. Yet one must wonder if beneath this inscrutable mask of discipline there was a longing to attain a more decisive verdict at sea. At that very moment, a second Russian Fleet was groping its way around the world to give him that opportunity.

V

On June 20, 1904, the task of leading the czar's Baltic Fleet to the Pacific was entrusted to Admiral Zinovi Petrovitch Rozhdestvensky. The admiral's troubles were many. He had to man and prepare the individual ships, amalgamate them into a cohesive battle fleet and make provisions for their 18,000 mile journey. The latter was particularly troublesome because it would require some 500,000 tons of coal, which had to be provided without the benefit of any Russian naval bases along the way. The problem was solved by contracting with Germany's Hamburg Amerikan shipline to use its colliers to fuel up in neutral ports whenever possible and directly at sea when it was not.

When the newly rechristened Second Pacific Squadron left the Baltic on October 17, the admiral's other problems had not been solved. Personnel was foremost on the list. The best Russian sailors were already in the Pacific, forcing Rozhdestvensky's ships to fill their complements with conscripts, reservists, or transferred merchant seamen. A Russian officer said of them, "One half have to be taught everything because they know nothing, the other half because they have forgotten everything; but if they do remember anything then it is obsolete."[30] Furthermore, there was a strong revolutionary strain in many of them, which would surface in numerous mutinies and disturbances during the voyage. Skilled officers might have salvaged the situation, for even the Russian seaman worked well under good leadership. But Russian officers were more concerned with personal pleasure than naval proficiency and were usually either too lax or too harsh in imposing discipline upon their crews. Rozhdestvensky's few good officers were spread so thinly throughout the fleet that they had no impact on its ability to function. The forty-two vessels that set out for the Pacific were not a fleet at all, but rather a collection of individual ships, united by neither purpose nor practice. They departed and proceeded in an atmosphere of typically Russian gloom and resignation to inevitable disaster.

The ships, at least, seemed impressive. Rozhdestvensky's First Division boasted four brand new battleships, *Suvorov*, *Borodino*, *Orel*, and *Alexander III*, each well armored and carrying four 12-inch and twelve 6-inch guns. His Second Division contained three older battleships, *Osliabya*, *Navarin*, and *Sysoi-Veliky* plus the armored cruiser *Admiral Nakhimov*. Seven lesser cruisers and nine destroyers rounded out the fleet's combat element.[31] But the ships, too, had their shortcomings. The new battleships included modifications that increased their displacement, making them top heavy and unstable, reducing their speed and submerging much of their belts of armor.[32] By mingling the new battleships with the older ship types, the top speed of the Russian battle line was reduced even further.

After nearly starting a war with England by mistakenly firing on fishing boats on Dogger Bank, the armada made its way to Tangier. There, Rozhdestvensky divided it, sending his older ships through the Mediterranean while taking the bulk of them around Africa. Their reunion at Madagascar was marred by the news of the fall of Port Arthur and of the dispatch of Rear Admiral Nicholas Nebogatov and the Third Pacific Squadron to reinforce them. Rozhdestvensky had no illusions about the value of his "reinforcements." The new squadron contained the old battleship *Nicholas I*, three coast defense ironclads, and an ancient armored cruiser that had originally been designed to carry sails. Their inclusion in the fleet would serve to reduce its already inadequate speed even further. This was especially detrimental because the fall of Port Arthur left Rozhdestvensky with no viable option other than a run for Vladovostok in the hope of establishing himself there as a threat to Japanese lines of communication and supply. Therefore, he decided to proceed without them, arriving at Singapore on April 8, 1905. Despite receiving direct orders to the contrary, the Russian commander again decided to move on. But a coal shortage on the *Alexander III* made this impossible. Rozhdestvensky, his energy dissipated from the travails of the voyage, gave up all thoughts of rebellion and pulled into Kamranh Bay to await his "reinforcements."

Togo had not been idle in the interval following his descent from 203 Metre Hill. After overhauling his ships, he put their crews through hours of gunnery drill. Japanese adherence to the British "hail of fire" doctrine accepted the view that the object of gunfire was to disable ships, whereupon their subsequent sinking or capture would follow as a matter of course. This required a heavy reliance on shells fused to explode on contact, with armor piecing projectiles reserved only for the final act. A Japanese naval engineer named Shimose developed an excellent "hot" powder for use in such shells. However, experience against the Russians had shown that the "Shimose powder" often exploded prematurely, sometimes while still in the barrel. During the weeks of practice, a new formula designed to rectify this problem was successfully test-fired, producing an understandable improvement in the sailors' morale.

Togo awaited his new adversary under circumstances that were more amenable to boldness than those that governed his earlier operations. The Baltic Fleet was Russia's last offering and Japanese experience against its predecessors was convincing evidence of Russia's inadequacies at sea. Additionally, although the Japanese had captured Port Arthur and won a series of land victories, they had failed to destroy the Russian army in a decisive battle of annihilation. After each defeat, the Russians had managed to fall back along their main line of communications, the Trans-Siberian Railway. This overburdened length of track was, to say the least, a clogged artery. Nevertheless, Russia's vast reserves of manpower were using it to flow east at a slow but steady pace. Time favored the czar if he had the will to continue the struggle. Japan, on the other hand, possessed a reservoir of spirit, but faced material exhaustion. Her army had no significant reserves left and her treasury was nearly bankrupt. She needed to end the war quickly to consolidate her territorial gains and avoid an impending fiscal collapse. The establishment of a Russian naval force at Vladovostok would not be conducive to this goal.

By May 1905, Togo anticipated the arrival of the Second and Third Pacific Squadrons with a fleet that was rested and battle-ready. When his fleet was fully assembled, the Japanese commander summoned his ships' captains to the *Mikasa* to prepare them for the coming event. He told them:

Those who have not often taken part in a modern naval battle are constantly apt, in the heat of action, to overestimate the enemy's strength and situation because they cannot perceive the damage wrought by our own fire in the enemy's ships, whereas the damage sustained by our own ships is tangible and visible. There are those who, seeing an enemy ship trying to escape by making its way through our line, believe her to be attacking us boldly; others, drawing near to a ship out of control and firing at random, receive the impression that her firepower has enormously increased. Such examples are not rare. And often, in the midst of an engagement, we think that we are losing whereas it is the enemy who has already lost. When we give our enemy seven chances of winning against our own three, the chances, in reality, are even. In a naval battle, there is never any occasion to think defensively, for a determined attack is always the best form of defense.[33]

Togo's main concern was finding the Russian fleet before it could slip by him and reach its obvious destination of Vladovostok. There were three possible routes to consider: the La Perouse Strait, the Strait of Tsugara, and the Strait of Tsushima. Because either of the first two would require the Russians to make a long journey around Japan's east coast, and proceed through narrow, heavily mined passageways, Togo deployed his entire fleet to intercept the Russians at Tsushima. This was somewhat risky, but his interior position coupled with the long sailing time required to reach the other passages would give him a chance to re-deploy to block them if necessary. Although both his subordinates and his superiors in Tokyo were entertaining thoughts that their fleet commander had guessed wrong, Togo remained firm in his conviction that the Russians would do as he supposed. His judgment was vindicated when he received intelligence reports that Russian auxiliaries, including colliers, had arrived at Shanghai. If he intended to make the long voyage around Japan, the Russian commander would need those vessels with him. Clearly, the Russians had shed their support baggage to make their run through the Straits of Tsushima. (In fact, Rozhdestvensky did retain some auxiliaries that he felt were necessary to support his operations at Vladovostok.)

The battle fleets that moved toward each other on May 27, 1905, each boasted twelve capital ships in their battlelines. Togo led with the battleships *Mikasa*, *Shikishima*, *Fuji*, and *Asahi* and the armored cruisers *Kasuga* and *Nisshin*. Kamimura followed with the Second Division's armored cruisers, *Izumo*, *Azuma*, *Tokiwa*, *Yagumo*, *Iwate*, and *Asama*. Rozhdestvensky led the four new battleships of his First Division from the *Suvorov*. His Second Division contained the three older battleships and one armored cruiser that had initially departed the Baltic the previous October. Nebogatov's Third Division, containing the battleship *Nicholas I* and the three coastal ironclads, struggled to keep up. In pure numbers, the Russians could hurl a broadside of more than 32,000 pounds from their twenty-six 12-inch, fifteen 10-inch, and 51 smaller caliber guns while the Japanese could produce about 28,400 pounds from their sixteen 12-inch, one 10-inch, and 110 secondary pieces.[34] However, the more modern and better manned Japanese guns could fire faster and more accurately, hit with more impact and send their shells farther than Russian guns of the same caliber. Furthermore, whereas the Japanese could sustain speeds of 15 knots, the Russians, burdened by their ancient Third Division and slowed by the barnacles attached to all their hulls, could make only 9.[35]

An auxiliary cruiser sighted the Russian ships steaming through a heavy pre-dawn fog and communicated their position by wireless. Togo was awakened to receive news of the sighting just after 5 a.m. As he read the message, his face broke into what his staff afterward insisted to be the first full, uninhibited smile that he displayed since the war had begun.[36] Other Japanese cruisers continued to shadow the Russian Fleet throughout the morning, despite the presence of a stubborn lingering mist, and kept their commander well informed of enemy movements. When the prospects for action became imminent, Togo's staff respectfully requested that he command the battle from the safety of the *Mikasa's* armored blockhouse. The admiral's reply gave his attendants a brief glimpse of his sense of humor. Togo dismissed their entreaties, saying he was too old to worry about dying, and then added, with a faintly mocking smile, that perhaps his young officers, with so much to live for, should go there instead.[37]

Shortly after noon, Rozhdestvensky ordered the ships of the First Division to turn in succession eight points (90°) to starboard and then eight points together to port. This maneuver, if properly executed, would have realigned his formation into an inverted "L," with the First Division leading line-abreast and the other two divisions trailing in a straight line ahead. It may have been intended to position the ships of the First Division where they would lead the rest of the battle line in a line-ahead formation to either port or starboard by merely executing another 90° turn in the chosen direction. Alternatively, the shift may have been the initial step in deploying the whole battle line in a line-abreast formation from which all twelve ships could quickly realign in either direction by executing an eight-point turn simultaneously. However, this explanation is suspect because a turn to port under such circumstances would place the Third Division's antiques at the head of the line. In any event, through a misreading of signals, the First Division made its second turn in succession rather than all together. This realigned the four modern battleships in their own line-ahead formation, slightly in front and to starboard of the other eight ships. When Rozhdestvensky ordered his lead ships back into line with the other two divisions, the latter's ships were forced to reduce speed or swerve to accommodate the First Division, creating a confused formation described as a "mob" by Admiral Nebogatov.[38]

At this moment, Togo's battle fleet appeared out of the mist. Slicing across the bow from starboard to port, he assumed a course that was parallel but opposite to that of Rozhdestvensky. Togo had sent his men into battle with the Nelsonian signal, "The fate of the Empire depends upon today's event. Let every man do his utmost."[39] In order to annihilate their enemy as the British had done at Trafalgar, the Japanese had to reverse their course. Otherwise, the Russians might well disappear into the mist after the initial exchange of broadsides.

Togo could have done so by executing a simultaneous turn movement in which each ship individually turns 180°. Such a maneuver would have placed the armored cruisers in the van and left the battleships trailing the pack. This realignment was unacceptable as it would force Japan's lightest armed and least protected capital ships to bear the brunt of the initial Russian salvoes. It would also place the Japanese commander in the awkward position of "leading" from the rear of his column. Alternately, Togo could maintain the order of his battle line by turning his ships in succession. A turn to starboard would allow the Japanese to change course beyond the range of the Russian guns, but might also give the Russians time to sort out their confusion and disappear into the poor visibility. Instead, Togo made his turn to port, toward the enemy. This course precluded Russian escape, but also entailed great risk to the Japanese. As each ship made its turn, it would present itself as a virtually stationary target for the Russian gunners. Because each ship turned at the same spot, the enemy would need only to find the range of the turn's "knuckle" and concentrate their fire at that point. Additionally, each Japanese ship would have its own guns masked by the preceding ships until it completed its turn.

No one knows how the Japanese commander calculated all the factors involved in his decision. Togo's pep talk prior to the battle shows that he was determined to press the issue from the outset but there is no evidence that the dangerous maneuver itself was premeditated. In later years, he would only comment, "The way to win a naval engagement is to strike hard at the right moment; the ability to judge the opportunity cannot be acquired from books, but only from experience."[40] Almost certainly Togo's prior experience against the Russians had convinced him that, like Nelson at Trafalgar, he had nothing to fear from his enemy except his escape.

As the *Mikasa* began to execute its turn, the Russians were momentarily stunned by a mixture of incredulity and anticipation. On the *Suvorov*, Captain Vladimer Semenoff overheard a young gunnery lieutenant exclaim, "How rash! Why, in a minute we'll be able to roll up their heading ships!"[41] "Please God we may," although Semenoff, who had fought in the Battle of the Yellow Sea and felt much less optimistic about his comrades' chances to

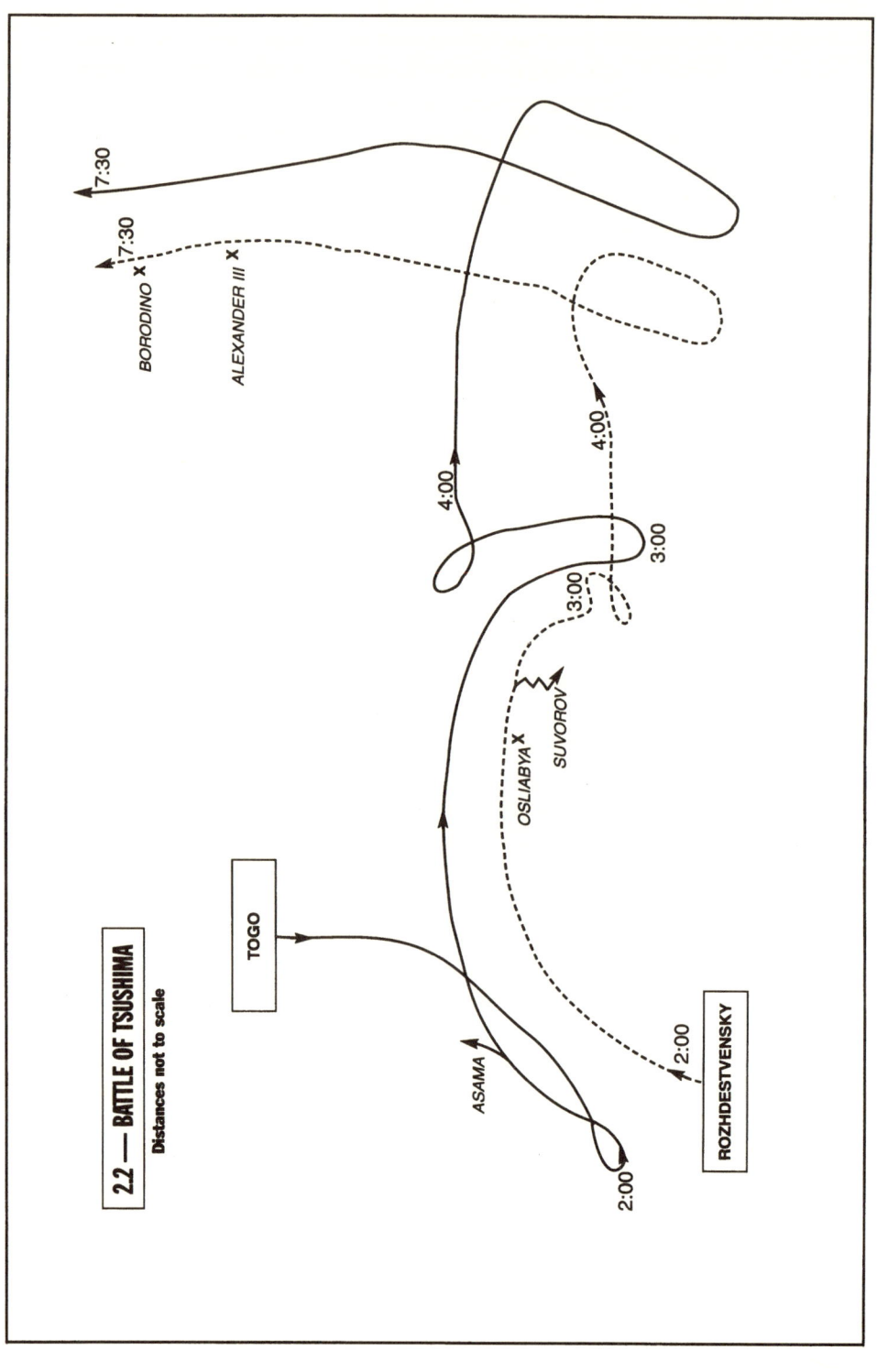

22 — BATTLE OF TSUSHIMA
Distances not to scale

deliver the results promised in the lieutenant's soliloquy.[42] The Russian ships soon began a rapid but generally inaccurate bombardment at a range of 6,500 yards. For nearly five minutes, they enjoyed open season on enemy vessels that must have seemed to be moving in slow motion. Their advantage declined steadily thereafter as each Japanese ship made its turn and began to reply. Although every member of Togo's battle line made the turn successfully, the armored cruiser *Asama* was soon forced to retire in order to repair its damaged steering mechanism. She would rejoin the Second Division some two hours later. The Russians had also scored multiple hits on the *Mikasa, Shikishima, Nisshin,* and *Yagumo*. Except for the loss of the *Yagumo's* forward 8-inch turret, these ships suffered no injuries that impaired their ability to fight. Oddly enough, most of this damage had been inflicted by the ancient guns of the Russian Third Division. But soon the inferior speed of these ships forced them to fall behind, out of the main action.

By 2:15 p.m., the battle lines were sailing on a parallel course and were locked in an intense gun duel. Togo's First Division concentrated on Rozhdestvensky's newer battleships, especially the *Suvorov*, whereas Kaminura's cruisers dealt with the Russian Second Division, directing their fire almost exclusively on the *Osliabya*. Unlike his conduct at the Yellow Sea, Togo now chose to heed the Japanese adage, "If your sword is too short, take one step forward."[43] Using his superior speed to dictate the course of battle, Togo closed on his enemy and took full advantage of his quick-firing secondary batteries. Semenoff noticed the difference and later reported,

On August 10th, in a fight lasting some hours, the *Tsarevitch* was struck by only 19 large shells, and I, in all seriousness, had intended in the present engagement, to note the times and places where we were hit, as well as the damage done. But how could I make detailed notes when it seemed impossible even to count the number of projectiles striking us? I had not only never witnessed such a fire before but I had never imagined anything like it. Shells seemed to be pouring on us incessantly.[44]

In addition to closing the range, Togo's speed advantage enabled him to gradually pull ahead of Rozhdestvensky's battle line and, by threatening to sail across its head, force it to veer east, away from its destination. Now fighting at distances of less than 3,000 yards, the Japanese gunners continued to rain shells on their opponents. Eventually, their battle line crossed the Russian "T", delivering the full weight of its broadsides to enemy ships that could only respond with those guns facing forward. The Russians wilted under this onslaught, scoring no significant hits of their own after the first half hour of the engagement.

Smothered by Kamimura's quick-firing artillery, the slab-sided *Oslia-bya* swung out of line with her upper works smashed and burning. She capsized and sank around 3 p.m., the first armored battleship ever sunk by gunfire alone. Next, the *Suvorov*, already a blazing inferno bereft of its forward funnel, fell out of line with a damaged rudder. The burning hulk remained afloat for many hours, providing an easy target for any Japanese ship that passed by. She was finally sent to the bottom by torpedo boats at around 7:20 p.m. Rozhdestvensky, *hors-de-combat* with serious wounds to his head and ankle, had long since been removed by a destroyer.

When the *Suvorov* drifted out of the fight, de-facto leadership passed to Captain Bukhovstov on the *Alexander III* by virtue of his position as next in line. Bukhovstov attempted to break away by cutting back across the Japanese wake, but Togo maintained contact by ordering the ships of the First Division to turn simultaneously to port. This expediency put the *Nisshin* at the head of the Japanese line and left the *Mikasa* trailing the pack. Kamimura did not follow immediately, but stayed on his original course long enough to put some shells into the *Suvorov*. From this point, his cruisers would operate independently, sometimes joining the battle line while other times functioning as a flying column that swooped down on cripples and other targets of opportunity. Meanwhile, the Japanese First Division reverted to its preferred order of battle when Bukhovstov repeated his maneuver. Togo again matched him with a simultaneous turn to port that not only blocked the escape attempt but also put the *Mikasa* back in the Japanese van. Shortly after 4 p.m., man's smoke and nature's mist gave the Russians a brief respite when the two fleets temporarily lost sight of each other.

Although the battle lines grappled in their death struggle, another fight was developing further south. Togo's cruisers looped around the main engagement and sought out Rozhdestvensky's cruisers, destroyers, and auxiliaries. (This force actually included fifteen protected cruisers and the obsolete battleship, *Chin Yen*, a relic that had been captured in the China War.) At 2:45 p.m., the Japanese Third and Fourth Divisions made contact with the First Division of Russian cruisers. As the auxiliaries scattered, the eight Japanese ships engaged the four Russian vessels at extreme range. The czar's ships gave a good account of themselves, partially because their number included two slow but powerful armored cruisers, *Dmitri Donskoy* and *Vladimir Monomakh*. Admiral Dewa's Third Division was cut in half when a hit on the *Kasagi*'s coal bunker started a serious leak and forced her to retire to port under escort of the *Chitose*. Two cruisers in Admiral Uryu's Fourth Division were also damaged, but these made repairs and continued to fight. At 4:45 p.m., the Fifth and Sixth Japanese Divisions entered the fray along with the Second Russian Cruiser Division. From that point on, the battle went decidedly against the Russians. The *Oleg* and the *Aurora* were raked by numerous hits that started small fires. Each of the four lighter cruisers in the Second Division was also hit. By 6 p.m., when the Japanese cruisers deferred to their approaching torpedo flotillas, the Russian cruisers were spent. Most followed the example of their auxiliaries and scattered to the four winds. The old *Dmitri Donskoy* stayed and fought into the night before limping away.

Meanwhile, Togo had rediscovered the enemy battle line and closed the range to begin the next round of the main event. This time, the *Alexander III* and *Borodino* were the main recipients of the Japanese gunners' attention. The period without combat had done nothing for the Russian gun crews as their return fire remained slow and inaccurate. Soon the *Alexander III* fell out of line and disappeared into the smoke of battle. Kamimura's cruisers noted her sinking a little after 7 p.m. No more is known of her fate because not one of her nine hundred crewmen survived to tell the tale. The fate of the *Borodino* was more publicized. She exploded and sank just before dusk, the victim of a parting salvo from the battleship *Fuji*. Next morning, a Japanese destroyer picked up her only survivor, who was clinging to a piece of a shattered lifeboat.

With the coming of night, the Japanese battle line withdrew and turned its prey over to the destroyers and torpedo boats. Togo's big ships had not achieved their success without cost. Among the battleships, the first two in line had predictably suffered the most. The *Mikasa* had been hit more than thirty times with a resulting 8 dead and 105 wounded while the *Shikishima* endured ten hits, leaving 13 dead and 25 wounded. Eight hits on the *Nisshin* destroyed three of her 8-inch guns, killed 5 of her crew and injured 90 more. (Among the wounded was ensign Isoruka Yamamoto who lost two of his fingers during his baptism of fire.) None of the other armored cruisers suffered serious damage or heavy casualties. The *Iwate* was struck by sixteen enemy shells, but incredibly had no one killed and only 15 wounded. Except for the *Kasagi*, all of the Japanese battleships and cruisers that faced the Russians on the morning of May 27 were still battle worthy by nightfall.[45]

Togo's twenty-one destroyers and thirty-seven torpedo boats had something to prove after their poor showing at the Yellow Sea. Throughout the night, they ruthlessly stalked their enemies and attacked them with reckless abandon. In terms of accuracy, the performance of the small ships was not impressive. Only seven of the one hundred torpedoes that they launched struck home.[46] However, in terms of damage inflicted, the torpedo flotillas were devastating. In addition to dispatching the *Suvorov*, they completed the destruction of the Russian Second Division, sinking the *Navarin* and damaging the *Nakhimov* and *Sissoi Veliky* so extensively that they were eventually scuttled. For good measure, a torpedo blew off the bow of the cruiser *Vladimir Monomakh*, which was subsequently scuttled just before dawn.

Morning found Admiral Nebogatov's *Nicholas I* leading the remnants of the czar's Second and Third Pacific Squadrons in some semblance of a battle line. In addition to his flagship, Nebogatov commanded the fast protected cruiser *Izumrud*, the battered *Orel*, and the coast defense ironclads *Apraksin* and *Seniavin*. (The third coast defense "flat iron," *Ushakov*, was badly damaged and languished far to the rear.) This ragged procession crawled along toward Vladovostok until smoke on the horizon heralded the arrival of the Combined Fleet.

Togo's First and Second Divisions approached the Russian ships in a crescent formation while his smaller cruisers and torpedo craft fanned out to complete the encirclement. The Japanese battleships then began a deliberate bombardment from 12,000 yards, a range that put them beyond the reach of the remaining Russian guns. When Nebogatov realized that he could offer no effective resistance, he ordered his signals officer to raise the international code flags XGE, meaning "We Surrender." But the Japanese fire did not abate so the Russian admiral ran a white tablecloth up his flag pole. This still did not produce the desired result. Finally, in desperation, Nebogatov had a Rising Sun hoisted to his masthead and ordered his ships to stop their engines.

The Japanese did not respond to the XGE flags because they simply did not recognize a signal that they would never have used themselves. After a code book was produced and a translation provided, Togo doubted the Russians' sincerity. In 1894, a Chinese warship had escaped his *Naniwa* by feigning surrender and then racing away. He remained unconvinced by the white flag and had his skepticism reinforced when the *Izumrud* struck its XGE pennant and sailed away at full speed. Togo sent two cruisers to pursue the runaway and allowed the bombardment of the encircled ships to continue.

However, Togo's operations officer, Commander Masayuki Akiyama, was troubled by the actions of his admiral and said, "Sir, the enemy has surrendered. Shouldn't you give the order to cease fire?" The Japanese commander gave no answer, but merely gripped his sword as he continued to observe the work of his gunners.

When the Rising Sun appeared on the masthead of the *Nicholas I*, Akiyama tried again, "Sir, doesn't the spirit of bushido compel us to stop firing?"

Togo's reply was that of an international lawyer, "Their ships are still in formation and still moving. If they mean to surrender, they should first stop their engines."[47]

This silenced the ethical young officer who was no doubt relieved that Nebogatov soon satisfied his commander's conditions for surrender. When the Russian ships became stationary, Togo finally called off his heavy artillery. Years later, he explained his feelings at that moment: "It was utterly beyond our expectations. We had opened fire with the strongest determination to annihilate them at once, but all in vain. It really was the strangest occurrence, and we were astonished and somewhat disappointed."[48]

Mopping up operations continued throughout the day. Three Japanese cruisers cornered the undergunned cruiser *Svetlana* and blasted her into oblivion. A little past 3 p.m., the destroyer *Bedovy* surrendered to two of her Japanese counterparts, yielding among others the injured Admiral Rozhdestvensky. Russia's final capital ship was accounted for not long after when the *Ushakov* was pounded into floating rubble by the armored cruisers *Iwate* and *Yagumo*. Her acting captain then ordered the seacocks opened and went down with his ship. The fate of the *Dmitry Donskoy* was also heroic. After engaging six enemy cruisers for nearly two hours, the ancient armored cruiser once again found safety in darkness. She proceeded to land the bulk of her crew on Matsushima Island, after which she was returned to deep water and scuttled.

When Togo called on the convalescing Rozhdestvensky at Sasebo, he was conciliatory and overly-generous in his praise. The victorious admiral told his former opponent: "There is no need for a warrior to associate an honorable defeat with shame. We fighting men suffer either way, win or lose. The only question is whether or not we do our duty. During the battle your men fought most gallantly and I admire them all and you in particular. You performed your great task heroically until you were incapacitated. I pay you my highest respects."[49]

It is doubtful that a defeated Admiral Togo would have been so sanguine in accepting duty over victory. His magnanimity sprang at least partially from the knowledge that he had produced a success worthy of his role model. Where Nelson had posthumously taken or destroyed eighteen of the thirty-three wooden ships that he faced at Trafalgar, Togo sank or captured all twelve of his enemy's battle line one hundred years later. Of the thirty-eight Russian ships present at Tsushima, only the auxiliary cruiser *Almaz* and the destroyers *Bravy* and *Grozny* reached their destination at Vladovostok. Four of the cruisers were lost, including the *Izumrud*, which escaped her pursuers only to run aground in a fog and be blown up by her crew. The fast cruisers *Oleg*, *Aurora*, and *Zhemchung* made it to Manila where they were interned along with two destroyers. Another destroyer was incarcerated at Shanghai, three were sunk, and one was captured. Most of the auxiliaries were also lost, although the *Anadyr* actually made it back to Russia by way of Madagascar! More than 12,000 Russian sailors were killed, captured, or interned. The cost to the Japanese was 117 dead and three torpedo boats sunk.[50]

VI

Strategically, Togo's victory at Tsushima eliminated any potential threat to Japan's maritime lifeline to the Asian mainland. Psychologically, its impact on the Russo-Japanese War was more far reaching. Despite all her reverses, Russia's situation on land was actually improving, as reinforcements continued to stream into Manchuria, completely immune from the material effects of Japanese seapower. Perseverance in the spirit of Peter the Great or Alexander I might still turn things around for Nicholas II. But news of the Tsushima disaster fanned the flames of an already burning Russian dissidence and helped transform it into a revolutionary fire that threatened the regime itself. This deterioration of domestic security finally compelled the czar to accept President Theodore Roosevelt's offer to host a peace conference to settle the matter.

The resulting Treaty of Portsmouth was not entirely satisfactory to the Japanese nation. By its terms, Japan acquired Port Arthur and its environs, the southern half of Sakhalin Island, fishing rights in Russian waters and "predominance" in Korea.[51] However, the treaty did not include the indemnity that had been sought to reimburse the bankrupt nation for the cost of the war. Its publication was met with outbursts of anger from the Japanese press and people, much of which was directed at the United States for its perceived role as dishonest broker. In fact, Roosevelt was sympathetic to Japan's position but had pushed them to drop their demand for an indemnity primarily because he felt that it was shifting world opinion against them and might even rehabilitate Russian morale sufficiently to allow the czar to prolong the war. Unfortunately, this was not apparent to the mobs who rioted and tried to storm the U.S. legation in Tokyo on the day the treaty was signed.

The battle of Tsushima was one of the most overwhelming victories ever won at sea. In terms of tactics and weaponry, its military significance would be short-lived. The ships that fought at Tsushima would soon be made obsolete by HMS *Dreadnought*, and their mode of fighting would pass into history with the development of air power and submarines. But to the officers and men of the Japanese navy, Tsushima was the moral equivalent of Trafalgar. Soon they would believe themselves capable of challenging even their mentors. Admiral Togo left to his service a legacy of invincibility that would remain intact for nearly four decades.

In December 1905, Togo addressed the officers of the Combined Fleet one final time before leaving to become naval chief of staff. He told them,

"Heaven gives the crown of victory to those who by habitual preparation are victorious even before they go into battle. But heaven forthwith deprives of that crown those who, content with one success, give themselves up to the ease of peace. In the hour of victory, tighten the straps of your helmet."[52]

Admiral Heihachiro Togo would remain a revered figure within the Imperial Japanese navy throughout its remaining forty years of life. However, in the ultimate contest for dominance of the Pacific Region, some of Togo's heirs would suffer a lapse of memory and forget his parting wisdom. But prior to the presentation of that tale, the theater of high naval drama shifts its focus back to European waters.

3

The Man Who Could Lose the Empire in an Afternoon

I

On June 28, 1914, in the Bosnian capital of Sarajevo, a disgruntled Serbian nationalist joined the ranks of those little men whose desperate acts give them claim to a disproportionate historical impact. Gavrilo Princip's two bullets not only ended the lives of Archduke Franz Ferdinand and his wife but also set off a conflagration that would consume three Imperial Dynasties and transform the world's political and social orders. As heir to the Austro-Hungarian throne, Franz Ferdinand had been viewed with a jaundiced eye by the notables of Vienna. He was too receptive to the aspirations of the Empire's subject nationalities and his wife's manners too clearly reflected her low social standing. Now, the deceased couple provided a pretext to crush Serbia and eliminate a major source of nationalistic agitation. But Russia's czar viewed himself as protector of southern Slavic peoples and intervened on Serbia's behalf. The German kaiser, whose nation was bound to Austria by alliance since 1879, backed Vienna to the hilt. This brought in France, which was pledged to support Russia when the latter was opposed by more than one other great power. Thus, Europe willingly marched into the conflict that would dissipate its wealth and manpower to such an extent that it would never recover its position of unassailable world predominance.

It was not a foregone conclusion that Great Britain would throw herself on the funeral pyre that was lit at Sarajevo. Unlike the other principals, England was not bound by any formal alliance that compelled her to participate in Europe's self-destruction. However, a deteriorating world position and more than a decade of antagonism toward Germany had set the stage for her involvement in the unfolding tragedy.

Great Britain had entered the twentieth century with a smugness befitting a nation at the apex of its power. She possessed the world's richest economy and held an empire that encompassed nearly one quarter of the planet's land and population. But the proud tower had fissures in its mortar. Its ruling class of gentlemen-amateurs, schooled more in the classics than in calculus, was proving itself either unwilling or unable to fully embrace the emerging technologies necessary to maintain the nation's preeminence. England's economy had peaked some thirty years before and was in the midst of a slow but steady decline. In 1870, the island nation had 32 percent of the world's manufacturing capacity and 25 percent of the world's trade. By 1900, its share of both items had fallen below 15 percent.[1] This trend continued into the new century, especially in the industrial sector. Britain's economy remained robust only because of the return on her foreign investments, the trafficking of goods by her merchant fleet, and her dominance in the banking and insurance fields.

Meanwhile, Germany's fortunes were clearly on the rise. The new century found her in the midst of an explosion of growth that would make her Europe's leading industrial economy. German steel mills exceeded the output of their British competitors in 1896 and by 1914 were turning out 14 million tons annually versus only 6.5 million tons in the United Kingdom.[2] (The United States was outproducing both combined but her geographic distance and disjointed foreign policy made her a secondary player in world affairs.) This material expansion was accompanied by an explosion of procreation, which increased the Second Reich's population by nearly 50 percent.[3] Unlike England, Germany sought to fully develop her human potential by establishing a system of education that was broad based and scientifically oriented. Thus, she added to her successes in manufacturing by also becoming a world leader in the chemical and electrical industries.

Yet, none of this was as threatening as Kaiser Wilhelm II's decision to challenge the British at sea. The architect of German Naval expansion was Admiral Alfred von Tirpitz. Although the kaiser wanted a navy, it was Tirpitz who convinced his sovereign and all concerned that Germany needed battleships. In a secret memorandum, composed almost immediately on becoming the Reich's naval minister, Tirpitz stated his case:

For Germany, the most dangerous naval enemy at the present time is England.

Our fleet must be constructed so that it can unfold its greatest military potential between Heligoland and the Thames.

The military situation against England demands battleships in as great a number as possible.

Only the main theatre of war will be decisive.

A German Fleet built against England requires: one fleet flagship, two squadrons of eight battleships each, two reserve battleships for a total of 19 battleships.

This fleet can be largely completed by 1905.[4]

Tirpitz secured the Reichstag's commitment to his build up in the German Naval Law of 1898. Two years later, when the legislation was amended to provide for thirty-eight battleships, England began to stir. The preamble of the Reich's new Naval Law included the following: "Germany must have a battle fleet so strong that even for the adversary with the greatest sea-power, a war against it would involve such dangers as to imperil his own position in the world."[5]

Even without access to the inner counsels of German government, the British admiralty recognized itself as the target of the kaiser's new navy. Germany had no need of a high seas fleet to fight its potential continental enemies, Russia and France. Her formidable army would decide that issue on its own. Furthermore, German ship design provided cramped living quarters and limited cruising ranges, clear evidence of an intention to operate strictly in the North Sea. This realization forced Great Britain to make changes in both her naval and diplomatic policies. Where the former was concerned, the nation was fortunate to find a match for Tirpitz in Admiral John ("Jackie") Arbuthnot Fisher.

In his tenure at the admiralty, Fisher transformed the British navy from a lumbering relic into a modern fighting force. As second sea lord, he completely revamped the method of training officers, devising a more uniform system that improved morale and professional skills. After spending one year as commander of Portsmouth's dockyard and training facilities, Fisher returned to Whitehall as first sea lord on October 21, 1904. His first act was to redistribute the fleet, concentrating a greater portion in home and Atlantic waters at the expense of Asia and the Mediterranean. He also instituted a nucleus crew system for the Reserve Fleet, which permanently assigned two fifths of each ship's complement, including all crucial officers and specialists. In time of war, the cadres of regulars would be quickly fleshed out with naval reservists. The additional personnel necessary to man the cadres were gleaned by scrapping 154 obsolete vessels whose main purpose had been to display the Union Jack in obscure places around the globe.

Fisher's many sea commands had convinced him that the Royal Navy paid too much attention to pomp and polish while neglecting practical combat skills, especially gunnery. To remedy that deficiency, he created the office of inspector of target practice and appointed Rear Admiral Percy Scott to head it. Scott had been a vocal advocate of better gunnery since his days as a junior officer. Largely on his own initiative, he had invented several devices to provide more realistic training, including the "dotter," which simulated the rolling conditions that would turn a ship into a bobbing target. Scott's innovations, which had already been perfected in ships under his captaincy, were now applied fleet wide. Accuracy improved almost immediately, despite the first sea lord's institution of "battle practice," which increased the firing range by 5,000 yards. Soon, most British ships were shooting better at 7,000 yards than they had been at 2,000 yards a few years before.[6] But Fisher's most profound impact would come from his role in the construction of HMS *Dreadnought*, a warship that represented a quantum leap in naval technology.

The intellectual foundation for an "all big-gun ship" can be traced to an Italian naval engineer named Vittorio Cuniberti. In 1903, *Jane's Fighting Ships* published Cuniberti's proposal for a battleship possessing the maximum number of big guns, a high speed, 12-inch armor, and no secondary armament. It postulated that the super battleship's overwhelming weight of shell could dispatch an opponent at extreme range and then use its superior speed to repeat the feat as often as was necessary.[7]

Fisher's proposed design was quite similar. His leviathan would carry ten 12-inch guns, steam at 21 knots, have an armored belt 11 inches thick, and carry no other armament except some light quick-firers for use against torpedo craft. These specifications would give the *Dreadnought* a clear superiority over contemporary battleships in long-range guns (ten vs. four) and speed (21 vs. 18 knots), while maintaining parity in armor protection. Her superior speed would come from turbine engines that also proved to be more reliable than the piston-driven power plants they supplanted. The first sea lord made no reference to Cuniberti and later claimed that he had formed his own idea independently while serving as commander of the Mediterranean Fleet in 1900.[8] (Perhaps the fecund Mediterranean climate coincidentally cultivated the same idea in both men.)

A swelling wave of revisionist scholarship adamantly purports that Fisher never wanted battleships at all but favored a fleet based on submarines and the battleship's faster but less heavily armored cousin, the battlecrusier.[9] This school holds that battleships were forced on him by the conservative members of the admiralty's committee on designs.[10] If this view is correct, the committee's traditional mindset must have been impregnable indeed, for Fisher was not inclined toward compromise. Furthermore, he considered the components of his reform program to be interlocutory and his mantra against opposition was "The Scheme! The Whole Scheme!

And nothing but the Scheme!"[11] Yet, despite his strident views and penchant for bombast, Fisher was a skilled political in-fighter who knew when to cut his losses. It is not inconceivable that he would have sacrificed part of his program to preserve the bulk of it.

Whatever his preferred form might have been, Fisher was unquestionably the prime mover in getting the turbine-driven, all big-gun warship to sea. On October 3, 1906, HMS *Dreadnought* was ready for her sea trials, one year and one day after her keel had been laid down at Portsmouth. The speed of her construction amplified the message conveyed by her superior capabilities: Britannia still ruled the waves. But Germany picked up the gauntlet and the naval race became steadily more expensive and acrimonious.

As she faced up to Germany's challenge, England found the need to look for friends. For nearly a century, the British government had shunned formal alliances and followed an aloof policy of independence that Lord Salisbury termed *splendid isolation*. This changed with the Anglo-Japanese Treaty of 1902. Britain's arrangements closer to home were less formal. Her ententes with France and Russia merely resolved colonial disputes and provided a basis for more friendly relations. However, military "conversations" with France did produce joint contingency plans for war against Germany should England become involved. France soon took British participation for granted, counting on the Royal Navy to protect her northern coastline and factoring in six British divisions to secure her army's left flank. To many political and military leaders in the United Kingdom, such reliance was reasonable because it was based on moral commitments made to the French, both expressed and implied. In the end, this attitude combined with alarm and outrage over German violation of Belgium's neutrality brought England into the war.

As Europe's diplomatic skies were darkening, the British battle fleet was undertaking a test mobilization at war strength. At its conclusion, first lord of the admiralty, Winston Churchill prudently kept the fleet concentrated and sent it to its war station at Scapa Flow in the Orkneys. There would be no Port Arthurs on Winston's watch. When war came, the fleet would be ready but its commander, the venerable Admiral George Callaghan, was considered too old to lead it. On August 3, 1914, Churchill sent the following communiqué to Admiral John Jellicoe, already chosen as Callaghan's successor but too respectful to present himself as such: "I am telegraphing to the Commander-in-chief directing him to transfer command to you at earliest moment suitable to the interests of the Services. I rely on him and you to effect this change quickly and smoothly, personal feeling cannot count now only what is best for us all, you should consult with him frankly, FIRST LORD."[12]

II

John Rushworth Jellicoe was born in Southampton on December 5, 1859. Love of the sea came to him at an early age, fostered by his maritime surroundings as well as his father's distinguished service with the Royal Mail Steam Packet Company. At age twelve, young John began two years of nautical training on HMS *Britannia*, an old three decker moored in the River Dart. There, he began to display the combination of mental ability and athletic prowess that still remain the cornerstones of a successful military career. Cadet Jellicoe took first honors in each of his terms and also overcame his slight physical stature to excel at cricket and rugby. He was the classic "all-rounder," described by his captain as "one of the cleverest cadets we have ever had."[13]

After serving four years at sea as a midshipman, Jellicoe returned to England for further study, earning first class certificates in torpedoes and gunnery. Now a lieutenant, he decided to specialize in the latter discipline once his next tour of sea duty was completed. That stint took him to Egypt where he saw his first "action" couriering dispatches across the Suez Canal while disguised as a native refugee. On returning to England, Jellicoe took courses at Greenwich and Portsmouth in order to qualify as a gunnery lieutenant. He achieved his customary top grades and also maintained his physical edge by playing wing-forward on the rugby team and perfecting his tennis game.

While at Portsmouth, Jellicoe caught the eye of Fisher, who was then captain of the navy's gunnery school housed on HMS *Excellent*. When Fisher was posted to sea duty the following year, he took Jellicoe with him as his staff officer. This choice assignment showed that, despite his junior grade and brief association with Fisher, Jellicoe was now a member of "the Fishpond," the nickname used by critics to describe the coterie of officers that Fisher had marked for future greatness.

Jellicoe's next two assignments kept him at sea for fifteen months as a gunnery lieutenant but he then spent more than five years in gunnery related staff positions. In December 1886, he was appointed experimental officer on the *Excellent* and supervised the development of new, quick firing 4.7-inch and 6-inch guns. After eighteen months in that capacity, Jellicoe was elevated to the *Excellent*'s senior staff, from which he vaulted after another sixteen months to the admiralty itself. Fisher was now director of naval ordnance and brought Jellicoe with him as his junior assistant, a position of detail-oriented drudgery that often required its holder to work past 11 p.m.

While toiling as Fisher's "details man," Jellicoe was promoted to commander and, after putting in thirty months at the admiralty, returned to sea duty in 1892 as executive officer on HMS *Sans Pareil*. His performance as first officer was so impressive that within one year's time he was transferred to the same billet on board HMS *Victoria*, the flagship of the Mediterranean Fleet. Shortly after assuming his duties on the flagship, Jellicoe nearly lost his life in one of the worst disasters ever experienced by the Royal Navy.

On June 22, 1893, Admiral Sir George Tryon's battle fleet was cruising in two columns off the Lebanese coast. Intending to reverse course while maintaining formation, Tryon ordered his ships to turn 180° inwards in succession, his own *Victoria* and HMS *Camperdown* heading the starboard and port columns, respectively. This maneuver was not dangerous provided there were ten cables (one mile) of ocean between the lines of turning ships. Unfortunately, the actual interval was closer to six cables. When apprised of this fact by his staff, the admiral merely confirmed the order, which was subsequently executed. Once the looming catastrophe finally became apparent, both ships reversed engines, but to no avail. The *Camperdown* rammed the *Victoria*, sending the flagship to the bottom along with 358 of her crew and Admiral Tryon.

When the crash occurred, Jellicoe was in his bunk with a fever of 103°. On feeling the impact, he came on deck and, on his own initiative, ordered the lifeboats to be lowered. He abandoned that task when he discovered that the boat hoist was out of action, soon seeking to abandon ship as well. As Jellicoe was climbing down the port torpedo nets, his vessel turned turtle, putting him under the water in a disoriented state. Training and athletic ability soon took over, however, allowing him to swim away before the ship sucked him down with it. Incredibly, what should have been a trauma served instead as a tonic. Jellicoe's fever was gone the next morning and he showed no signs of the despondency which gripped his fellow survivors. On the ship back to England, he passed time by leading a group of midshipmen in daily calisthenics.

Jellicoe's physical incapacity at the time of the collision between the *Victoria* and the *Camperdown* shielded him from any blame for the tragedy. But the ensuing investigation of the incident provided a window on the cult of obedience that dominated the officers of his service. The inquiry revealed that two ships' captains, as well as Rear Admiral Albert Markham, who commanded the Second Division from the *Camperdown* had dutifully followed an order which was prima facie disastrous. Although Markham had initially hesitated, he promptly executed the command after being prodded by Tryon's signal, "What are you waiting for?"[14] The court of inquiry "regretted" that Markham did not follow through on his doubts and seek clarification, but nevertheless placed full responsibility for the accident on the shoulders of the late Admiral Tryon. It felt that it would be "fatal to the best interests of the service" to blame a subordinate for carrying out the directions of his commander in chief.[15]

Some solace might have been salvaged for the *Victoria* fiasco if it had prompted corrective action within the Royal Navy. Certain officers saw the necessity for this, including one admiral who wrote, "The one lesson to be learned is the necessity for every officer to cultivate belief in his own judgment, so as not to be afraid of acting correctly when the day of trial comes."[16] But the majority view was probably best expressed by another officer, who would one day command the Channel Fleet, "Unconditional obedience, no matter at what cost, is, in brief, the only principle on which those in the service must act."[17] With such eloquent proponents, the mindset that sank the *Victoria* would certainly survive well into the new century.

Jellicoe next spent three years as the executive officer of the brand new battleship *Ramillies* with, in his words, "a complement of officers second to none in the service."[18] In his later years, Jellicoe would describe this period of his life in almost idyllic terms. Yet, it was also at this time that he began to decry the fact that his service did not share his passion for proficiency with sea-born artillery, writing, "Gunnery efficiency in the modern sense was I fear non-existent. An annual competition prize firing was carried out off Malta at a range of some 1,600 yards and fire control was unheard of, as was long-range practice. . . . Gunnery work took rather a back seat in considering the smartness and efficiency of a ship's company."[19]

On the first day of January 1897, Jellicoe was promoted to captain and after serving a year on the joint Army–Navy Ordnance Committee, received the command of HMS *Centurion*, flagship of the China Squadron. The young flag captain's stay in the Far East provided him with a horizon-broadening experience of the first magnitude, weaving sports, travel social contact, and professional achievement into his tapestry of personal development. He played cricket on a regular basis, won the squadron tennis tournament at Hong Kong, and beat the kaiser's brother in a rifle shooting match. Jellicoe traveled to Japan where he admired the manners of Japanese women and, on his second visit, was formally received by the emperor. He also paid close attention to the foreign naval contingents he encountered, finding Dewey's Americans shockingly undisciplined but acquiring a deep respect for the efficiency of the Germans.

During the Boxer Rebellion, Jellicoe saw his first real combat, ironically on land, when he led the British contingent in the naval brigade that attempted to relieve the besieged legations at Peking. The international relief column met heavy resistance and gave up its quest when the Boxers severed the rail connection to its base at Tientsin. The rescuers were now themselves besieged and had to fight their way to safety. With no land transport available, the column loaded its supplies on river junks and began a laborious retreat along the banks of the waterway. Each village in its path presented a fortified obstacle that had to be overcome with the bayonet. While leading one of these desperate assaults, Jellicoe was wounded in the chest and experienced internal bleeding so severe that he deemed it prudent to draft a will. The column's situation was no less perilous, with ammunition running low and little prospect of covering the remaining distance to friendly lines. However, salvation came the very next day with the capture of Hsiku Arsenal, where the Europeans found rifles, machine guns, and millions of rounds of ammunition. Although still unable to force its way through the hostile countryside, the column was able to hunker down and defend itself until it was rescued by another relief force. Meanwhile, Jellicoe's condition had stabilized by virtue of Hsiku's medical supplies and his own tough constitution. He was evacuated and recovered on ship but retained a bullet in his lung, which brought him occasional cramps and rheumatism for the remainder of his life.

Jellicoe returned to England for two tours at the admiralty, with the captaincy of an armored cruiser in between. In July 1903, he married Gwendoline Cayzer, second daughter of Sir Charles Cayzer, and set up housekeeping in London. Jellicoe was doubly blessed by the union, which widened his social contacts and gave him a happy domestic life. Fisher's patronage continued to be a key ingredient in his rise, but Jellicoe's industry and innate abilities were in themselves sufficient to impress most everyone he came into contact with. Also in his favor was the fact that, unlike his mentor, Jellicoe combined his overwhelming professional competence with an equally overwhelming likeability. He made few enemies and was polite almost to a fault with all ranks. A description of the aura surrounding England's coming man was provided by a correspondent who met him in China.

A man below the middle height, alert, with that in the calm brown eyes which spoke of decision and a serene confidence in himself, not the confidence of the over sure, but that of the real leader of men. A man whose features would have been unpleasantly hard but for the lurking humor of the eyes and for certain humorous lines about the mouth that on occasion could take the likeness of a steel trap. A man to trust instinctively and one to like from the beginning . . . he inspired me with the same feeling of affection with which he was regarded by everyone with whom he had occasion to come into close contact. There was, and is, a magnetism about the man which stamps the personality of one who is indeed a commander.[20]

In February 1907, Jellicoe was promoted to rear admiral and made second in command of the Atlantic Fleet. After a year at sea, he came once again to the admiralty, this time as controller. In this capacity, he raised two issues that would later prove him quite prophetic. Throughout the naval race, Great Britain built dreadnoughts that were more heavily gunned than German ships of the same generation. Jellicoe cautioned against the complacency this engendered by pointing out that the German ships were equal in displacement, thus indicating their potential advantage in other characteristics. (This advantage later showed up in the German vessels' heavier and more complete armor protection.) Jellicoe also warned that the British superiority in guns was somewhat negated by inferior shells that tests had shown to burst on impact when striking a target at an oblique angle. He urged the development of an armor-piercing shell with better powers of penetration but went off to command the Atlantic Fleet before he could see the matter through.

By this time, it was becoming accepted among Britain's naval establishment that Jellicoe was destined to command the Home Fleet, quite possibly in the eventual showdown with Germany. Fisher had no doubt whatsoever that his protégé should hold the fleet's reigns at the hour of decision. Although he was officially in retirement, the seventy-year-old dynamo remained the most influential naval authority in the United Kingdom. In 1911, he wrote to Winston Churchill at the admiralty: "I hope you have seen Jellicoe. He has all the Nelson attributes: 1) Self-reliance, 2) Fearlessness of Responsibility, 3) Fertility of Resource, 4) Power of Initiative. It won't be victory that Jellicoe will accomplish! It will be annihilation."[21]

Later that year, Churchill jumped Jellicoe over twenty more senior vice admirals and placed him in command of the Home Fleet's Second Division. Fisher's advocacy was unquestionably a major factor in the decision. Jellicoe needed this posting as a prerequisite to overall fleet commander because up to that point he had had no operational experience with dreadnought battleships. In addition, it was hoped that the time spent with England's largest fleet would cure one of Jellicoe's few apparent weaknesses: reluctance to delegate. First Sea Lord Sir Francis Bridgeman summed up the problem in a letter to Fisher:

[Jellicoe] has had no experience of fleet work on a big scale, and is so extremely anxious about the work in it that he really does too much. He must learn to work his captains and staff more and himself less! At present he puts himself in the position of, say, a glorified gunnery lieutenant. This will not do when he gets with a big fleet. He must trust his staff and captains and if they don't fit, he must kick them out![22]

Surprisingly, Nelson's anointed successor acted as if he was completely oblivious to the honor being bestowed on him. Jellicoe expressed a desire to remain with the Atlantic Fleet and accepted the new posting only after being told that he had no choice in the matter. His most pleasant duty with the Home Fleet turned out to be conducting tests of Percy Scott's new "director firing," whereby a ship's entire main battery was aimed and fired electronically by a single officer in an elevated observation post. Jellicoe was an instant convert but his enthusiasm was not universally shared within the service. Only eight battleships would be converted to director firing by the war's outbreak.

After spending a year with the dreadnoughts, Jellicoe became second sea lord. He repeatedly locked horns with Churchill on a variety of issues, including the adequacy of the Royal Navy's oil reserve. Although most of Britain's large ships still burned coal, oil powered her destroyers, submarines and the new "Queen Elizabeth" class battleships, then under construction. Churchill strongly resisted Jellicoe's "extravagant" proposal to increase naval oil reserves from three months war consumption to six months. A compromise of four-and-a-half months' supply was reached after the second sea lord threatened to resign over the dispute. None of these disagreements interfered with Jellicoe's marked destiny, however. In late July 1914, he was appointed second in command of the newly designated Grand Fleet and was then ordered to assume overall command once war became a certainty.

III

The Royal Navy faced a multitude of missions in the coming struggle. Defensively, it was charged with protecting the homeland from invasion and guaranteeing the flow of cargo and communication across her sea lanes. Although the specter of a sudden seaborne assault haunted many Englishmen for the war's duration, cooler heads rightfully concluded that no such operation was possible as long as the Grand Fleet maintained its superiority over the enemy's High Seas Fleet. England's true Achilles heel lay in her dependence on maritime commerce. On the eve of World War I, Great Britain imported 86 percent of her raw materials, 55 percent of her grain, and 40 percent of her meat. Fisher was right on the mark when he concluded, "It's not invasion we have to fear if our Navy's beaten, it's starvation."[23] At the war's outset, surface ships rather than submarines were viewed as the greatest threats to the British lifeline. The admiralty judged German capabilities based on those of their own boats, whose limited speed and range relegated them primarily to coastal defense. But this lack of vision also extended to the Germans. Tirpitz was surprised by the early success of his submarines, whose attacks were largely desultory. A coordinated strategy of undersea warfare against Britain's commerce was not formulated until early 1915.

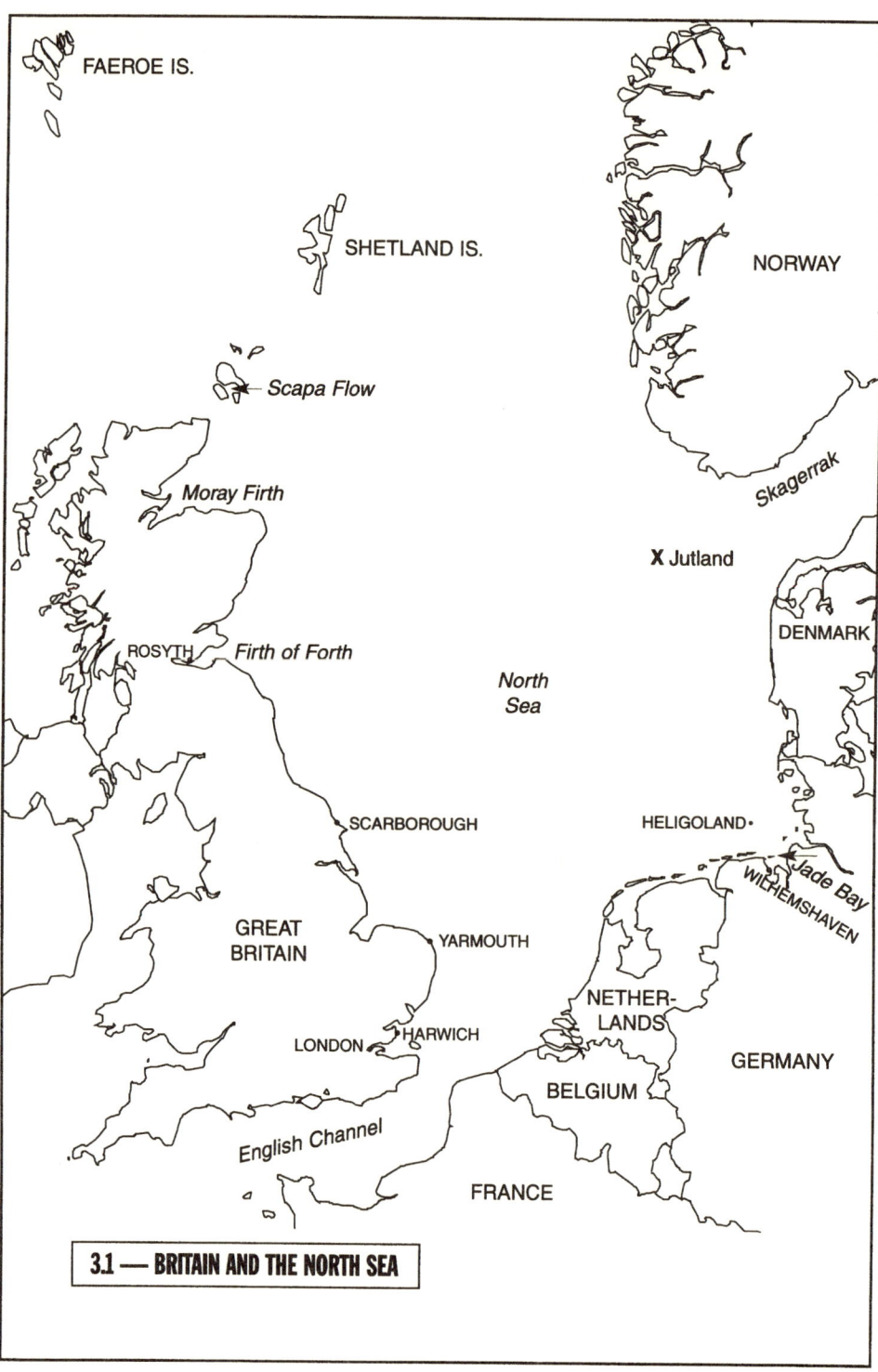

FAEROE IS.

SHETLAND IS.

NORWAY

Scapa Flow

Moray Firth

Skagerrak

X Jutland

ROSYTH Firth of Forth

DENMARK

North
Sea

SCARBOROUGH

HELIGOLAND •

Jade Bay

WILHEMSHAVEN

GREAT
BRITAIN

YARMOUTH

NETHER-
LANDS

LONDON   HARWICH

GERMANY

BELGIUM

English Channel

FRANCE

3.1 — BRITAIN AND THE NORTH SEA

Offensively, the Royal Navy's paramount task was the projection of British land forces onto the continent. Jellicoe felt that conditions favored any German attempt to disrupt the British army's transit of the Channel because of the great distance separating its crossing points from the main concentration of British naval strength in northern Scotland. He feared that the High Seas Fleet might risk some of its numerically superior destroyer force to dash in, inflict losses, and then withdraw before the Grand Fleet could intervene. But the Germans chose not to contest the passage of the British Expeditionary Force to France, intending instead to destroy it along with its Gallic allies in the *Kesselschlacht* planned by von Schlieffen and then entrusted to von Moltke. But quick victory was foiled by the realities of time, space, and logistics as well as Moltke's faint heart. When the war degenerated into a four-year ordeal of attrition, Britain's ground commitment escalated to a level that would have been unimaginable in 1914. Nevertheless, her navy unfailingly maintained the army in France throughout the struggle.

The navy also mounted its own strategic assault on Germany in the form of its blockade. Traditionally, an effective blockade required the establishment of a continuous naval presence in close proximity to an enemy's ports. However, an admiralty study concluded that submarines and surface torpedo craft made a blockade of this nature "impossible."[24] British naval thinkers may have underestimated the U-boat's potential against merchant ships in open ocean but they had already developed a healthy respect for the sub's potency against loitering warships. Therefore, a long-range blockade was initiated that essentially aimed at sealing the exits from the North Sea. The English Channel was closed by a mine barrier, a destroyer flotilla at Dover, and four squadrons of pre-dreadnoughts with the Channel Fleet. Northern exits were blocked by cruiser patrols between the Shetlands, Iceland, and Norway with the Grand Fleet at Scapa Flow in close support. Two destroyer flotillas and a few cruisers based at Harwich guarded the Channel's eastern approaches and could theoretically join the Grand Fleet in any major operation in the North Sea.

Every British seaman from Jellicoe down to the lowest rating eagerly anticipated the navy's remaining mission: engagement of the German High Seas Fleet. The Grand Fleet had good reason to face such an encounter with optimism. When Jellicoe raised his flag aboard the battleship *Iron Duke* on August 4, he commanded twenty dreadnoughts and four battlecruisers against the thirteen and three with Admiral von Ingenohl at Wilhelmshaven in Jade Bay. He also had the eight first-class pre-dreadnoughts of the 3rd Battle Squadron at his disposal and would soon get four on temporary assignment from the 6th Battle Squadron of the Channel Fleet. These served as a counterweight to the sixteen old battleships possessed by the Germans.

However, because their top speed was three knots less than the dreadnoughts, these ships could not maneuver with the rest of the battlefleet and were assigned to the Channel Fleet in early November. The battlecruiser *Invincible* would soon come over from Ireland, followed by her sister, the *Inflexible*, up from the Mediterranean by the end of the month. Three new battleships, built for other navies but requisitioned by England, began arriving at Scapa Flow in early September and were all present by mid-October. During this same period, the High Seas Fleet would be augmented by two new battleships and one new battlecruiser.[25]

But Jellicoe's ardor for combat was dampened by the burden of his role as the guarantor of all the other missions. It was British superiority at the highest level of potential conflict that prevented the German Fleet from lingering at sea long enough to support an invasion, interdict the flow of soldiers to France or break up the blockade. And the same blockade that denied the ocean to Germany's merchantmen also denied it to her commerce raiders, thus limiting them to cruisers already on foreign station when hostilities commenced. (The significance of the last point would diminish once the U-boats asserted themselves.)

Of course, the surest way to prevent interference from the High Seas Fleet was to destroy it in a decisive battle. In Jellicoe's own words, "The fleet exists to achieve victory."[26] But Jellicoe doubted from the war's onset that the kaiser would be so cooperative as to expose his Gordian Knot to England's sword. He felt it more likely that any German offer of battle would be a ploy to lure the British Fleet into a minefield or the torpedoes of lurking submarines. This threat had to be taken seriously, for Jellicoe had no doubt about the capabilities of his enemy. He retained his healthy respect for the quality of German naval personnel and still believed unequivocally, and quite correctly, that their capital ships were better protected than his own. He was acutely aware that the High Seas Fleet had been granted a generous allowance of ammunition for gunnery practice and that it possessed a well-developed safe haven in Kiel Bay to expend it. Because Britain's strategic objectives could be achieved by merely containing the German Fleet, Jellicoe decided that he would accept battle only on his own terms. He intended to assume an offensive posture by keeping his ships at sea as much as possible and engaging them in training exercises or broad "sweeps" of the North Sea. However, these activities were restricted to waters above the 54th parallel of latitude in order to minimize the danger from mines and submarines. To safeguard against piecemeal destruction, Jellicoe issued very un-Nelsonian battle orders that stressed the need to keep the fleet concentrated, under central control and in a single line of battle. Although squadron commanders were given theoretical authority to act independently after the fleet's initial deployment into line, the instructions heavily favored the single line as the best method that could be devised to fight a fleet action.[27]

IV

First blood in the naval war would be drawn by the battlecruisers under Vice-Admiral Sir David Beatty. Fisher had conceived the battlecruiser as the Dreadnought Age's successor to the armored cruiser, with greater speed but thinner armor than modern battleships. But the new ships differed from their predecessors in that they were given main batteries with guns as powerful as those of their dreadnought contemporaries, albeit two barrels fewer in number. This combination of speed and power made the battlecruiser an unbeatable trump card against commerce raiders, theoretically allowing it to destroy hostile corsairs without ever coming within the range of their guns. When attached to the battle fleet, Fisher's battlecruisers formed a flying column that could stiffen friendly scouting forces or envelop the enemy's main body. At the war's beginning, the Royal Navy possessed nine of these vessels, five in home waters, three in the Mediterranean, and one in the Pacific. Germany had three full-fledged battlecruisers in the Jade, plus the *Blucher*, rated as a battlecruiser but really a hybrid armored cruiser with 8.2-inch guns. (Her remaining battlecruiser, the *Goeben*, began the war in the Mediterranean but made its way to Constantinople where its presence helped convince the Sultan to bring Turkey into the war on the side of the Central Powers.)

On August 28, 1914, Beatty took his battlecruisers to sea in support of the Harwich Force's raid into the Heligoland Bight. The admiralty hoped that an attack on German destroyer patrols near the island would bring some heavier ships into the sights of eight British submarines operating nearby. When Jellicoe heard of the plan, he requested permission to include the entire Grand Fleet but was allowed to commit only the battlecruisers and Commodore William Goodenough's 1st Light Cruiser Squadron. The British light forces sank a destroyer and a light cruiser but were soon confronted by a swarm of additional enemy cruisers that threatened to overwhelm them. At this point, Beatty's *Lion* led England's seaborne cavalry to the rescue. His battlecruisers obliterated two German light cruisers and scattered the rest, allowing all British ships to extricate themselves safely.

The luster of the Heligoland victory was dimmed somewhat by the failure to engage any of the kaiser's bigger ships. Rear Admiral Franz Hipper's battlecruisers had been ordered out, but they were slow in raising steam and then delayed by low tides. By the time Hipper arrived at the scene of battle, the British were long gone. But the consequences of Heligoland far exceeded Germany's material losses of three light cruisers and one destroyer. Beatty's audacity in the face of potential mines and submarines gave his nation a tremendous morale boost and convinced his opponents that the British retained their unshakable confidence and offensive spirit at sea. Accordingly, the kaiser explicitly instructed his admirals that the German Fleet was "to hold itself back and avoid actions which can lead to greater losses."[28]

After Heligoland, the commander of the Grand Fleet entered a time of troubles that did not fully abate until the next year. Jellicoe's main problem was his base. Scapa Flow was a dismal, wind-blown anchorage with inadequate shore facilities and nonexistent submarine defenses. A major point in its favor had been the mistaken belief that it lay beyond the U-boat's effective range, but sightings of German subs near the Orkneys dispelled that illusion during the first week of war. Jellicoe relied on expedient measures while awaiting the installation of the booms, nets, and mines that would provide a proper antisubmarine barrier. He blocked Scapa's lessor entrances with sunken merchant ships, guarded the main entrances with batteries of 12–pounders taken from battleships and kept the fleet at sea as much as possible.

The last solution exacerbated another of the admiral's problems: the destroyer shortage. Only forty-two such ships were present at Scapa, an amount that Jellicoe found inadequate to both screen the capital ships and serve as an offensive torpedo arm. As early as August 18, he had requested that one flotilla from Harwich be permanently attached to the Grand Fleet. The admiralty replied that such a move was unnecessary because the entire Harwich Force would simply join him at sea during any prospective fleet action. (Such a link-up never in fact occurred during the entire war.) Further complicating the matter, the destroyers' low fuel capacity and high maintenance requirements gave them considerably less sea stamina than the battleships and cruisers they were charged with protecting. Jellicoe's persistent pleas eventually brought him some additional destroyers, pulled from flotillas assigned to patrol England's east coast. In the meantime, he was often forced to keep his big ships at sea without escorts, although they understandably remained as far north as possible. One of his expediencies placed a pre-dreadnought from the 6th Battle Squadron at the head of each of the other four battle squadrons, earning those expendables the nickname "Mine Bumping Squadron."[29]

On September 1, a reported periscope sighting within the fleet's anchorage set off a flurry of shooting that became known among fleet wags as the "First Battle of Scapa." Although the intruder was probably a seal, this was not apparent at the time and would not have been accepted in the prevailing atmosphere in any event. In response, Jellicoe moved the fleet to Loch Ewe on the west coast of Scotland, where it remained for nearly three weeks. The Royal Navy's subhysteria rose even higher when three armored cruisers were sunk by U-9 off the Dutch Coast on September 22. Thus, when another phantom sighting set off the "Second Battle of Scapa" on October 7, Jellicoe took the battle fleet all the way to Loch Swilly on the Irish coast. This was so far away from the main theater of operations that it provided little more than a haven for coaling, keeping the British ships at sea for even longer periods of time. After a slight nudge from the admiralty, Jellicoe returned to Scapa on November 9. However, the base was still not fully secure from submarines, a fact that wore constantly on the Grand Fleet's commander. Fortunately for the British, the Germans had no idea of Scapa Flow's vulnerability and never mounted an underwater assault against it.

Jellicoe's level of anxiety rose even further during this period because of a drastic reduction in the ranks of his capital ships. On October 27, one of his most powerful dreadnoughts, the *Audacious*, struck a mine and sank in full view of the liner *Olympic*. Published photographs taken from the passenger ship prevented Churchill from concealing the loss. Additionally, the grueling pace of operations exposed flaws in machinery that, along with scheduled refits, put four battleships and one battlecruiser in the docks by the end of the month. Worse yet, the four afflicted battleships were all second-generation dreadnoughts, each carrying ten of the fearsome 13.5-inch guns that no German ship could match. Although the arrival of the new battlecruiser *Tiger* was imminent, and the battleship *Canada* was working up to fighting trim, Jellicoe's margin of superiority at that moment was only seventeen to fifteen in dreadnought battleships and five to four in battlecruisers.[30] It would soon be reduced even further.

On November 1, 1914, Vice-Admiral Maximilian von Spee's Pacific squadron met Rear Admiral Christopher Cradock's smaller force off the Chilean coast. Von Spee's veterans easily disposed of Cradock's outgunned reservists, sinking two British armored cruisers, and killing more than one thousand men, including the admiral. Four days later, Fisher, just out of retirement and back as first sea lord, sent Vice-Admiral Doveton Sturdee to the South Atlantic with the battlecruisers *Invincible* and *Inflexible* to avenge the defeat. On November 11, the battlecruiser *Princess Royal* was also detached from Beatty's command in order to block von Spee's possible transit through the Panama Canal. Jellicoe accepted his initial loss without comment but sharply protested the diversion of the *Princess Royal*. Its departure would momentarily leave Beatty with only three battlecruisers until the *New Zealand* returned from dock and the *Indomitable* could be re-deployed from the Mediterranean.

Most disturbingly, the diminution came on the heels of Hipper's bombardment of Yarmouth on November 3, in the first of his "tip and run" raids. Although the attack had no strategic significance whatsoever, it caused a public outcry over the lack of protection for England's east coast. Meanwhile, Jellicoe's protest availed him nothing other than the transfer of the 3rd Battle Squadron's eight pre-dreadnoughts back from the channel to Rosyth in the Firth of Forth. The admiralty's choice of location did not sit well with the Grand Fleet's commander, who promptly communicated his preference that the "King Edwards" be based at Scapa, as they had been before their move to the Channel. Churchill's reply curtly informed Jellicoe that not only must the 3rd Battle Squadron remain at Rosyth but the Grand Fleet must detach a group of destroyers to provide it with a screen! Additionally, Beatty's battlecruisers would henceforth be based at Cromarty in order to be closer to the threatened coastal towns. The moves of the large ships were all carried out, but Jellicoe did manage to browbeat the admiralty into assigning destroyers from Harwich to serve as a screen for the 3rd Battle Squadron. However, these vital little ships did not move north until late February 1915, and the Grand Fleet's destroyer arm remained stretched thin until that time.

Sturdee would annihilate von Spee's squadron off the Falkland Islands in December, thus vindicating Churchill and Fisher for further diluting their strength in home waters. However, the British were fortunate that the High Seas Fleet was not more aggressive or the weakness of the Grand Fleet might have been exposed. Admiral von Ingenohl, handcuffed by the kaiser's directive to preserve the fleet, remained relatively inactive and let the opportunity pass. The balance of capital ships would never again be as favorable to Germany as it was in the final months of 1914.

In the midst of his time of troubles, Jellicoe composed a statement of the principles that would govern his conduct in any future fleet action. His memorandum to the admiralty stated, in part:

The Germans have shown that they rely to a very great extent on submarines, mines and torpedoes, and there can be no doubt whatever that they will endeavor to make the fullest use of these weapons in a fleet action, especially since they possess an actual superiority over us in these particular directions. It therefore becomes necessary to consider our own tactical methods in relation to these forms of attack.

If, for instance, the enemy battle fleet were to turn away from an advancing fleet, I should assume that the intention was to lead us over mines and submarines, and should decline to be so drawn. I desire particularly to draw the attention of Their Lordships to this point, since it may be deemed a refusal of battle, and indeed might possibly result in failure to bring the enemy to action as soon as is expected and hoped. Such a result would be absolutely repugnant to the feelings of all British Naval Officers and men, but with new and untried methods of warfare new tactics must be devised to meet them. I feel that such tactics, if not understood, may bring odium upon me, but so long as I have the confidence of Their Lordships I intend to pursue what is, in my considered opinion, the proper course to defeat and annihilate the enemy's battle fleet, without regard to uninstructed opinion or criticism.

The situation is a difficult one. It is quite within the bounds of possibility that half our battle fleet might be disabled by underwater attack before the guns opened fire at all, if a false move is made, and I feel that I must constantly bear in mind the great probability of such attack and be prepared tactically to prevent its success.[31]

Jellicoe's memorandum, although indisputably an epistle of caution, nevertheless reveals something of the moral courage of its maker. Both Fisher and Churchill valued boldness above all else and were apt to confuse prudence with timidity. Yet, the admiralty was fully aware of the temporary unfavorable ratio in capital ships, which probably accounts for its expression of "full confidence" in Jellicoe's proposed conduct. Additionally, Fisher and Churchill may have failed to focus on the memo because they were too involved in concocting schemes for peripheral actions to break the deadlock on the Western Front.[32] (Fisher's proposal for a landing on the Baltic Coast was so ludicrous that it resurrected Bismarck's joke about arresting Britain's tiny army if it ever set foot in Germany. Churchill's grand scheme for the Dardanelles was yet to come.) In any event, Jellicoe feared a short memory at Whitehall and entrusted the positive reply to his banker for future reference.

Although it restimulated British fears of invasion, the shelling of Yarmouth was actually a mere hit-and-run raid used to cover a mine-laying operation. Because Britain's long-range blockade strategy deprived the U-boats of easy targets, Germany relied on indiscriminate mining of the open ocean as its method of reducing enemy naval strength. The *Audacious* met its fate off Ireland through this tactic. When Sturdee's victory in the Falklands revealed the absence of at least two battlecruisers from home waters, von Ingenohl judged the time ripe for another raid. He also decided to support Hipper with the entire High Seas Fleet, in direct contravention of his monarch's stricture against taking such risks.

This time, the British knew the Germans were coming. Allied intelligence had received a windfall late in August when the cruiser *Magdeburg* wrecked in the Gulf of Finland and yielded its code books to Russian scavengers. These were soon passed on to London where the admiralty set up a special operation to exploit them. By December, decoders in "Room 40" could decipher enough wireless traffic to know when a German naval sortie was about to occur. However, they could not always tell much more than that with any degree of certainty. Regarding the coming raid, intelligence knew that the enemy's battlecruisers would come out on December 16, but was not aware that they would be followed by the rest of the High Seas Fleet. Therefore, Jellicoe was once again denied permission to go to sea with his entire force. The admiralty's response would come from Beatty's four battlecruisers, Goodenough's light cruisers, and the Harwich Force, supported by the 3rd Battle Squadron, and one squadron of dreadnoughts from Scapa.

Unknown to him, von Ingenohl had been presented with precisely the scenario he had longed for since the war began. A major portion of British seapower would be exposed to destruction by a superior German force. But von Ingenohl tossed away his chance when he interpreted an early morning destroyer contact as a herald of the entire Grand Fleet. No doubt feeling the invisible hand of the kaiser on his shoulder, the German commander promptly reversed course and returned to the Jade. Hipper's battlecruisers, also in retreat after their bombardment of Whitby, Scarborough, and Hartlepool, were now the ones in danger as four battlecruisers and six dreadnoughts were in position to cut them off. But this opportunity also passed when rapidly deteriorating weather and Goodenough's misreading of a vague signal from Beatty allowed Hipper to escape.

The British public was outraged by the shelling of Scarborough, Whitby, and Hartlepool, which killed or wounded more than five hundred civilians. Their criticism of the navy's incompetence was nearly as severe as their diatribes against the enemy's perfidy. In response, the battlecruisers and the lst Light Cruiser Squadron were moved further south to Rosyth where they got an opportunity to redeem themselves early in the new year. On January 23, Room 40 determined that Hipper was about to lead a reconnaissance-in-force to the Dogger Bank, anticipating his arrival early next morning. The admiralty decided to meet him there with Beatty's battlecruisers, Goodenough's scouts, and the Harwich Force. Jellicoe was also ordered out with the whole Grand Fleet but received his directive so late that he could not possibly reach the projected point of contact in time to participate.

Hipper sortieed on the evening of January 23 with the battlecruisers *Seydlitz, Moltke, Derfflinger,* and *Blucher* (*Von der Tann* was in dock), four light cruisers, and eighteen destroyers. Beatty's battlecruisers were now organized into two squadrons. He led the first, composed of the *Lion, Tiger,* and the recently returned *Princess Royal,* while Rear Admiral Sir Archibald Moore led the 2nd Squadron's *New Zealand* and *Indomitable.* (The *Queen Mary* was also in local waters but was laid up in dock.) Beatty's screen was provided by Goodenough's four light cruisers plus the cruisers and destroyers of the Harwich Force.

British intelligence had plotted Hipper's course with uncanny accuracy, allowing Beatty to make contact just after dawn. The first duel between dreadnought battlecruisers began at 9 a.m. when the British opened fire at the previously unheard of range of 20,000 yards. (Pre-war "battle practice" took place at about half this distance.) Beatty signaled his ships to engage the corresponding ones in the enemy line, intending them to pair off front-to-rear. But the *Tiger's* captain counted rear-to-front, thinking it better that he and Beatty should gang up on the flagship, *Seydlitz*. This left Hipper's second ship in line, *Moltke*, without an opponent and gave it the opportunity for unmolested target practice. The British received no benefit from the *Tiger's* guns because she fired wild high and failed to compensate because her spotter took the *Lion's* more accurate splashes to be those of his own ship.

At approximately 9:30 a.m., with the range down to 17,000 yards, a 13.5-inch shell from the *Lion* hit the aftermost turret of the *Seydlitz* at the level of its working chamber. It ignited the chamber's cordite charges, sending flames up into the gunhouse, down to the magazine, and through an open door into the next turret's magazine as well. The flagship was saved from destruction only by its executive officer's instantaneous decision to flood both magazines. Meanwhile, the *New Zealand* made its presence felt at the other end of the line, raking the *Blucher* until she lost speed and fell out of column.

To this point, the British battlecruisers had suffered no serious damage and seemed to be poised on the verge of an annihilating victory. However, when the *Lion* received three 12-inch shells from *Derfflinger*, she too lost speed and Beatty soon lost control of the battle. He ordered the *Indomitable* to finish off the *Blucher* just before another hit destroyed the *Lion's* last dynamo and left him totally dependent on signal flags for communications. Beatty used these to order his nearest three ships to "attack the enemy's rear," intending that they pursue Hipper. But his previous flag, "Course NE," was still flying and the combined signals sent all the British ships toward the *Blucher* whose bearing was, unfortunately, to the northeast. Beatty could then only watch in frustration as four British battlecruisers pummeled the crippled hybrid while the rest of Hipper's flock escaped over the horizon.

Dogger Bank was another tactical victory for England who lost no ships and less than fifty men in exchange for a German battlecruiser and more than one thousand German sailors. Photographs of the capsizing *Blucher* were jubilantly received by the British public, now satisfied that the civilian deaths of the previous December had been avenged. But the affair left a sour taste with the Royal Navy as once again their quarry escaped due to botched communications. At the admiralty, Fisher railed about the lack of initiative displayed by Beatty's second in command, and pushed for an inquiry. Churchill demurred on the grounds of morale, disposing of the matter instead by discretely reassigning Admiral Moore to command a cruiser squadron in the Atlantic. In the long run, it was the Germans who profited the most from Dogger Bank. The near destruction of the *Seydlitz* led to the installation of anti-flash protection throughout the High Seas Fleet. Cordite charges were encased in metal containers until they were loaded, hoists were equipped with automatic shutters and doors connecting the magazines of adjacent turrets were locked shut. The British remained unaware of the problem and would pay a high price for its discovery when the fleets next met.

The war so far had been a constant mental grind for Jellicoe, with anxieties over enemy submarines, the destroyer shortage, and the revolving door at the dockyard working unremittingly on his psyche. Inadequate gunnery practice also continued to be a problem, especially among the battlecruisers. (The *Tiger's* atrocious shooting at the Dogger Bank is understandable because she went into the fight without ever having fired her guns at a moving target.) Jellicoe's fatigue was aggravated by the fact that his hectic schedule prevented him from using his customary sports and exercise as an emotional outlet. Near the end of January, a bad attack of piles brought on a breakdown that was remedied by a minor operation and a month's convalescence. On his return to duty, Jellicoe's mental state received a further boost from the steady improvement in his ship situation. By April 1, he held an advantage of twenty-three to seventeen in battleships, nine to four in battlecruisers, and had increased his destroyer total to fifty-four.[33] The Grand Fleet's margin of superiority would continue to increase through the next year as the building programs of 1912 and 1913 brought in their dreadnought dividends and the crash program of destroyer construction kicked into full gear.

Operationally, the first part of 1915 was dominated by the ill-fated Gallipoli Campaign. Churchill's brainchild was aimed at forcing the Dardanelles in order to open a supply line to beleaguered Russia and take the war to Germany's Turkish ally. It had only a slight impact on the home theater because it relied mainly on pre-dreadnoughts, although the brand new battleship *Queen Elizabeth* was included to provide some utilitarian drill for her virgin 15-inch guns. Gallipoli was a brilliantly conceived but ineptly executed enterprise whose failure can be attributed to a host of causes, including poor interservice cooperation and vacillating local commanders. By May, the operation was being viewed as such a fiasco that it provided a catalyst for the removal of the already controversial and recently feuding duo of Churchill and Fisher. Their successors, Arthur Balfour and Sir Henry Jackson, proved less abrasive but a great deal more sedentary. Jellicoe's major source of dissatisfaction with the new regime would come from its failure to speed up new naval construction, especially of light cruisers, destroyers, submarines, and mine sweepers.

For the remainder of his second year at war, Jellicoe devoted a great deal of his attention to improving the accuracy of his gunners. The Grand Fleet's shooting proficiency was substandard, handicapped by a shortage of targets as well as the need to conduct drills at sea where the submarine threat severely limited their duration. Jellicoe's entreaties soon produced a sufficient number of targets but the efficiency of his dreadnoughts did not noticeably improve until he began conducting more lengthy exercises in the relative safety of Moray Firth. Later, after the targets were moved to the closer and more secure confines of Pentland Firth, the British battleships finally met the high standards established by their commander. Beatty's ships did not show a similar improvement, however. Rosyth had no facilities for target practice and the battlecruisers could not vacate their station to use the facilities near Scapa Flow. Although Beatty did put his ships through some gunnery drill in the North Sea toward the end of November, Jellicoe continued to be vexed by doubts about the battlecruiser's combat efficiency.

During this period, Jellicoe also spent a great deal of energy to improve the mental well-being of the 60,000 officers and men in his charge. Fleet morale was drooping due to the bleak surroundings and inability to get at the enemy. A wardroom song summed up the prevailing attitude: "We hate this bloody war; it gives us all the blight; we cannot go ashore; and yet we cannot fight."[34]

Jellicoe saw boredom as the most dangerous enemy and made every effort to banish it from Scapa Flow. Besides employing the men on military construction projects, he set up football fields, target ranges, and a golf course, the latter strictly for officers, of course. Jellicoe, the keen sportsman, actively promoted intership sailing and athletic competitions, officiating whenever possible. He even pledged to turn out for a game of rugby against the *Iron Duke's* gunroom but was dissuaded from doing so after much haranguing by his staff.[35] A major weapon in the war on melancholia was the canteen-ship *Gourkho* with its theater, lecture hall, and boxing ring. The vessel's facilities were used for both entertainment and education. Ship's companies put on lavish stage productions, officers lectured on popular topics, and naval schoolmasters held night classes. Jellicoe's morale-boosting programs were eminently successful as no unrest or insubordination surfaced during his tenure as commander in chief.

Meanwhile, at Wilhelmshaven, the High Seas Fleet was showing symptoms of the same disease that Jellicoe had worked so hard to prevent at Scapa Flow. In some respects, the German sailor had a better lot than his British counterpart. He slept in barracks rather than on ship and did his drilling undisturbed in the Baltic, which was accessible through the near-by Kiel Canal. But the lack of organized sports or entertainment gave rise to perpetual boredom within the German navy and the segregated living arrangements on shore served to isolate its officers from their men. The worst influence on morale was the fleet's continued inaction. Admiral von Ingenohl lost his job after the Dogger Bank and was replaced by Admiral von Pohl, whose policy was even more cautious than that of his predecessor. He took the fleet to sea only five times, never venturing more than 120 miles beyond Heligoland.[36] This lethargy produced a creeping discontent that enveloped officers and men alike. Ship captains, driven to the very un-German practice of ignoring channels, sent their demands for more action directly to the chief of naval staff. Lower ranks, more concerned with life's basics, grumbled among themselves about a cut in food rations, knowing that its cause was a blockade wrought by ships that they were not allowed to fight.[37]

V

Germany's battle fleet remained dormant until January 1916 when the terminally ill von Pohl was replaced by Admiral Reinhard Scheer. The new commander almost instantly produced a blueprint for a more aggressive strategy. He planned to use the "systematic and constant pressure" of surface sweeps, shore bombardments, mine laying, and Zeppelin raids to goad the British into rash countermeasures that would offer the Germans "favorable possibilities of attack."[38] Remarkably, the kaiser quickly agreed to give his admiral a free hand in carrying out the proposed strategy. Scheer also lobbied for the commencement of unrestricted submarine warfare, a position shared by Tirpitz at the Naval Ministry. After first expressing his agreement, the kaiser backed off from the submarine offensive due to its likelihood of bringing America into the war on the side of England. This abrupt retreat was too much for Tirpitz who resigned in disgust.

Scheer's initial surface sweeps netted little, but the bombing of British cities struck a nerve, resulting in an unsuccessful seaplane raid on the Zeppelin's hangers. Jellicoe had long been concerned about the German airships, giving them a greater value as aerial scouts than as bombers. He now became even more concerned that they would provide the admiralty with a pretext to order him to pursue a "more active policy" that would expose his fleet to unnecessary risks and still not bring out the enemy fleet on any terms favorable to a decisive British victory.[39] Although Beatty favored more air raids for their harassment value, he agreed wholeheartedly with his commander in chief about the need to avoid imprudent risk of the fleet. Beatty termed the pressure from the admiralty "deplorable" and flatly stated, "The German Fleet will come out *only* on its own initiative when the right time arrives."[40]

For Scheer, the time was next right on April 24, when Lowestoft and Yarmouth were bombarded in an operation timed to coincide with an uprising by Irish nationalists in Dublin. German shells failed to win Ireland's independence but did succeed in bringing out the Grand Fleet in support of another fruitless air attack on the Zeppelin hangers. More significantly, Scheer's ability to hit and run with impunity convinced the admiralty that its ships were concentrated too far north. Accordingly, the 3rd Battle Squadron and its attendant cruisers were redeployed to Sheerness in the Thames estuary. The *Dreadnought* herself accompanied them to round out the squadron, now down to seven battleships since the loss of the *Edward VII* to a mine. It was further decided to move the entire Grand Fleet to the Firth of Forth, but this would not be done until anti-submarine defenses were constructed to protect its outer anchorage. In the meantime, the 5th Battle Squadron's five "Queen Elizabeths" came to Rosyth, temporarily trading places with the 3rd Battlecruiser Squadron, whose three ships went to Scapa for some desperately needed gunnery practice.

Meanwhile, Scheer had formulated plans for a trap using Hipper's bombardment of Sunderland as the lure with the battle fleet and eighteen U-boats providing the snare. He intended to avoid being trapped himself by employing his Zeppelins and submarines to report the movements of the Grand Fleet. The surface portion of the operation was initially scheduled for May 17, but bad condensers on seven battleships and the *Seydlitz's* slow recovery from mine damage forced its postponement until May 30. By that time, one submarine had been sunk, others had been chased off their stations and the rest were near the end of their endurance. So when gusty crosswinds grounded the Zeppelins, Scheer concluded that his original plan was too risky. Instead, he would bait his trap further east near Norway's Skagerrak by threatening the cruisers that formed Britain's northern cordon. (It was ironic that Jellicoe had just finished planning his own scheme to lure the High Seas Fleet to the same vicinity using two light cruiser squadrons as bait.) In the early morning hours of May 31, Hipper left the Jade on the *Lutzow* leading his four other battlecruisers, five light cruisers, and thirty destroyers. Scheer followed on the *Friedrich der Grosse* at the head of fifteen other dreadnoughts, six pre-dreadnoughts, six light cruisers, and thirty-one destroyers.[41]

At the admiralty, the wizards in Room 40 overheard enough enemy wireless traffic to know that something was up. Forewarned, the Grand Fleet was at sea four-and-a-half hours before Hipper's departure. Beatty's Battlecruiser Fleet included his flagship *Lion*, five additional battlecruisers, four-

teen light cruisers, twenty-seven destroyers, and the seaplane carrier
Engadine. Rear Admiral Hugh Evan-Thomas' 5th Battle Squadron accompanied them with the battleships *Barham*, *Valiant*, *Warspite*, and *Malaya*
(the *Queen Elizabeth* was in dock). On board the *Iron Duke*, Jellicoe commanded an armada of twenty-four dreadnought battleships, three battlecruisers, eight armored cruisers, twelve light cruisers, and fifty-one destroyers.[42] The Royal Navy's air arm went unrepresented among the battle fleet
because the seaplane carrier *Campania* missed the signal to get underway
and sailed two hours late. Jellicoe then decided to order the unescorted carrier back to Scapa rather than risk it to submarine attack.

   The two fleets steaming toward their only wartime confrontation deserve
some comparison. Numerically, England had a clear advantage in every
class of surface warship except pre-dreadnoughts, and the presence of the
latter merely emphasized Germany's inferiority in modern battleships. In
firepower, Jellicoe possessed 264 heavy guns against Scheer's 200, whereas
Beatty outnumbered Hipper in the same category by 80 to 44.[43] Moreover,
British main batteries ranged from 12- to 15-inch in calibre, with 200 guns
of 13.5-inch or greater, giving them a much heavier weight of shell than the
ll- and 12-inch barrels of their opponents. This was tremendously significant due to the disproportionate increase in throw weight that can be obtained by a relatively small increase in diameter. For example, while the
shell of a 12-inch gun weighed 850 pounds, that of a 13.5-inch gun weighed
1,400 pounds, and 15-inch shells tipped the scales at 1,920 pounds.[44] Thus,
the Grand Fleet's twenty-eight battleships and nine battlecruisers could
hurl a combined broadside of 401,000 pounds compared to the 167,000
pounds that the 27 German capital ships could fire back.[45] (The calculation
excludes half of any ship's wing turrets because only those on one side of
the ship could fire in a broadside.) However, this edge was offset somewhat
by the superiority of German armor-piecing shells that did not share their
counterparts' proclivity to break up on impact.

   The Germans were roughly equal to the British in the number of torpedo
tubes and superior in the thickness of their ships' armor, especially in the battlecruisers.[46] But the British came out on top in the category of speed. Jellio-
ce's dreadnoughts could steam about one knot faster than their German
counterparts and Scheer conceded another three knots by including six pre-
dreadnoughts in his battle line.[47] Beatty's four most modern battlecruisers
were faster than any of Hipper's capital ships, but the inclusion of the 5th Battle Squadron in the British vanguard presented some tactical problems.
The "Queen Elizabeths" were the finest fighting ships then afloat, combining the power of eight 15-inch guns with a 24 knot speed. However, the fast
battleships were still slower than the battlecruisers they would have to sup-

port. Beatty had campaigned to obtain Evan-Thomas' ships, and was happy to have them, but time would tell if his force could operate together under battle conditions.

Both sides went into battle nearsighted as they were almost wholly dependant on light cruisers for reconnaissance. Five of Scheer's sausage-shaped scouts did finally take off around noon but saw nothing due to low clouds and a gathering mist. Thus, the German commander remained completely unaware that any British heavy forces were at sea. Jellicoe was not only virtually blind, but also misled thanks to a major foul-up by his director of operations in London. On the morning of May 31, Captain Thomas Jackson asked Room 40 for the position of call sign DK, which he knew belonged to Scheer. Once informed that DK was placed at Wihelmshaven, he assumed that the High Seas Fleet was still in port and transmitted the erroneous information to the *Iron Duke*. If Jackson had elaborated on the purpose of his inquiry, Room 40 would have told him that DK was only a harbor call sign and that Scheer used a different one when at sea. But Jackson was not only ignorant in the ways of intelligence but also contemptuous of those who gathered it. He regarded the occupants of Room 40 as rank amateurs fit only to provide raw facts and dealt with them as infrequently as possible. Relying on the misinformation, Jellicoe decided not to close on Beatty and instead maintained his interval some 70 miles to the northwest in order to cover the blockading cruisers. Meanwhile, Beatty steamed along on an eastward course under orders to fall back on the battle fleet if no contact was made with the enemy by 2 p.m. The Germans were heading north, almost at a right angle to Beatty's vector, with Hipper in the van and Scheer about 50 miles behind.

The Battle of Jutland was brought about by a chance encounter between the British light cruiser *Galatea* and two German destroyers, all of whom were investigating smoke from what turned out to be a Danish tramp steamer. When he received his scout's report of the incident, Beatty was already heading north for his scheduled rendezvous with Jellicoe but promptly doubled back toward the "sound of the guns." Unfortunately, Evan-Thomas missed the signal to turn and continued to travel north. Although urged by his ship's captain to follow Beatty on his own initiative, Evan-Thomas remained on his divergent course for nearly eight minutes and only turned around after receiving orders by searchlight. By that time, the 5th Battle Squadron was 10 miles astern of the *Lion*. Shortly after Beatty's change in course, the *Engadine* sent up a seaplane that managed to sight enemy cruisers before being forced down with a ruptured gas pipe. Although the carrier tried repeatedly to pass on its information to both the *Lion* and the *Barham*, neither Beatty nor Evan-Thomas ever received it. No more

British seaplanes went aloft during the day because the *Engadine's* inadequate speed soon left it far out of the action.

Visual sightings made each commander aware of the other's presence by 3:30 p.m. After identifying the British battlecruisers, Hipper assumed his role as bait and sped south in an attempt to lead them into the jaws of the German battle fleet. His foxes ran in the following order: *Lutzow, Derfflinger, Seydlitz, Moltke,* and *Von der Tann.* Beatty, the huntsman, formed his battlecruisers into a line-ahead formation and pursued at full speed, leaving Evan-Thomas to catch up as best he could. The *Lion* was the lead hound, followed by the *Princess Royal, Queen Mary, Tiger, New Zealand,* and *Indefatigable,* in that order. At 3:48, with the range down to 15,000 yards, battle was joined when the German guns spoke in a simultaneous roar. Less than one minute later, the British ships began to reply one by one.

During the first few minutes of combat, the range fell below 13,000 yards but then rose to more than 16,000 after each antagonist felt the heat of the other's fire. Early honors in the gun duel went to the Germans largely because their stereoscopic range finders could acquire a target faster than the British coincidence types but also partially due to prevailing winds that blew British funnel smoke into their gunners' line of fire. Addditionally, the British repeated their mistake made at the Dogger Bank by failing to engage the *Derfflinger* for nearly 10 minutes. By 4 p.m., Hipper's ships had scored at least twelve times compared to only four times for Beatty's.[48] One 12-inch shell penetrated the *Lion's* "Q" turret (midships), peeling back its roof and igniting the cordite charges inside. Major Francis J. Harvey of the Royal Marines, although mortally wounded with both legs blown off, saved the ship by ordering the magazine doors shut and the magazine flooded. A few minutes later, the *Indefatigable* did not have the benefit of such quick and courageous action. She was struck by two successive salvoes from the *Von der Tann's* 11-inch rifles that started fires in her forward turret and aft superstructure. When the fire in her turret reached the magazine, the ship exploded in a sheet of flames and disappeared in a cloud of black smoke. Only two of her one thousand man crew survived the demolition.

Although the smoke from their stricken comrade was rising over the North Sea, England's struggling battlecruisers received formidable reinforcements. Evan-Thomas had pushed his four dreadnoughts to their maximum 24 knots and had closed the distance enough to join the fight with his 15-inch guns. Reaching out from 19,000 yards, the *Barham* smote the *Von der Tann* below the waterline, damaging its steering gear and causing flooding. As the remaining battleships came into range, they justified their squadron's reputation for crack shooting by hammering the last two ships in the German line. Beatty's feeling of deliverance must have been lessened, however, by a hit from the *Lutzow* that destroyed the *Lion's* wireless transmitter. His signals to Jellicoe would now have to be laboriously relayed by blinker through the *Princess Royal*.

The *Lion* now landed a salvo on the *Lutzow* but in turn received a counter-punch to its mess deck, which caused several fires. Beatty's flagship was so completely enveloped by the resulting smoke that some of the German ships incorrectly assumed that it had dropped out of line. Thinking that the *Lutzow* would take on the *Princess Royal*, the *Derfflinger* now shifted its fire to the *Queen Mary*, already engaged in a spirited tilt with the *Seydlitz*. The *Queen Mary* had done the day's best shooting among the British battle-cruisers and continued to fire fast and accurately despite the attentions of two opponents. Then, at 4:24, three 12-inch shells from *Derfflinger* landed near her "Q" turret, followed two minutes later by an additional pair in almost the same location. Seconds later, the *Queen Mary* was racked by spectacular internal explosions that blew off her masts and funnels and broke her in two. The *Tiger* was pelted with debris as she swerved to avoid the wreck and the *New Zealand*, doing likewise, caught a glimpse of the dying ship's stern jutting 70 feet out of the water with propellers still turning. A massive smoke cloud and twenty survivors were all that remained of the once proud battlecruiser and her crew of 1,286 officers and men. At this juncture, Beatty earned his place in British naval lore when he casually remarked to his flag captain, "There seems to be something wrong with our bloody ships today."[49] Legend further states that he then altered course two points toward the enemy, but recent sources claim that he actually turned two points away.[50]

In either case, Beatty had good reason to maintain contact and continue the pounding match. Despite his twin disasters, the British commander could see that his superior weight of metal was grinding down the enemy ships and noticeably suppressing their return fire. *Seydlitz* and *Von der Tann* had only five working guns between them, and the shooting of all the German battlecruisers was becoming increasingly erratic. Hipper now turned away to escape the unrelenting deluge of English steel. He also wished to give his torpedo craft some room to grapple with on-rushing enemy flotillas. In the melee that followed, each side lost two destroyers and the *Seydlitz* sustained inconsequential damage from a single torpedo hit. As the torpedo duel was tailing off, Beatty received two signals from Goodenough's *Southampton*. First, "Battleships S.E." and then, "Have sighted Enemy battle fleet bearing approximately S.E., course of Enemy N."[51] Beatty sailed on until he saw Scheer's funnels with his own eyes, then immediately counter-marched and began to run north at full throttle. He was now the hunted, but if he could bring the Germans under the guns of the Grand Fleet, he would play turnabout yet once again.

Meanwhile, Jellicoe had altered course to the southeast upon the receipt of the *Galatea's* report and then went to 20 knots when he learned that Beatty was about to engage Hipper. He also detached Rear Admiral Horace Hood's 3rd Battlecruiser Squadron and sent its three ships flying ahead to provide immediate support to the Battlecruiser Fleet. Jellicoe learned of Scheer's presence at sea through Goodenough's "Enemy battle fleet" transmission of 4:38 p.m. A few minutes later, the British commander signaled his fleet to prepare for battle and informed the admiralty that a fleet action was imminent.

Jellicoe's major concern at this point was information. His battleships were steaming in six parallel columns of four ships each and would require more than twenty minutes to deploy into a single line ahead. At the moment of deployment, Jellicoe would have to choose between forming on his port wing behind Vice-Admiral Sir Martyn Jerram's *King George V* or on his starboard wing behind Vice-Admiral Sir Cecil Burney's *Marlborough*. Because the dreadnoughts were extremely vulnerable during this maneuver, it was imperative that the battle line be formed at the earliest possible moment. However, the decision could not be made without definite knowledge of the enemy's position, course and speed. Jellicoe's latest battle instructions stressed the need for constant and accurate reporting but, except for Goodenough, his ships' captains acted as if they had never read them. Between 4:38 and 5, the Grand Fleet's commander in chief received five reports, three of which came from the *Southampton*, and then endured a complete news blackout for forty minutes.

The commander of the armada that dominated Jellicoe's thoughts was chasing Beatty at full speed, oblivious to the fact that his prey was running north rather than west. Hipper's battlecruisers led the pursuit in the same order in which they had entered the battle. Rear Admiral Paul Behncke's *Konig* was at the head of the German battle line leading the six other dreadnoughts of the 3rd Squadron. Next came Scheer's *Friedrich der Grosse* followed by eight older dreadnoughts in Vice-Admiral Schmidt's 1st Squadron. The six "Deutschland" pre-dreadnoughts in Rear Admiral Franz Mauve's 2nd Squadron were already falling behind. Beatty's battlecruisers outstripped their pursuers by 5:10, but the slower battleships of the 5th Battle Squadron did not escape the German firing range for a further twenty minutes. This was at least partially attributable to another botched exchange of signals that delayed the battleship's turn to the north. Beatty's signals officer was almost certainly to blame for tardiness in this instance, but Evan-Thomas is also suspect for failing to turn on his own initiative, despite the rapidly narrowing distance toward disaster. Although Evan-Thomas' ships bore the brunt of British suffering during the run north, they also gave as good as they got. Multiple hits on the *Warspite*, *Barham*, and *Malaya* were answered by numerous blows to the *Lutzow*, *Derfflinger*, and *Seydlitz,* as well as one apiece to the battleships *Markgraf* and *Grosser Kurfurst.*

Throughout his flight, Beatty remained cognizant that sanctuary was not his only objective. Therefore, at 5:35, he altered course to the northeast in order to re-engage the German van for the purpose of either masking Jellicoe's approach or driving the Germans closer to Jellicoe's assumed center of gravity. This time, British shooting was accurate from the start, forcing Hipper to turn away under cover of a torpedo attack. More weight was added by the timely arrival of the 3rd Battle Cruiser Squadron on Hipper's previously unengaged eastern flank. Hood's ships crashed through the German scouts, crippling the *Wiesbaden* and badly damaged two other light cruisers. The *Invincible*, *Inflexible*, and *Indomitable* then brought Hipper's big ships under fire so heavy and accurate that it caused him to retire completely and to re-route his destroyers toward the new arrivals. They were met by Hood's two light cruisers and four destroyers that broke up the German torpedo attack at a cost of one British destroyer sunk and another incapacitated.

Hipper retreated under the impression that he had been assaulted by some battleships, but still had no inkling that he was in the proximity of the entire Grand Fleet. Thus, Beatty had indeed reversed the situation once again by bringing the German battle fleet to the edge of the abyss. Unfortunately, Beatty's bravura performance as a decoy was not matched in his role as scout. After a garbled signal at 4:45 that identified twenty-six to thirty "probably hostile" battleships, he made no more reports during the entire run north. This inflated estimate of the size of the enemy force was not nearly as disturbing to Jellicoe as Beatty's failure to provide updates concerning its location. Goodenough broke the silence at 5:40 to begin a series of three reports but these did not provide enough information to be of much help. Finally, at 6:01, with the tension level steadily rising, Jellicoe spotted the *Lion* as it emerged from the mist off the *Iron Duke's* starboard bow. The *Lion's* proximity told Jellicoe that the enemy was closer than his scant intelligence data had indicated but it did not reveal the precise direction of Scheer's approach. Using search lights, the British commander twice requested the information from Beatty before receiving the reply that the enemy battle fleet was within visual range on a bearing of south by southwest.

Faced with the need to deploy immediately, Jellicoe made his decision in twenty seconds. His first impulse was to form on Burney's starboard wing (*Marlborough*) in order to bring the battle fleet into action as soon as possible. However, he quickly dismissed this thought because it would expose the fleet to attack while deploying, put its weakest squadron at the head of the line, and leave Scheer in position to cross the British "T" and/or escape to the south. Jellicoe decided instead to deploy on Jerram's port wing (*King George V*) despite the fact that doing so would increase the distance from the enemy and delay the moment of contact. But his chosen alternative would protect the fleet during its moment of vulnerability, place the powerful 2nd Battle Squadron at the head of the line, and position the fleet to cross Scheer's "T" while also blocking his escape route. Additionally, Jellicoe's choice would submerge his ships in a steadily blackening background while giving them targets framed by the bright southwestern horizon. This last benefit did not come by chance. During his approach to battle, the Grand Fleet's commander in chief had his flag captain take ranges on various bearings to determine the direction of optimum visibility for gunnery.[52]

At 6:15 p.m., the *King George V* turned one point to port followed in succession by the *Ajax*, *Centurion*, and *Erin*. The leaders of the other five divisions swung 70° to port together, with the remaining three ships in each column following in succession. In order to reach their position in the van, Beatty's battlecruisers raced across the front of the twisting line, forcing some of its ships to reduce speed. Hood's three vessels attached themselves to the head of Beatty's force and became the tip of the spear. Jellicoe's battle instructions placed his "Queen Elizabeths" slightly ahead of the battle line's engaged bow where their superior speed could be best exploited. However, Evan-Thomas soon realized that he was too far astern to reach that station and instead moved to his alternate station at the rear of the line. During this maneuver, the *Warspite's* already damaged helm jammed and the ship made two complete circles within range of the German guns. Despite receiving some thirteen hits, the *Warspite* righted herself and followed her squadron, only to suffer a similar breakdown at 7 p.m., which finally forced her to retire to Rosyth.

As the Grand Fleet was forming for battle, its 1st Cruiser Squadron under Rear Admiral Sir Robert Arbuthnot dashed forward to finish off the *Wiesbaden*. This brought the four British armored cruisers into the sights of the German battle fleet, now emerging from the haze less than 8,000 yards away. In moments, the *Derfflinger* and four German battleships opened up on Arbuthnot's *Defence*, obliterating the flagship along with its admiral and all nine hundred of its crew. German shells also ravaged the *Warrior* and the *Black Prince* but they escaped destruction when Scheer's dreadnoughts shifted their focus to the circling *Warspite*. The *Warrior's* salvation was only temporary, however, for she sank next morning in swelling seas off the Scottish coast.

Although it took more than twenty minutes for the Grand Fleet to fully deploy into line of battle, its dreadnoughts began shooting as soon as they had a target. The *Marlborough* opened fire at 6:17 with its ten 13.5-inch guns and was soon followed by a full salvo from the fourteen 12-inch guns of the singularly designed *Agincourt*. Once again, the struggle between the battlecruisers was especially bitter, often taking place over a distance of less than 9,000 yards. Paced by the exemplary shooting of the 3rd Squadron, the British battlecruisers scored nine hits on the *Lutzow* and four on the *Derfflinger*.[53] But at 6:33, the *Invincible* was done in by a shell that pierced the roof of the apparently magnetic "Q" turret and set off its cordite charges. When the flash reached the turret's magazine, it set off a series of quick explosions that broke the *Invincible* in two, killing Hood and more than one thousand English seamen. The two halves rested on the shallow bottom, leaving each end sticking up out of the water. As an indication of the already deteriorating visibility, many of the British sailors cheered wildly as they passed the grotesque sight, thinking it was the remains of an enemy vessel.

By this time, the whole British battle line was blazing away at an average range of 12,000 yards. Jellicoe's dreadnoughts actually formed a 6-mile crescent, concave toward the enemy, putting Scheer into a cup rather than crossing his "T." Because of the limited visibility, Jellicoe gave no fire distribution signal, allowing his ships to fire at "what they could see when they could see it."[54] All that the Germans could see was a ring of flashes along a dark horizon, which accounts for their failure to score a single hit on the British dreadnoughts during this phase of the battle. The British were scoring often, especially among the enemy battlecruisers. With hits too numerous to count, the *Lutzow* fell out of line sinking by the bow, forcing Hipper to board a destroyer to shift his flag. Because *Derfflinger* and *Seydlitz* were both taking in water and *Von der Tann* had no working turrets, the *Moltke* was the only viable alternative. Due to the machinations of battle, Hipper was unable to make the transfer for over three hours, leaving Captain Hartog on the *Derfflinger* in de-facto command during that period. The British fire storm also reached the battleships *Konig*, *Markgraf*, and *Grosser Kurfurst* as well as the doomed *Wiesbaden*, which miraculously stayed afloat for several hours before sinking during the night.

With his ships being battered and his formation beginning to break up, Scheer now resorted to a desperate maneuver. He ordered the fleet to execute a *Gefechtskehrtwendung,* or "battle turn," whereby his rear battleship would immediately turn around 180° and each succeeding vessel would put its helm over as soon as it saw the ship next astern begin to turn. In order to cover the retreat, German destroyers put up a smoke screen and launched a halfhearted torpedo attack that did no damage. Although Scheer completed his maneuver by 6:45, the British ships had already stopped firing for lack of targets in the smoke and thickening mist.

When Jellicoe realized that his adversary had withdrawn, he turned the Grand Fleet south to stay between Scheer and his base. Before the turn, the *Marlborough* was struck by a torpedo, fired by either the *Wiesbaden* or a lingering destroyer, which reduced her speed to 17 knots. At 7:04, Jellicoe received word from his terrier on the *Southampton* that Scheer had executed another sixteen-point turn-around and was coming back. The German commander's claim that he did so in order to "deal the enemy a second blow" is refuted by both common sense and his subsequent conduct. More likely, he was trying to slip by Jellicoe's rear, based on bad information that put the British further southeast than their true position. Instead, Scheer sailed into a second hail of fire from a nearly invisible assailant. By 7:15, the entire British battle line was raking the German column at ranges varying from 11,000 to 14,000 yards. This exchange was as one-sided as the first, with the High Seas Fleet scoring only two hits while receiving between twenty-three and thirty-seven.[55] At the head of the line, the battlecruisers and the 3rd Battle Squadron were again punished severely. The *Lutzow* began to burn and crawled away to be finished off by her own destroyers during the night. Several battleships were seriously damaged, including the *Konig* in which Behncke himself was wounded.

Faced with his second glimpse of Armageddon, Scheer executed yet another *Gefechtskehrtwendung*, this one covered by the suicide charge of his battlecruisers in addition to the usual smoke and torpedoes of his flotillas. Although the battlecruisers' death ride was called off almost as soon as it had begun, the destroyers pressed their attack enough to launch thirty-one torpedoes. Jellicoe responded by turning his big ships away four points (45°) and sending his own light forces into the breech. The net result was one German destroyer sunk and two badly damaged with no hits on any British ships. But the turnaway also helped Scheer to break contact and once again extricate himself from the jaws of destruction.

Scheer was out of harm's way and sailing on a southwest course by 7:35. Jellicoe had reformed his line and was steaming on a parallel course about five minutes later. Light was now becoming a major concern as sunset occurred at 8:19 and darkness would fall by about 9 p.m. At 8 p.m., shortly after receiving Beatty's report that the enemy was 10 miles to the northwest, Jellicoe turned west to intercept. However, due to Beatty's lack of wireless and the need for decoding, nearly thirty minutes elapsed between the signal's origin and its receipt. In that interval, Scheer had altered course to the south and was positioned to escape by crossing ahead of the British battle fleet.

Not long after changing course, Jellicoe received another signal from his battlecruiser commander that read, "Submit van of battleships follow battlecruisers. We can then cut off whole of enemy's battle fleet."[56] Beatty's exhortation purely was based on "feel" because he had lost sight of the Germans by the time it was sent. After a few minutes of deliberation, Jellicoe informed Beatty of the Grand Fleet's recent course change and then instructed Jerram to follow the battlecruisers. But because Beatty had not transmitted his position and the two groups of ships were not in each other's sight, Jerram could do nothing but continue sailing west while his lookouts scanned the horizon in search of the friendly vessels he was supposed to follow. Meanwhile, Beatty was still traveling southwest on a converging course with the enemy. When his light cruisers collided with some hostile scouts, Beatty sped toward the gunfire and drove back the German van with some crisp jabs to the *Seydlitz* and *Derfflinger*. Mauve's pre-dreadnoughts then intervened to save their battlecruisers and both sides soon lost contact in the deteriorating visibility.

In the meantime, Jellicoe had heard the noise from Beatty's guns and altered course to the southwest to investigate. At 8:45, the light cruisers *Caroline* and *Royalist* caught a glimpse of three enemy battleships, but their torpedo attack proved ineffective at the extreme range of 8,000 yards. On the *King George V*, Jerram also sighted the apparitions some 10,000 yards away, within easy range of his squadron's 13.5-inch main batteries. But he did not open fire because he believed the vessels to be Beatty's battlecruisers, which were in reality about 6 miles further south. The ships were also spotted from the bridge of the *Orion*, flagship of Rear Admiral Arthur Leveson's Second Division. After identifying them as German, the admiral's flag lieutenant turned to him and said, "Sir, if you leave the line now and turn towards, your name will be as famous as Nelson's." But, in a response that evoked the spirit of the *Victoria* rather than the *Victory*, Leveson demurred, saying, "We must follow the next ahead."[57] The German dreadnoughts soon disappeared into the dim twilight, taking with them the Grand Fleet's last opportunity for a daylight engagement.

Jellicoe adamantly refused to seek a night action because he felt that his fleet's inferior searchlights and lack of star shells put it at a great disadvantage in such combat. Also, unlike the Germans, the British had not yet fitted their secondary armament for director firing. This would be a major handicap in the confused close quarters of night combat and cast serious doubt on the Grand Fleet's ability to repel torpedo attacks in the dark. Jellicoe therefore decided to parallel Scheer until morning and then close for the kill. Since his most recent intelligence indicated that the High Seas Fleet was heading southwest, Jellicoe altered course from southwest to south in order to remain interposed between Scheer and his base. Shortly thereafter, the Grand Fleet went into its night cruising order, which formed the battle line into three columns abreast, 1 mile apart, with the 5th Battle Squadron 5 miles astern. The battlecruisers steamed slightly ahead and 12 miles to starboard. Light cruisers were disposed forward and to starboard while the flotillas were grouped 5 miles to the rear of the battleships.

Jellicoe's task now devolved into a guessing game concerning Scheer's chosen path of retreat. In order to return to port, the High Seas Fleet would have to negotiate its way through the massive British mine fields in the Heligoland Bight. Jellicoe was aware that the Germans maintained a swept passageway at each end of the Bight. The northern route ran along the Schleswig-Holstein coast, emerging about 15 miles southwest of Denmark's Horns Reef while the southern route ran past the mouth of the River Ems and then along Holland's north Frisian coast. He also knew that the British left a wide gap near the center of their mine barrier and had to contend with the possibility that the Germans knew of it too. (A fourth passageway that ran just northwest of Heligoland was unknown to the British at the time of Jutland.) Based primarily on Beatty's latest report that had the German Fleet still sailing southwest, Jellicoe decided to steer for a position that would allow him to cover both the Ems route and the gap in the mine fields. He hedged his bet slightly by sending the minelayer *Abdiel* to thicken the minefield south of the British submarine patrol line near Horns Reef.

The course that Beatty reported was merely Scheer's attempt to open the distance after his run-in with the battlecruisers. The German commander had long since resolved to seek sanctuary via Horns Reef and had already altered course to the southeast by the time Jellicoe received Beatty's signal. At 9:46, he turned more sharply to the southeast and began to move across the British rear. The German battle line was now led by the 1st Squadron with the *Wesfalen* at the head, followed by the battered 3rd Squadron and pre-dreadnoughts of the 2nd Squadron. The *Derfflinger* and *Von der Tann* tagged along behind Mauve's ships while the stricken *Seydlitz* and *Moltke* as well as the doomed *Lutzow* all made their way independently.

Scheer had no qualms about possible night actions because his ships were well equipped and trained for them. He also had an advantage due to his scouts' acquisition of the enemy's recognition code as it was being passed from the *Princess Royal* to the *Lion*. After two brushes with British destroyers, the German cruiser screen tangled with Goodenough's squadron in a brief but sharp fight that left the *Frauenlob* sinking and the *Southampton* badly damaged. Goodenough's usual prompt reporting was delayed for an hour by the destruction of the *Southampton's* wireless and the scattering of his remaining ships. The Germans next ran into the 4th Destroyer Flotilla and smashed their way through it after a violent engagement that lasted nearly an hour. This donnybrook cost Scheer two more light cruisers but

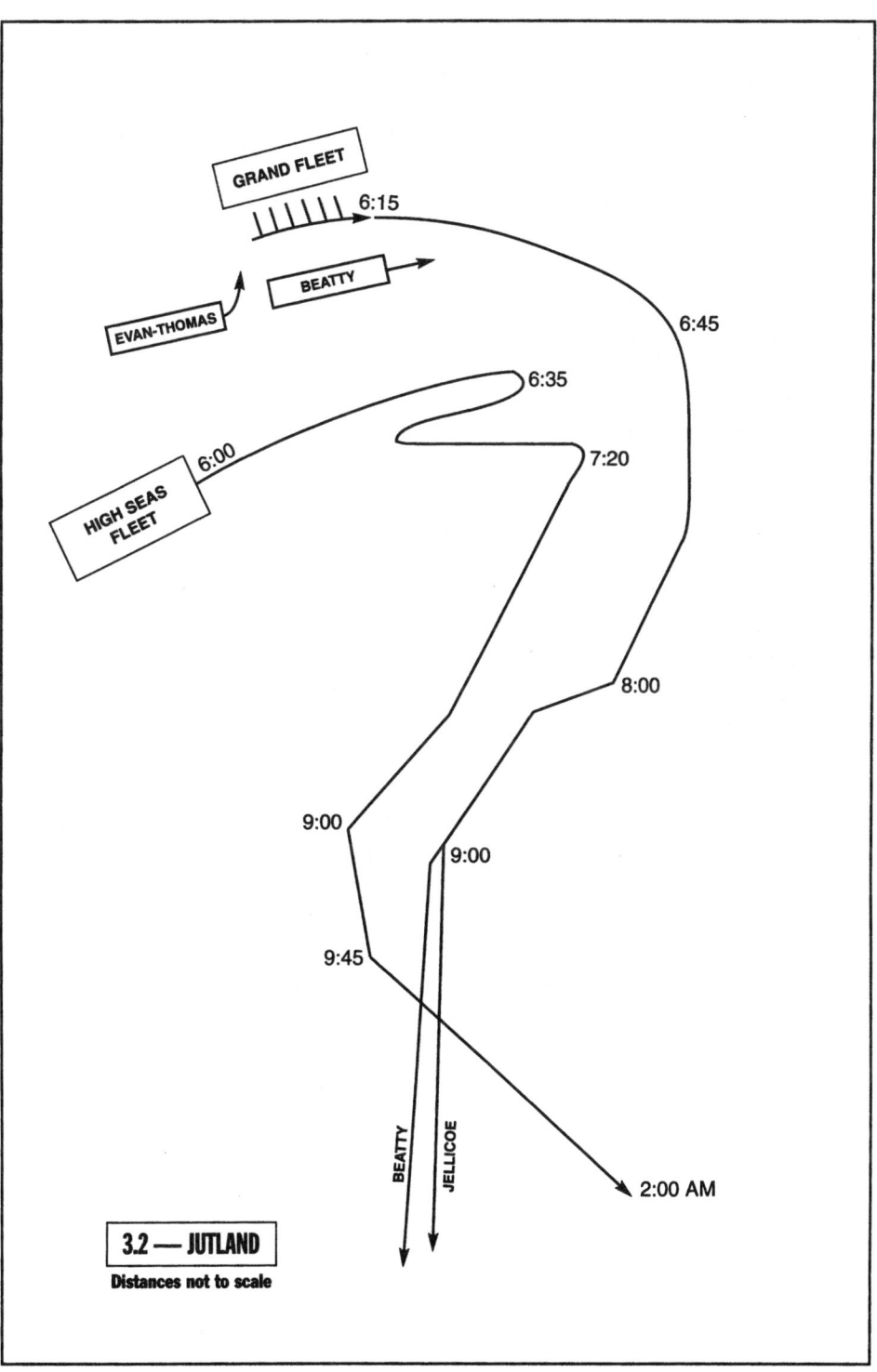

GRAND FLEET 6:15

BEATTY

EVAN-THOMAS

6:45

6:35

HIGH SEAS
FLEET 6:00

7:20

8:00

9:00 9:00

9:45

BEATTY JELLICOE

2:00 AM

3.2 — JUTLAND

Distances not to scale

effectively destroyed the 4th Flotilla, which had four destroyers sunk and three more seriously damaged. The armored cruiser *Black Prince* also met its end around this time when it blundered into the middle of the German formation and was obliterated by the battleships *Ostfiesland* and *Thuringen*. Incredibly, not one of the British destroyers nor any of the nearby ships that viewed the action made a report to their commander in chief.

However, at about 11:30, Jellicoe did receive the following message from the admiralty, sent at 10:41: "German Battle Fleet ordered home at 9:14 p.m. Battlecruisers in rear. Course SSE 3/4 E. Speed 16 knots."[58] This communiqué was a summary of several intercepts deciphered by Room 40 between 9 and 10:10 p.m. Once plotted, its course and speed pointed the enemy toward Horns Reef and placed him almost directly astern at that very moment. Ordinarily, this would have been viewed as vital information but the admiralty's credibility was low among those on the *Iron Duke's* bridge. Jellicoe's mistrust of Whitehall stemmed not only from its midday signal that put the High Seas Fleet in the Jade but also from a recent report on Scheer's position that was too patently wrong to be taken seriously. Also, the admiralty's information was soon contradicted by Goodenough's tardy report and a signal from the *Birmingham* that supported Jellicoe's inclination that the High Seas Fleet was still heading south. (These were based on the observation of German warships that were following temporary courses necessitated by the aforementioned engagements with Goodenough's cruisers and the 4th Flotilla.)

The dilemma presented by this conflicting information should never have arisen. Room 40 had also deciphered Scheer's urgent request for early morning Zeppelin reconnaissance at Horns Reef, an obvious indication of his chosen route home. But Captain Jackson did not see the significance of Scheer's plea nor did he deign to discuss it with the "amateurs" in Room 40. Consequently, he omitted it from his communiqué to the *Iron Duke*, thereby denying Jellicoe a kernel of knowledge that would have resolved all doubts as to German intentions. Jackson compounded his error by neglecting to pass on subsequent intercepts of Scheer's communications, including one which ordered all German torpedo flotillas to assemble near Horns Reef at 2 a.m. Without these crucial details, Jellicoe chose to rely on his ships on the scene and took the lack of further reports as proof that the pyrotechnics to the north were only manifestations of skirmishes between opposing light forces. Shortly before midnight, the Grand Fleet's commander retired for a brief sleep, completely unaware that his quarry was slipping through his grasp.

While Jellicoe grabbed his forty winks, the men of the Grand Fleet remained at their action stations, sleeping in shifts and sustaining themselves on the Royal Navy's traditional cocoa. By 2 a.m., Scheer's main body was well across Jellicoe's wake and the kaiser's crews enjoyed their own repast of corned beef and coffee. The only remaining barrier to their safe passage was the 12th Destroyer Flotilla led by Captain A.J.B. Stirling on the *Faulknor*. Stirling spotted a line of ships off his starboard bow and shadowed until identifying them as German battleships. His force then charged in and launched torpedoes, one of which hit the pre-dreadnought *Pommern* and atomized it with the loss of all hands. During the melee, Stirling sent off three dispatches to his commander in chief, uncharacteristic behavior for a British destroyer captain that night. Although the bulk of the German Fleet was now uncatchable, an immediate change of course would probably have allowed Jellicoe to net some stragglers. But none of Stirling's signals got through to the *Iron Duke*, either because of enemy jamming or the *Faulknor's* damaged antenna. Scheer arrived at Horns Reef by 3:30 and shepherded his bruised survivors into the swept passageway for home. Briefly thereafter, Jellicoe received information that told him of this occurrence and after a brief sweep to the north in search of stragglers took his own force back to port.

VI

The Battle of Jutland cost England three battlecruisers, three armored cruisers, eight destroyers, and 6,097 dead, compared to Germany's bill of one battlecruiser, one pre-dreadnought battleship, four light cruisers, five destroyers, and 2,551 dead.[59] To those who find historical truth purely in statistics, Jutland comes out a German victory. On further reflection, however, it is hard to see exactly what the Germans won. The strategic situation remained unchanged, with the British in command of the sea and the blockade still in place. Tactically, the exchange of one battlecruiser for three of the enemy's could be considered a victory of sorts, but Scheer's inability to follow up greatly diminished its importance. When it returned to the Jade, the German Fleet had only twelve battleships and *no* battlecruisers which were seaworthy. Jellicoe, on the other hand, reported twenty-six battleships and six battlecruisers fit for duty within twelve hours of reaching Scapa Flow.[60] In addition, German damage was more severe, requiring longer periods of repair. The *Seydlitz* would be out of action until September 16 and the *Derfflinger* would not be ready until the beginning of December. By the time these ships returned, the Grand Fleet would have replaced its losses with the brand new *Renown* and *Repulse*, plus the *Australia*, back from the docks.

Jutland's most significant result was produced during the forty-five minutes that the High Seas Fleet was exposed to the broadsides of the British battle line. It convinced all informed participants that the German Fleet could not put up with such encounters and expect to survive. Scheer claimed to his dying day that the imminent destruction of his fleet was a "myth" but his actions proved that he believed otherwise. Even if we accept his dubious claim that a desire for battle created the second meeting of the battle lines, it is indisputable that after his second turnaway his exclusive preoccupation was flight. Jellicoe was extremely irritated by the claims of victory that flooded the Teutonic Press after what their kaiser termed the "Battle of the Skagerrak." In a moment of pique, he wrote his wife, "If they had been so confident of victory, they would have tried to go on fighting instead of legging it for home."[61] Despite his public pronouncements and post-war writings, Scheer seemed to agree. He took the High Seas Fleet to sea only three more times during the remainder of the war and did not vigorously press for a confrontation on any of those occasions. This inactivity was the true indicator of who won at Jutland.

Nevertheless, Jellicoe's "victory" is itself diminished by the need to find it in explanation. The fact that the British commander failed to annihilate an inferior foe naturally raises questions about the quality of his leadership. Certainly, no fault can be found with his mode of deployment. Churchill conjectured in his post-war chronicle that a better alternative would have been to deploy on the *Iron Duke's* center column, thereby forming the battle line 4,000 yards closer to the enemy while still giving it a degree of protection.[62] But tactical studies had long since concluded that the battle line must be commanded from the middle rather than the front. Therefore, deployment on a center column had not been practiced before the battle and was not considered at the moment of decision. (The Germans seemed to agree with the Royal Navy's tactical assessment since Scheer's flagship was the eighth vessel in a line of sixteen dreadnoughts.) Jellicoe's choice crossed the enemy's "T," blocked his retreat and made him an optimum target. When one considers that Jellicoe made his decision in twenty seconds and without knowing the precise course of the opposing fleet, his first move rates as a masterstroke.

The wisdom of Jellicoe's turnaway from enemy torpedoes during the battle fleet's second encounter is more questionable. Scheer's flotillas launched only thirty-one torpedoes, all of which were easy to dodge because their wakes made them visible over 2 miles away. Relinquishing contact with the enemy seems a disproportionate response to the threat. It is easy to conclude that Jellicoe suffered from torpedo psychosis, especially because the *Marlborough* was his only capital ship that received torpedo damage in the battle. But this conclusion does not hold up in light of what Jellicoe knew when he knew it. The torpedo had become a more lethal weapon since Tsushima, with a larger warhead, increased speed, and longer running time. Furthermore, the Germans practiced an aggressive doctrine of its use, evidenced by their continued use of the term *torpedo boat* rather than destroyer. Jellicoe had every reason to expect massed torpedo attacks at Jutland and he had no inkling whatsoever that German torpedoes would be clearly visible during their runs. Furthermore, it is only fair to suggest that the ineffectiveness of the German torpedo arm was at least partially attributable to Jellicoe's countermeasures. By turning away, he increased the range that the hostile torpedoes had to run, presented them with more difficult targets and probably prevented additional launchings from the more distant German flotillas. As it was, six British battleships experienced close calls with the twenty-odd hostile torpedoes that actually reached their battle line.[63] Finally, his planned response to such a maneuver was well known at the admiralty and throughout the fleet from the October 1914 memorandum. Because his policy was accepted with almost no dissent, the rest of England's naval leadership must have shared Jellicoe's conclusions as to the potency of the underwater weapon.

The confusing exchange of communications that preceded Jutland's final clash between capital ships gave rise to a post-war myth that Jellicoe passed up the chance for victory by ignoring Beatty's "follow me" signal, thereby forcing the British battlecruisers to fight unsupported. This fable can be summarily dismissed for two reasons. As previously noted, Jellicoe did in fact order Jerram to follow the battlecruisers but Beatty's failure to give his position prevented Jerram from complying with the directive. More significantly, the question was moot in any case because it was physically impossible for Jerram's ships to reach the point of contact in time to make a difference. The 2nd Battle Squadron was 6 miles northeast of Beatty when his signal reach the *Iron Duke's* bridge and they could not have closed on the battlecruisers before dark even at their top speed of 20.5 knots.[64]

The decision to avoid night combat was definitely sound although as commander in chief, Jellicoe is at least partially accountable for his fleet's deficiencies in this mode of fighting. His actions during the night itself are not so easily judged. The failure to cover the route to Horns Reef can rightly be attributed to flawed intelligence. Reports from ships on the scene were scanty, vague, and often downright wrong. For instance, Stirling's first message was the only nocturnal signal that mentioned the magic word "battleship." The admiralty was even more at fault by being so stingy in its communiqués. It is probable that either the request for Zeppelin flights or the order for the assembly of the flotillas at Horns Reef would have provided a sufficient "smoking gun" to prove Scheer's intentions. But despite these shortcomings, Jellicoe did receive the admiralty's report telling him the correct enemy course and was soon treated to a rising cacophony from his rear to verify it. A great commander must sometimes rely on intuition to transcend the known and seize the unknown. Jellicoe's intuition failed him miserably that night in the North Sea.

Yet, the real reason for the British failure to annihilate the German Fleet does not lie in any one decision made in the heat of battle but rather in the guiding principles laid down by both sides before the battle commenced. On the eve of Jutland, Jellicoe's battle instructions limited his fleet exclusively to a daylight gun duel fought at long range in single line ahead under central command. (The "hail of fire" doctrine had long since been laid to rest in recognition of the improved accuracy and proliferation of big guns on capital ships.) Although his battle orders included provisions for more flexible divided tactics that would have allowed squadron commanders to fight independently, they also strongly implied that such tactics should be used only to conform the squadrons' movements to those of the commander in chief when the latter maneuvered without signals. Jellicoe's intentions were made crystal clear by the following: "In all cases the ruling principle is that the *Dreadnought* fleet as a whole keeps together, attempted attacks by a division or a squadron on a portion of the enemy line being avoided as liable to lead to the isolation of the ships which attempt the movement, and, so long as the fleets are engaged on approximately similar courses, the squadrons should form one line of battle."[65]

These rigid rules of engagement coupled with the policy of turning away from potential mines or torpedoes virtually precluded a decisive victory unless the Germans stood and slugged it out. Instead, the High Seas Fleet proved unwilling to fight but very adept at flight, thereby sealing the battle's result. Furthermore, on both occasions during which the battle fleets exchanged broadsides, the Germans were able to successfully complete their battle turns before the British knew they had begun. It is not outrageous to propose that Scheer's second *Gefechtskehrtwendung*, skillfully executed under a shroud of smoke, mist and failing daylight, may have been sufficient in itself to secure his escape. The first prerequisite for winning a match is that one's opponent shows up ready to play. Jellicoe never found his own adversaries to be so accommodating.

Jellicoe's post-war explanation for holding such a tight reign was "the necessity for not leaving anything to chance in a Fleet Action, because our Fleet was the one and only factor that was vital to the existence of the Empire, as indeed to the Allied cause."[66] Divided tactics might have helped the Grand Fleet get at the enemy during deployment and would certainly have enhanced its ability to maintain contact during a pursuit. But such tactics also presented a concentrated German Fleet with the opportunity to turn on one of the British squadrons and overwhelm it before it could be supported by its mates. Jellicoe's restrictive strategic environment forced him to put a premium on the firm control of his fleet while the fleet's size and inadequate communications precluded him from exercising that control in any manner that allowed tactical flexibility. When confronted with a choice between flexibility and control in the fluid atmosphere of combat, his analytical mind ruled in favor of the safer route offered by control.

Jellicoe held few illusions as to the likelihood of Scheer standing fast to assist in his own fleet's demise. But he fully realized that the war would be decided, in Churchill's words, by "its tendencies rather than its episodes."[67] In order for the tendencies to run in England's favor, the blockade must be enforced, the sea lanes must be kept open and the British army in France must be supplied and reinforced. Therefore, although Jellicoe undoubtedly felt that the destruction of the enemy fleet was desirable, he was correct in concluding that the preservation of his own fleet in superior strength was the only true imperative. Such a cautious doctrine seems out of place in a navy inculcated with Nelson's dictum that "something must be left to chance." But Nelson operated in an era of technological certainty and never led more than one fourth of his nation's ships-of-the-line into combat. Jellicoe's time was one of technological ambiguity and he was entrusted with the entire first line naval strength of the British Empire. Although Churchill was lavish in his post-war criticism of Jellicoe, he also provided his former subordinate's most eloquent defense by terming him "the only man on either side who could lose the war in an afternoon."[68]

VII

In many ways, Jutland was a bloody shakedown cruise for the Grand Fleet, which revealed numerous flaws in its methods and material. Afterward, Jellicoe focused his attention on fixing those flaws by appointing committees to examine the various aspects of the battle and make recommendations. Their reports led to the installation of anti-flash protections, the introduction of star shells, the revision of fire control techniques, and the extension of director firing to cruisers and destroyers as well as the secondary armament of capital ships. Because the Germans had already taken these actions prior to Jutland, Jellicoe's remedial measures could not be matched by any corresponding improvements in the High Seas Fleet and would indisputably widen the margin of England's superiority in any future clash. Jellicoe later wistfully summed up the situation after Jutland with an uncharacteristic boast, "Had the German Fleet come out to battle a terrible punishment awaited it!"[69]

Jellicoe's rising confidence was not reflected in any radical new battle orders. He basically retained his tactical doctrine but modified it somewhat to give his squadron commanders more discretion to maneuver independently while supporting the flagship or when avoiding torpedoes. Jellicoe also added a flag signal for the deployment of the battle fleet into line on its center column. There were no changes in strategy and none were seriously considered at any level of British naval leadership. Even the audacious Beatty felt obliged to remind his commander in chief of the old proverb, "When you are winning risk nothing."[70]

As his fleet's ability to fight on the surface was being improved, Jellicoe began to suspect that England's major peril had shifted underwater. Germany intensified its submarine campaign in October, partially because Scheer convinced the kaiser that no favorable decision could be achieved in future fleet actions. By the end of the month, increased sinkings of merchant ships motivated Jellicoe to write the admiralty to flag the threat. He prophetically warned that at the current rate of loss, England would be faced with starvation by summer, and emphasized his concern by offering to give up a flotilla of his precious destroyers for anti-submarine duty. Due in part to his memo, Jellicoe was summoned to the admiralty to meet the threat head on. He turned the Grand Fleet over to Beatty on November 28 and assumed his new post as first sea lord a few days later.

It would be fitting to end the story with Jellicoe's defeat of the sub menace, but this was not to be the case. Germany's announcement of unrestricted submarine warfare on January 31, 1917 sanctioned the indiscriminate destruction of any vessel within the war zone designated to exist in the coastal waters of England and France, the western half of the North Sea, the English Channel, and 400 miles west into the Atlantic Ocean. True to the fears of his civilian advisors, the kaiser's draconian policy brought the United States into the war on April 6, 1917. In the meantime, however, Allied ship losses soared into the stratosphere, confronting England with the prospect of defeat before a single U.S. division landed in France. The U-boats were eventually overcome by a convoy system that massed merchant ships and shepherded them to their destination under the protection of destroyers. This was not truly an innovation because small convoys of troopships and essential materials had been in use since 1914. But the implementation of a general convoy system for all merchant traffic was a massive undertaking that was opposed by the first sea lord. Jellicoe did not believe that merchant ships could keep station in such formations, especially at night, and felt that there were insufficient destroyers available to provide escorts. Instead, he favored a continuation of the "hunter–killer" strategy that sent patrol groups searching the seas for targets they seldom found. This unproductive approach also rendered the patrolling destroyers unavailable for convoy duty, thereby fulfilling its proponents' prophesy of a shortage of escorts. Jellicoe continued to have reservations about the convoy doctrine despite its successful trial application to ships in the Channel and Scandinavian trades. His endorsement of a general convoy system on April 27, 1917 was more an act of desperation than conversion.

Jellicoe's overall performance at the admiralty was indifferent at best. His one clear accomplishment was the production of an improved armor-piercing shell for the fleet. Throughout his tenure, Jellicoe was severely hampered by an inability to delegate that often left him overwhelmed by detail. An even greater nemesis was failing health, brought on by the twenty-eight months of unremitting tension he endured while at the helm of the Grand Fleet. Jellicoe was perpetually fatigued and was periodically laid up from attacks of influenza and neuritis. The beleaguered first sea lord began to present an image of pessimism and inactivity, reinforced by the undercurrent of recriminations over his failure to annihilate the enemy at Jutland. Finally, on Christmas Eve, 1917, he was asked to relinquish his office and retired in January with the title Viscount Jellicoe of Scapa.

A stream of sympathetic correspondence began flowing in Jellicoe's direction when the news of his resignation became public. It included a warm personal note from King George V as well as an indignant letter from Beatty, who categorized the turn of events as "the usual way they have at the Admiralty of dispensing with the service of officers who have given their whole lives to the service of the country."[71] Perhaps the most touching of all was a telegram from a group of enlisted men serving with the Grand Fleet:

We heard with regret of your retirement and would wish to know what was the cause, you know of course that we have implicit trust in you and please do not take it lying down. We want you back. Don't take any notice of armchair critics, what do they know of our wants and desires? Sir, you might ask for a naval election, they can do it in France, why not in the Fleet? You are our Idol and one who we would follow to Death, you have shown us the way to possess ourselves in patience, you have always been one with us in our sports and you are the Man we want. . . . Come Back is the message from the Lower Deck to you.[72]

In 1918, Europe's tournament of attrition finally played itself out. Russia had already collapsed in spasms of internal upheaval, freeing masses of German troops for Field Marshall Erich Ludendorff's last roll of the dice on the western front. Employing new tactics of infiltration and concentrated artillery barrage, the Germans cut wide swaths through Allied lines but still came up short of victory. The blockade's toll of deprivation contributed to Ludendorff's failure to deliver a knockout blow. On several occasions, advances petered out when soldiers broke ranks to gather captured food and wine. The significance of the stuffed enemy larders was not lost on the exhausted German infantrymen who began to believe that their country was losing the war. When the Allies went on the offensive, bolstered by the stream of reinforcements from America, they moved unspectacularly but steadily forward. In truth, the German army never collapsed but its slow crumbling convinced German's military and civilian leaders to seek an armistice. Scheer planned to show his disagreement by sending out the fleet for one last apocalyptic sortie but his disgruntled sailors declined the honor and mutinied. When the mutiny sparked insurrections throughout Germany, the tottering Reich was forced to accept an armistice with terms so severe that it was tantamount to an acknowledgment of defeat.

One condition of armistice was that a portion of the High Seas Fleet be interned at Scapa Flow while a formal treaty was being negotiated. At dawn on November 21, 1918, nine battleships, five battlecruisers, seven light cruisers, and forty-nine destroyers left their prison in the Jade and sailed to their new jail in Scotland. But the man who had given so much of his health and reputation to stage the procession was not present to witness it. Sir John Jellicoe had not been asked to attend the surrender and felt it improper to go uninvited.

Admiral Heihachiro Togo. (*U.S. Naval Institute*)

The Battleship *Mikasa*, just after Tsushima. (*Naval Historical Center*)

Admiral Sir John Rushworth Jellicoe. (*U.S. Naval Institute*)

HMS Iron Duke. (Naval Historical Center)

Plebe Halsey. (*U.S. Naval Institute*)

Admiral William F. Halsey, Jr. (*U.S. Naval Institute*)

Midshipman Ray Spruance. (*U.S. Naval Institute*)

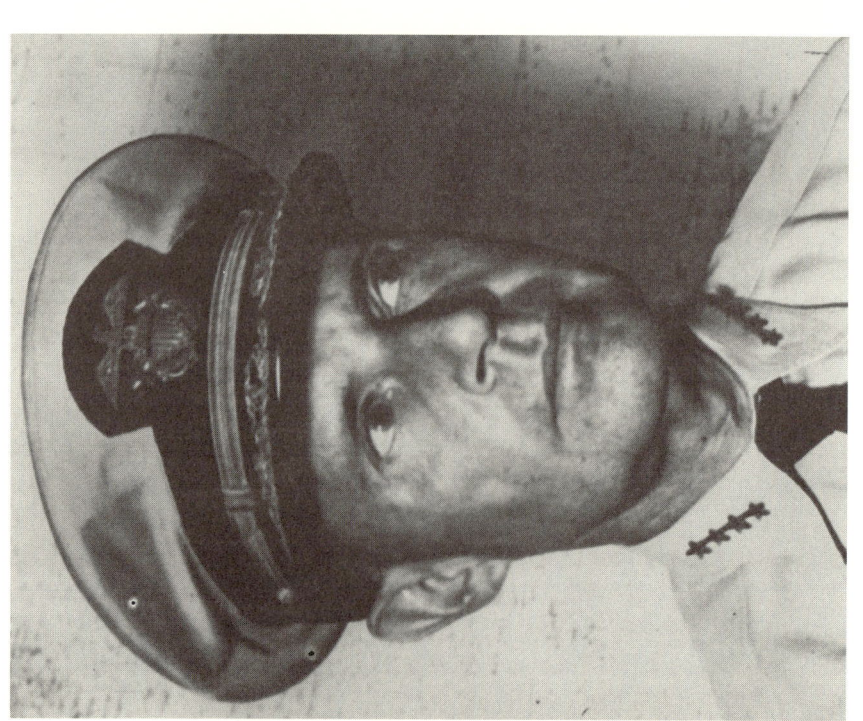

Admiral Raymond A. Spruance. (*Naval Historical Center*)

U.S.S. *New Jersey. (U.S. Naval Institute)*

U.S.S. *Enterprise*. (*U.S. Naval Institute*)

4

The Fighter and the Strategist

I

On December 7, 1941, Japanese naval air units attacked the U.S. Pacific Fleet at Pearl Harbor. Once again, Japan had begun a war by launching a naval assault prior to its formal declaration of hostilities. This time, the political and economic stakes were much more significant. In 1904, Japan had sought to keep Russia out of Korea and to ensure her own ability to exploit China on an equal basis with the European powers. By 1941, Japan's growing military power and territorial acquisitions had put her on the road to regional hegemony. Admiral Isoroku Yamamoto's pre-emptive strike reflected the raised ante. While Togo risked only ten destroyers at Port Arthur, Yamamoto sent Vice-Admiral Chuichi Nagumo's six fleet carriers and the cream of Japan's naval air force against Pearl Harbor. His results were proportionate to his boldness. In a few hours, the Japanese sank or disabled eight battleships and effectively destroyed U.S. land-based air forces in Hawaii.

Fortunately for the United States, no aircraft carriers were present at Pearl Harbor when Nagumo's raiders struck. One carrier, the U.S.S. *Enterprise* (Big E), was in the process of delivering twelve F4F Wildcat fighters to Wake Island. Although scheduled to return on December 6, bad weather delayed the Big E's arrival until after the danger had passed. On board the *Enterprise* was the senior carrier commander in the Pacific, Vice-Admiral William F. Halsey, Jr. When the *Enterprise* returned to Pearl Harbor on December 8, its officers and men saw a panorama of destruction depressingly framed in the twilight of dusk. Halsey viewed the carnage from the bridge with a steadily deepening scowl. He finally growled to no one in particular, "Before we're through with 'em, the Japanese language will be spoken only in hell."[1]

Accompanying Halsey to Wake Island was Rear Admiral Raymond A. Spruance, commander of Cruiser Division 5. A dwindling fuel supply had forced Spruance's cruisers to return to Pearl Harbor on the morning of December 8. As Spruance surveyed the devastation from the bridge of the *Northampton*, his only recorded reaction was silence. This stoicism was as characteristic to Spruance as bombast was to Halsey. However, Spruance was deeply shaken by what he saw in the harbor. He was a battleship admiral whose icons had just been shattered. Spruance only revealed this despair to his wife and daughter that evening. By the next morning, he regained his composure and never spoke of it again.[2]

These two officers would serve with distinction over the next four years and contribute mightily to the legacy of the U.S. Navy. But a greater study in contrast could not be found outside the realm of fiction. "Bull" Halsey was a born fighter, a two-pack-a-day smoker, and an aficionado of alcoholic beverages. His nickname reflected a colorful and aggressive personality that endeared him to the lower ranks and the general public. Halsey took war personally and was inclined toward extremes, both in his hatred of the enemy and his defense of his staff. Spruance, on the other hand, was an intellectual who drank sparingly, avoided tobacco, and was not inspirational in any sense other than the magnitude of his abilities. He took a balanced approach to warfare that allowed him to admire the Japanese fighting man even as he ruthlessly destroyed him. To his small circle of intimate associates, which included Halsey, Spruance was a warm family man with a wry sense of humor. But he was also the consummate professional officer whose personality seldom permeated his mask of cool detachment. In 1944, these men would lead the U.S. Fleet in the two greatest sea battles in history. Each man would preside over a victory that served to eliminate the Japanese Fleet as a factor in the Pacific War. But each victory would also raise controversial questions concerning the leadership of the U.S. commanders.

There was a grim irony to Yamamoto's success at Pearl Harbor. Although America's material superiority over Japan was never in question, her political will most certainly was. Japan's only hope for victory was to strike while she had local superiority, consolidate her gains, and negotiate from a position of strength. The presumption was that the American people's internal divisions and pacifist sentiments would force her leadership to recognize a *fait accompli*. Yamamoto, who never favored war with the United States, saw dubious prospects for even this grand strategy. His statement that Japan "would have to march into Washington and dictate the terms of peace in the

White House" was a warning not a boast.[3] Nevertheless, when war became inevitable, he conceived the Pearl Harbor raid in the belief that the initial blow should be struck with maximum force. In fact, the sneak attack provided the perfect emotional stimulus to galvanize the American public into supporting a policy of total war and unconditional surrender.

The air raid on Pearl Harbor also served to resolve a question of doctrine that had been debated in the world's navies for twenty years. At issue was the essence of modern naval warfare. Had the aircraft carrier become the centerpiece of the fleet or was it to be used only in support of the battle line? The destruction of U.S. battleships in Hawaii coupled with the subsequent sinking of HMS *Repulse* and *Prince of Wales* off Malaya clearly showed the dreadnought's vulnerability to air attack. More importantly, the shift in the balance of naval power meant that the U.S. Navy could only respond in a hit-and-run fashion. Even when the least damaged battleships were returned to service, they were too slow to operate with the carriers. While the admirals awaited the arrival of the new fast battleships, the carriers would prove themselves in the crucible of battle. Although the carrier versus battleship debate would continue, circumstances had already rendered it moot.

These long-term benefits were not readily apparent to the officers and men of the U.S. Pacific Fleet. Morale was understandably low and leadership was bewildered and indecisive. This began to change on December 31, 1941, when Admiral Chester W. Nimitz assumed command of Pearl Harbor. Nimitz was a submariner whose appointment jumped him over a host of more senior admirals. He had evidently made quite an impression on the higher ups in Washington during his recent duty as chief of the Bureau of Navigation. (Despite its title, the agency was essentially the navy's personnel office.) His day of promotion was not necessarily a joyous occasion for the new commander in chief of the Pacific Fleet (CinCPAC). When congratulated by his wife, he responded, "But sweetheart, all the ships are at the bottom."[4] Nimitz found the atmosphere of depression that pervaded Pearl Harbor to be even more daunting than the physical tasks required to rebuild the shattered fleet. He immediately improved morale by assuring his top commanders of his confidence in their abilities and his intention to keep them on the job. Spruance later said this was like a "breath of fresh air in a stuffy room."[5] Nimitz also made it clear that he expected the Pacific Fleet to assume a more aggressive posture. This last edict was especially pleasing to his senior carrier commander.

II

Halsey was born in Elizabeth, New Jersey, on October 30, 1882. His family had strong ties to the sea that dated back to colonial times. In the admiral's own words, many of his ancestors were "seafarers and adventurers, big, violent men, impatient of the law and prone to strong drink and strong language."[6] His father's naval credentials were more savory, having graduated from Annapolis in 1873. As a young man, Halsey faced considerable difficulty following in his father's footsteps. His grades were poor and the perpetual motion of a navy family prevented the establishment of any strong political connections. After all attempts to secure an appointment to Annapolis came up empty, the Halseys decided to pursue a more elliptical strategy that would get their son into the service as a medical officer. Thus, in the fall of 1899, Bill entered the University of Virginia with the avowed goal of a degree in medicine. He had a great time in Charlottesville but his aversion to the disciplines of the classroom made it highly unlikely that he would ever become a doctor. Fortunately, Congress had, in the meantime, authorized five additional presidential appointments to the Naval Academy. Bill received one of these, but only after his mother wangled an audience with President William McKinley.

Cadet Halsey continued his indifferent academic performance at Annapolis. He graduated forty-third out of sixty-two in the class of 1904, concentrating mainly on football and social activities. In addition to holding every class office at one time or another, Halsey was first string fullback on the mediocre teams that the academy fielded during his junior and senior years. Halsey's first duty assignment was aboard the battleship *Missouri*, rather appropriate considering his presence some forty years later at the Japanese surrender aboard its namesake. He later served on the battleship *Kansas* during its participation in the circumnavigation of the globe by Theodore Roosevelt's "Great White Fleet" from December 1907 to February 1909. During the journey, Halsey's physical stature and self-assured manner made him a valuable commodity on shore patrol duty where he collared many a drunken sailor. The worst transgressions with alcohol took place during stops in Austria and New Zealand, where the persistent offers of friendly locals to buy rounds of drinks enticed even some of Halsey's own shore patrolmen.

A crucial stop in this worldwide parade of U.S. naval power was Japan, still basking in the stature acquired from its recent defeat of Russia. While in Japan, Ensign Halsey attended a reception hosted by Admiral Togo, the architect of Japan's naval victory. Halsey was not thrilled by the meeting because he considered Togo's attack at Port Arthur to be dishonorable. He also distrusted the Japanese in general and regarded their universal courtesy as a veil over devious intentions. Nevertheless, Halsey participated in giving Admiral Togo the ceremonial three tosses, writing later, "We were big and he was a shrimp, so instead of tossing him gently, we gave him three real heaves. If we had known what the future held, we wouldn't have caught him after the third one."[7]

Halsey passed his lieutenant's exam shortly after the world cruise ended, skipping the junior grade because the exigencies of an expanding navy had created a shortage of senior lieutenants. His first command was the torpedo boat *DuPont*, a tiny vessel of 165 tons, whose like was soon to disappear from the service. He soon began receiving commands from a new source when he married his fiancée, Fanny Grandy, a southern belle whose uncle had been chief engineer on the Confederate ironclad *Virginia*. In August 1912, Halsey was given command of his first proper ship, the destroyer *Flusser*, the beginning of a twenty-year stretch where his sea duty would take place almost exclusively on destroyers. Halsey's first opportunity to see action came during the spring of 1914 when, as skipper of the *Jarvis*, he participated in President Woodrow Wilson's Mexican intervention. Assigned to the landing force, the young lieutenant envisioned himself part of a fierce amphibious assault in the spirit of his lusty forbearers. In fact, the landing proceeded with no opposition and Halsey had to content himself with the mundane details of evacuating American civilians.

The outbreak of World War I found Halsey still on the *Jarvis*, which he took on several of Wilson's so-called "neutrality patrols." He was assigned to the staff of the Naval Academy in 1915 and made lieutenant commander in the fall of the same year. Halsey was still at Annapolis when the United States entered the war in April 1917. His old flotilla commander, William S. Sims, was already in England on a mission to determine how the U.S. Navy could best aid its new allies. Admiral Sims found a nation whose lifelines were being severed by German U-boats and concluded that Britain's most immediate need was American destroyers for convoy duty. He also concluded that Halsey should command one of those destroyers. Navy politics stifled that recommendation for many months but orders directing Halsey to the destroyer base at Queenstown, Ireland, finally came through on the day after Christmas, 1917.

Halsey was scheduled to sail from the port of New York on January 7, which gave him a few days to take in the town with his wife Fan. One day, while standing on the corner near a department store in which Fan was shopping, the fully uniformed lieutenant commander was accosted by a well-dressed woman and told to fetch her car! Before his wife returned, eight other people approached him and asked where they could find various items within the store. Halsey was not amused that a nation at war could mistake a naval officer for a doorman. He got a degree of revenge by telling each shopper, "Go to the top floor, walk to the opposite side of the store, then turn right and go as far as you can. There's your department."[8]

Glory in the North Atlantic would have provided a neat literary counterpoint to the humiliation in New York, but this was not to be the case. During his months at Queenstown, Halsey never even had a confirmed sighting of a German U-boat, let alone a sinking. After the war, he changed oceans and commanded a division of six destroyers operating out of San Diego. It was here that Halsey began his association with Spruance, the best skipper in his division and soon a close friend. Halsey did not always receive such warm feelings from the officers of the battle force, however. His division was tops in the flotilla but it earned its status from its commander's aggressive and often unorthodox tactics, which exposed the vulnerabilities of the Navy's cherished dreadnoughts. During one mock exercise, while temporarily in command of his entire squadron, Halsey's destroyers "sank" three battlewagons and caused more than $1 million worth of damage with dummy torpedoes. Next day, Halsey was chewed out and told to tone down his tactics, one suspects as much to soothe bruised egos as to avoid the expense of future damage.

Halsey made full commander in June 1921 and departed San Diego a few months later for duty with the Office of Naval Intelligence. The next three years of paperwork were not especially pleasing to the man of action, but it did give him the benefit of a close look at his former enemies during his assignment as naval attaché in Berlin. His most notable achievement during his stay in the German capitol was to serve as middleman in the U.S. Navy's acquisition of the excellent stereoscopic range finder that had performed so well at the Battle of Jutland.

After Berlin, Halsey spent three years in more desirable surroundings, first on destroyers and then as executive officer of the battleship *Wyoming*. When his promotion to captain made the latter assignment inappropriate, he left the *Wyoming* and went back to Annapolis for his second tour on the staff of the Naval Academy. His jurisdiction at the academy included command of the navy's brand new aviation detail, headed by Lieutenant Dewitt C. "Duke" Ramsey. Halsey became chummy with the aviators, flew with them as a passenger whenever he could, and eventually began taking the controls himself. He decided to go to flight school but gave up the idea after flunking the rigorous eye examination three times. Instead, he took command of a destroyer squadron in the Atlantic, a very well-received consolation prize. After concluding what would turn out to be his last assignment on destroyers, Halsey got the rare privilege of attending both the Naval War College and the Army War College in successive years.

In the spring of 1934, near the end of his tenure as a student, Captain Halsey was offered command of the aircraft carrier *Saratoga*. This required a trip to Pensacola, Florida, for training as an aviation observer. But Halsey

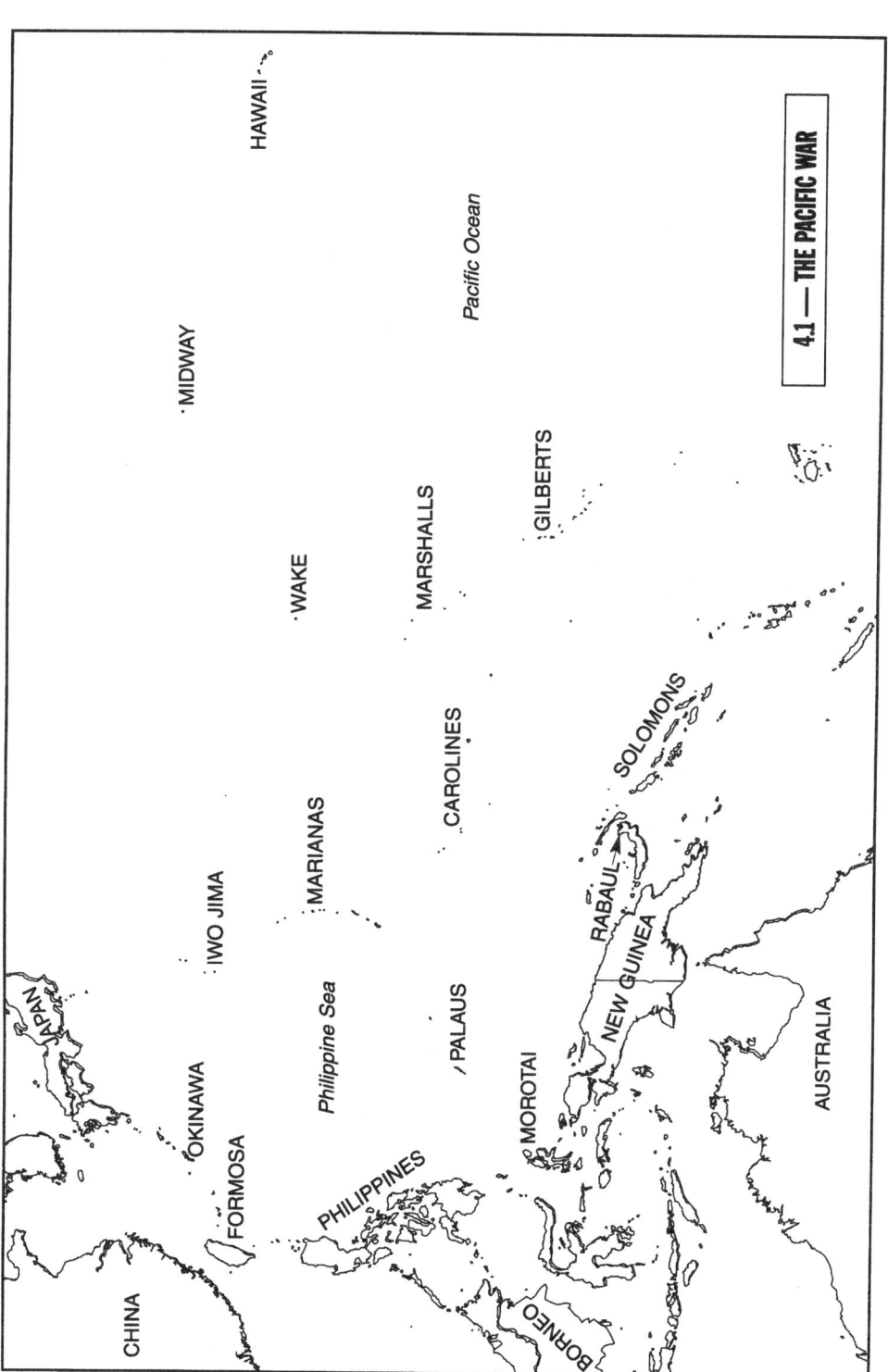

CHINA · JAPAN · OKINAWA · FORMOSA · PHILIPPINES · IWO JIMA · MARIANAS · PALAUS · MOROTAI · BORNEO · NEW GUINEA · RABAUL · SOLOMONS · AUSTRALIA · CAROLINES · MARSHALLS · GILBERTS · WAKE · MIDWAY · HAWAII · Pacific Ocean · Philippine Sea

4.1 — THE PACIFIC WAR

was determined to go further and become a pilot, despite eyesight too poor
to pass any unrigged physical examination. Evidently, those running the
program conveniently developed some bad eyesight of their own because
Halsey was admitted. The best synopsis of his flying ability came from an
instructor who said, "The worse the weather, the better he flew."[9] Halsey
earned his wings at age fifty-two and took command of the *Saratoga* soon
thereafter. He skipped the "Sara" for two years before returning to Pensacola as commandant of its Naval Air Station, during which service he received his rear admiral's stars. Halsey returned to flattops in 1938 as
commander of Carrier Division 2's brand new *Enterprise* and *Yorktown*,
and then took his flag back on board the *Saratoga* to lead Carrier Division 1.
He made vice admiral in June 1940, accompanying his elevation to commander, aircraft, battle force, which put him in charge of all of the navy's
carriers and carrier air groups. When war came, Halsey still held the title
and was nominally in command of all carrier-based naval aviation. However, because the U.S. Navy had officially been organized into Atlantic and
Pacific fleets earlier that year, his more accurate title was commander,
carriers, Pacific.

III

The Pacific Fleet's new aggressive posture would keep Bill Halsey at sea
for the greater part of the next five months. Task Force 16, built around the
Enterprise conducted raids against Japanese bases in the Marshall Islands
in January and then against Wake and Marcus Islands during late February
and early March. Despite some exaggerated claims to the contrary, these attacks inflicted little material damage on the enemy. But they definitely
helped build morale by removing the feeling of impotence that pervaded the
fleet and the nation after Pearl Harbor.

In April, Halsey embarked on the ultimate morale builder when his task
force was joined at sea by the new carrier *Hornet* and sixteen army B-25s
under the command of Lieutenant Colonel James H. Doolittle. The mission
required each bomber to deliver one ton of bombs to the Japanese mainland
and then shuttle to friendly bases in China. Doolittle would lead twelve of
the planes to hit Tokyo while one each dusted Yokohama, Nagoya, Osaka,
and Kobe. Because the twin-engine aircraft could not fit on the *Hornet*'s ele-
vators, they had to be crammed on her flight deck for the entire journey. This
kept the *Hornet*'s own planes inactive in her hangar deck and left the protection of Task Force 16 up to the air group on the *Enterprise*. Doolittle's original mission plan called for takeoff at a distance of 500 miles from the target
but detection by an enemy patrol boat required the bombers to be launched

from more than 100 miles further out. Despite the warning, the Japanese were unable to intercept the incoming aircraft nor strike back at the rapidly departing U.S. carriers, cruisers, and destroyers. Unaware of the B-25s, they failed because they focused their search within a 300-mile radius in the belief that no carrier could strike from beyond that range.

After returning from the Doolittle Raid, Task Force 16 made only a brief stop at Pearl Harbor before racing south in an attempt to assist Rear Admiral Frank Jack Fletcher in the Coral Sea. Fletcher's Task Force 17 was in the South Pacific to counter a Japanese threat to Port Moresby on New Guinea's southern coast. The resulting flattop duel was not entirely satisfactory to the Americans, costing them the venerable carrier *Lexington* in exchange for the light carrier *Shoho*. But the Japanese high command considered the presence of enemy carriers sufficient cause to scratch their invasion, thereby giving the U.S. Navy its first strategic victory of the war. Halsey did not arrive in time to participate but something even bigger was now brewing and Task Force 16 was ordered to expedite its return to Hawaii to deal with it.

By the spring of 1942, Japan's initial war objectives had all been obtained. Her drive south had seized the oil and natural resources in the Dutch East Indies as well as eliminated Allied bases in the Philippines and Malaya. Her defensive perimeter had been extended by the conquest of Northern New Guinea and the capture of various islands in the Central Pacific. Japanese military leaders now faced the necessity of planning the next phase of the war. It was agreed that Japan's presence in New Guinea should be strengthened by seizing Port Moresby on the island's southeast coast. (This thrust would be parried in the Battle of the Coral Sea on May 7–8, 1942.) There was little agreement as to what should follow. The army considered itself already overextended and would not agree to any new initiatives. The naval general staff focused on Australia and proposed cutting its lifeline to the United States by taking Fiji and Samoa. Admiral Yamamoto's Combined Fleet favored an assault on Midway Island, in the Central Pacific.

The blueprint that emerged from this dispute was mainly attributable to Admiral Yamamoto. He argued persuasively that the U.S. Fleet would surely sortie to defend Midway and be annihilated in the ensuing naval battle. His persuasive abilities were enhanced by the not-too-subtle hint that he might resign if his plan was not adopted. They received a further boost by the Doolittle Raid that focused attention on Midway as a potential launching pad for U.S. bombers. Therefore, it was decided that the main body of the Combined Fleet would capture Midway while a task force simultaneously captured the western Aleutians. Following the inevitable destruction of the American Fleet, Nagumo's carriers would bomb Australia while other naval units seized Fiji and Samoa. The Combined Fleet would then be reunited to attack and neutralize Hawaii.

Yamamoto counted on the element of surprise to ensure that he would face the U.S. Pacific Fleet after he had seized Midway. But his *coup de main* was foiled by U.S. naval intelligence. Commander Joseph Rochefort's cryptanalysts had broken the Japanese code and given Nimitz a clear picture of enemy intentions. Pearl Harbor's cryptanalysts had the work habits of Trappist monks, putting in an average of twenty hours a day on the job. Some were so good that they could identify a particular Japanese ship by the idiosyncrasies of its wireless key operator. By early May, intelligence knew that Yamamoto was massing his ships to seize a place designated as "AF." Rochefort was certain that their destination was Midway but lacked any hard evidence to support his contention. In order to resolve all doubts, he had Midway send a phony message concerning the failure of its distillation plant. Soon, Japanese commanders were being advised that AF was short of water.

Rochefort's ruse clinched the decision as far as Nimitz was concerned. He ordered that Midway be reinforced to its capacity and instructed his operations section to begin formulating a plan to support the island with the fleet. Nimitz gave his intelligence officer, Captain Edwin T. Layton, the job of conjuring Japanese tactical intentions. Layton pored over three weeks of reports, cross-referencing them and conferring often with Rochefort, but still expressed a reluctance to be specific. When Nimitz pressed the matter, his intelligence chief got more specific than the admiral anticipated. Layton told him, "I've previously given you the intelligence that the carriers will probably attack Midway on the morning of the 4th of June. . . . They'll come in from the northwest on bearing 325 degrees and they will be sighted at about 175 miles for Midway, and the time will be about 0600 Midway time."[10] A satisfied and slightly bemused Admiral Nimitz promptly ordered the information to be passed on to Midway and to his operations officers.

When the Combined Fleet reached Midway, the U.S. carrier force would already be there. But it would not be led by its colorful senior commander. All his years of experience had not taught Halsey how to pace himself. He continued to have only one speed: flat out. During his recent months at sea, Halsey had pushed his endurance to the limit, sustaining himself on coffee and cigarettes. He paid for it with a 20-pound weight loss, chronic dermatitis, and general exhaustion. Nimitz took one look at him and ordered him into the hospital. Before departing, Nimitz solicited Halsey's recommendation for a replacement to command Task Force 16. He unhesitatingly recommended Ray Spruance.

IV

Raymond Ames Spruance was born on July 3, 1886, in Baltimore, Maryland. He showed intellect and ability at an early age, often earning the ire of his teachers by achieving good grades despite never taking home books. Neither Raymond nor his family had any special attraction to the sea. They looked toward the Naval Academy because financial reverses made college tuition unaffordable. Spruance's road to Annapolis was much smoother than young Bill Halsey's. While his mother secured an appointment through political connections in Indiana, Ray won another through competitive examinations in New Jersey. He was in New Jersey because his neglectful mother had long ago dumped him on her family, where he was raised by his grandmother and three aunts. The experience had made the young man fiercely independent, so it was not surprising that he decided to accept the appointment, which he had earned on his own. But his aunts thought otherwise and badgered him into taking the Indiana appointment as a token of appreciation to his mother.

Spruance hated the discipline at the academy and was extremely dissatisfied with the school's quality of education that he blamed on a rigid curriculum, poor instructors, and low academic standards. On his first summer cruise as a midshipman, he also discovered that he was prone to seasickness. Nevertheless, he conformed to his surroundings and graduated 25th of the 209 members of the Class of 1907. Although undistinguished in competitive sports, Spruance also toughened himself physically at the academy by taking marathon swims and hikes in the worst of weather. After initial duty on the *Iowa*, he participated in the global promenade of the "Great White Fleet" aboard the battleship *Minnesota*. Spruance's attitude toward Japan was quite different from that of Halsey. He mingled with the locals as much as possible and left with a very favorable impression of Admiral Togo's nation. The world cruise was a positive experience for Spruance and convinced him to stay in the navy.

Spruance decided that his future lay in mastering the Navy's mushrooming technology, so he applied for postgraduate training and received one year of instruction in electricity at the General Electric plant in Schenectady, New York. He then went on the battleship *Connecticut* where, despite a personality clash with the captain, he was promoted to lieutenant (junior grade). Spruance's next stop was the Far East, first as engineering officer on a cruiser and then as commanding officer of the destroyer *Bainbridge*. Based in the Philippines, the U.S. Asiatic Fleet was best known for its old ships and shady characters. Although the conservative Spruance did not fit the mold of his rough and ready comrades, he turned the previously troubled *Bainbridge* into a happy and efficient ship. His ensigns appreciated the fact that as long as their work was satisfactory, he took no notice of their extracurricular activities ashore. Spruance became popular with his enlisted men by showing interest in their work, giving them swimming lessons and, perhaps most importantly, making it his personal crusade to see that they received good food. Spruance made full lieutenant in October 1913 and left the *Bainbridge* the following spring for an assignment at the Newport News Shipyard. While traveling cross county, he detoured long enough to propose to his long-time love interest, Margaret Dean. The two were married that December.

When the United States entered World War I in April 1917, Spruance was serving as electrical officer on the battleship *Pennsylvania*. Like many officers schooled in the glory of the battleship navy, he looked forward to a contest with the kaiser's dreadnoughts. But Spruance's recognized expertise in electrical engineering was in demand elsewhere. He was transferred to a billet on shore and spent the war in unglamorous activities involving the development and installation of new gunnery fire control systems. The disappointed warrior was consoled somewhat by two rapid promotions that made him a full commander by the time the armistice was declared.

In 1920, Spruance was placed in command of the destroyer *Aaron Ward*, the assignment that began in association with Halsey. The friendship expanded when Fan Halsey and Margaret Spruance hit it off as well as their husbands. Soon, the couples were socializing on a regular basis. The relationship thrived despite decidedly different attitudes about alcohol. Halsey had a seaman's affection for liquor and a constitution to match. Spruance occasionally drank to excess but the resulting hangover then induced a long period of abstinence. After a few binges with Halsey, however, Spruance resolved on enforced moderation and alcohol virtually disappeared from his home. Halsey, of course, constantly jibbed Spruance about his inability to hold liquor. During one of the Halseys' frequent unannounced late night visits, their host was hard pressed to find them a drink, producing only a tiny bit of cognac. Bill declined the offer, saying, "Not at this time of night, Spruance. You still haven't learned how to drink."[11]

Spruance left San Diego in the summer of 1921 for duty in Washington, D.C., as head of the Bureau of Engineering's Electrical Division. He was then assigned to the naval force based in European waters where he served as the admiral's assistant chief of staff until relieving Halsey as commander of the destroyer *Osborne*. The contrast in the two men became immediately apparent to the ship's crew. Halsey's style of command was informal, boisterous and theatrical. Spruance ran what was known as a "quiet bridge," always calm and collected. Once, while in a French harbor, an excited lieutenant rushed into Spruance's cabin to report that a depth charge had fallen over-board. Used to Halsey's emotionalism and casual profanity, the young offi-cer was expecting an eruption from the new captain. Instead, Spruance responded in his usual monotone, "Well, pick it up and put it back."[12]

In the summer of 1926, Spruance traveled to Newport, Rhode Island for a year of study at the Naval War College. He enjoyed his stay at the War Col-lege where he finally found a robust academic environment that gave him intellectual stimulation. His studies at Newport added military history, strategy, tactics, and international relations to his vast array of technical knowledge. Spruance put his new wisdom to use first at the Office of Naval Intelligence in Washington and then as executive officer on the battleship *Mississippi*. He returned to the War College in the fall of 1931 as the direc-tor of the Correspondence Courses Department and made captain while serving in that capacity.

As his tour at Newport was winding down, Spruance received the unwel-come news that he was slated to command the repair ship *Vestal*. The newly promoted captain viewed this as a giant step backward and resolved not to accept it without protest. It is not clear exactly what strings he pulled, but his orders were changed at the last minute and he was assigned instead to the Pacific Destroyer Force at San Francisco as the admiral's chief of staff. His first task was to supervise navy experiments with the new underwater detec-tion device later known as SONAR. Spruance spent two years of adminis-trative drudgery and frustration in San Francisco, struggling to keep antiquated destroyers operational with inadequate resources. He earned an exemplary fitness report, however, and then headed back to Newport for a senior staff position at the War College.

Spruance made his third trip to Newport against his will. He had instead requested duty at the Naval Mine Depot in Yorktown, Virginia. His criteria for choosing Yorktown was that it would be easy duty and allow him and his wife to reaquaint themselves with the part of the country where they spent their honeymoon. This gives us a vivid illustration of Spruance's state of mind at this point. Mentally fatigued from his previous labors and pessimis-tic about his chances of making admiral, he was looking to play out the re-mainder of his career in the most comfortable manner possible. But the president of the War College specifically asked for him so off he went for another three years at Newport.

Spruance shook off his disappointment and put in a solid if uninspired performance at the War College. Following his stint in Rhode Island, he re-alized his one remaining career ambition, command of a battleship. On the last day of April 1938, Spruance returned to the *Mississippi* as its captain, some seven years after finishing his tour as her executive officer. The crew

found him to be demanding but fair and responded to his leadership by taking first place in both gunnery and communication during the fleet exercises
of 1939. His sparkling record on the *Mississippi* was instrumental in earning him his rear admiral's stars several months after he had relinquished the
ship's reigns and taken his new post as commandant of the Tenth Naval Dis-
trict in the Caribbean. Spruance desired next to lead a division of battleships
but instead received orders in September 1941, to proceed to Pearl Harbor
and take command of the four ships in Cruiser Division 5.

V

It may seem curious that a nonaviator would be placed in command of a
carrier task force on the eve of the most important battle of the war. Halsey's
recommendation was partially based on personal loyalty. But Spruance's
reputation was well known to Nimitz and to Admiral Earnest J. King, the
chief of naval operations. Nimitz had already received permission from
Washington to make him his chief of staff. Spruance was informed of this at
the same meeting in which Nimitz gave him command of Task Force 16. It
is not difficult to imagine the resulting flow of emotions which might have
overwhelmed a less disciplined personality. Spruance's anxiety and excite-
ment over the approaching battle must have co-mingled with disgust and
disappointment over the prospect of coming ashore when it was over.

Admiral Yamamoto was deploying most of the Combined Fleet against
Midway and the Aleutians. However, he was spreading it over 1,000 miles
of ocean. Vice-Admiral Moshiro Hosogaya was assigned two aircraft carriers, six cruisers, and twelve destroyers for his attack on the Aleutians. A
"Guard Force" built around four old battleships was available to support
Hosogaya if necessary. Vice-Admiral Nobutake Kondo's Midway Invasion
Force would tackle its objective from the southwest. It included five thousand troops on twelve transports, escorted by ten destroyers and a light
cruiser. Kondo's surface support was impressive, totaling two battleships,
eight heavy cruisers, three light cruisers, and twenty destroyers. But his air
cover was limited to the twenty-four planes of the light carrier *Zuiho*. The
bulk of Yamamoto's air strength was contained in Admiral Nagumo's Carrier Strike Force, which approached Midway from the northwest. Nagumo's four fleet carriers possessed 261 planes and a screen of two battleships,
three cruisers, and 12 destroyers. Yamamoto himself sailed some 300 miles
behind the carriers. His Main Body contained Japan's three most powerful
battleships accompanied by a light carrier, nine destroyers, and a light
cruiser.[13] The designation of this force as the Main Body was not due
merely to the presence of its exalted passenger. It also reflected the linger-

ing belief among much of Japan's naval leadership that the battleship was still the arm of decision at sea.

Conspicuously absent, however, were the carriers *Shokaku* and *Zuikaku*. The former had been damaged in the Coral Sea battle and both ships needed to replace planes and air crews. Even without these ships, Japan enjoyed overwhelming material superiority. She also possessed many qualitative advantages. Japan's "Zero" fighter planes could fly rings around anything the Allies could put in the air. Her Long Lance torpedoes were vastly superior to American types in range, reliability and striking power. Japanese naval aircrews were the most experienced in the world and the night-fighting techniques of Japan's surface ships were unmatched. In the spring of 1942, it would not have been hyperbole to proclaim Japan's navy as the best on the planet.

The U.S. Navy's only effective opposition to Yamamoto's onslaught would come from the 233 aircraft on the *Enterprise*, *Hornet*, and *Yorktown*. The three carriers would be protected by a paper-thin screen of eight cruisers and fifteen destroyers.[14] It required extraordinary measures to assemble even this tiny force. The *Yorktown* had returned from the Coral Sea so badly damaged that it would normally have taken three months to repair her. But 1,400 workmen laboring around the clock made the battered flattop seaworthy in just two-and-a-half days. Fletcher would exercise overall command from the *Yorktown's* bridge while Spruance led Task Force 16 from the *Enterprise*. Because reigning doctrine required that carrier task forces be dispersed, Spruance would operate with wide latitude. Nimitz directed his commanders to be guided by "the principle of calculated risk" that meant "avoidance of exposure of your force to attack by superior enemy forces without good prospect of inflicting greater damage on the enemy."[15] In his discussion with Spruance, Nimitz made it clear that Midway was to be held, but not at all costs. The preservation of the carriers was even more important.[16]

On the morning of June 4, 1942, Admiral Nagumo sent 108 planes to soften up Midway for the invasion troops. He also ordered a single-phase search of seven aircraft to seek out any enemy ships that might be lurking nearby. Four of the search planes were late in departure, including the two assigned to cover the sections containing the U.S. task forces. Nagumo's remaining attack planes, half of which were armed with torpedoes, were poised to deal with any enemy vessels that turned up. The Japanese air assault on Midway made mincemeat of the island's fighter cover but failed to destroy its airstrips or coast batteries. Flight leader Lieutenant Joichi Tomonaga informed the flagship *Akagi* that there was need for a second attack. His opinion was soon supported by the appearance of U.S. land-based aircraft. These attackers scored no hits but convinced Nagumo that Midway remained a potent threat. He concurred in Tomonaga's recommendation and ordered the planes carrying torpedoes to be re-equipped with bombs. Then, at 7:40 a.m., Nagumo received a vaguely worded dispatch from one of his tardy scouts that indicated the presence of enemy ships. He quickly suspended the switchover to bombs and sent off a terse request for more specific information.

Nagumo received several follow-up reports, one of which identified five cruisers and five destroyers but made no mention of carriers. As he sifted through the incoming information, Japan's carrier leader was continuously distracted by more attacks from Midway's air group. Mere distractions they were, for the mishmash of Marine and Army aviators did not hit a single ship. Finally, at approximately 8:30 a.m., the search plane confirmed that the U.S. naval force included at least one carrier. By that time, the planes from the Midway strike were circling their mother ships with nearly empty fuel tanks. Nagumo decided to clear his flight decks and allow the returning aviators to land. The planes of his second echelon were taken below deck to be armed for their sortie against the American ships. Nagumo planned to send them aloft as soon as the recovery operation had concluded. Unfortunately for the Japanese commander, the U.S. Navy did not acquiesce in his scheduling.

One of Midway's patrol planes (PBYs) located Nagumo's force at approximately 5:55 a.m., Midway time. (Incredibly, Layton's "guess" was off by only five minutes, five degrees, and five miles.) On the bridge of the *Enterprise*, Admiral Spruance conferred with the staff he had inherited from Halsey. His chief of staff, Captain Miles S. Browning, calculated that an immediate U.S. attack might catch Nagumo in the process of recovering the planes from his Midway strike force. Although only two Japanese carriers were positively identified, Spruance decided to launch an attack with nearly every dive bomber and torpedo plane at his disposal. Fletcher gave him the go ahead and promised to follow suit as soon as he recovered his morning air search. At 7 a.m., Spruance's two carriers turned into the wind and commenced flight operations. The *Hornet* sent aloft thirty-five Dauntless dive bombers, fifteen Devastator torpedo bombers and ten Wildcat fighters. The *Enterprise* contributed thirty-three Dauntlesses, fourteen Devastators, and ten Wildcats. About ninety minutes later, the *Yorktown* launched its contingent of seventeen dive bombers, twelve torpedo planes, and six fighters. Fletcher held twenty Dauntlesses in reserve.[17]

The planes of Task Force 16 flew under directions that assumed that the Japanese carrier force would maintain the course it was following when first sighted. In fact, Nagumo altered his course shortly before he recovered the last planes from the Midway strike. Although the PBYs observed the change in course, no one on Midway bothered to inform either task force commander. Thus, the U.S. pilots found nothing at the projected point of interception and were forced to "dead reckon" their way into battle. *Hornet's* fighters and dive bombers missed the target completely. Most of the Dauntlesses returned safely, landing either on their own flight deck or on the airstrips at Midway. Every one of the Wildcats ran out of fuel and had to ditch. The fighters from the *Enterprise* found the Japanese carriers but not the attack planes they were supposed to escort. They all returned to their mother ship without engaging the enemy.

The torpedo bombers displayed a better sense of direction. *Hornet's* squadron attacked first and lost all fifteen of its planes without scoring any hits. Fourteen Devastators from the *Enterprise* followed them in and lost ten planes for the same empty payback. Meanwhile, the dive bombers from the *Enterprise* had arrived at their projected point of contact and found empty ocean. Lieutenant Commander Wade McClusky turned his flight to the northwest and then spotted a lone Japanese destroyer that led him to the big boys. The *Yorktown's* air group found Nagumo's carriers at about the same time. Their air officer had anticipated the course change and gave directions that brought them right to the target. This time, U.S. torpedo planes attacked with some fighter cover. But six Wildcats could not alter the fate of the slow, obsolete Devastators. All twelve were destroyed without so much as scratching an enemy vessel.

At this point, the battle had the makings of a great Japanese victory. Midway's fighters had been shot out of the sky by the Japanese Zeroes and her attack planes had suffered heavy losses in their ineffective efforts against the Japanese ships. Three U.S. torpedo squadrons had been annihilated. No Japanese ships had been damaged and only a few planes had been lost. The American carriers had been located and their airborne executioners were now massed on deck, ready for takeoff. But even as the first Zero began its run down the *Akagi*'s flight deck, Dauntlesses came diving out of the sun to turn Japan's world upside down. McClusky's gang made two hits on the *Akagi* and four on the *Kaga*. Lieutenant Commander Max Leslie's bunch from the *Yorktown* chipped in with three hits on the *Soryu*. The damage inflicted by their bombs was amplified by exploding armaments and gasoline. In minutes, the three Japanese carriers were blazing wrecks. All would eventually sink.

On Nagumo's remaining carrier, *Hiryu*, Rear Admiral Tamon Yamaguchi struck back with two attack waves. Lieutenant Tomonaga led the second group even though his aircraft was leaking fuel so badly that he knew it could not make the return flight. The Japanese counterpunch hit the *Yorktown* with three bombs and two torpedoes. This damage rendered Fletcher virtually incommunicado and put Spruance in de-facto command. The

Americans had only a vague idea of the *Hiryu's* location, but Halsey's former staff urged Spruance to act on it and launch an attack. Spruance refused to send his planes until he had more definite information. He felt that his reduced air wings must not be further dispersed on wild goose chases. Because Yamaguchi maneuvered extensively after each of his launches, the decision was probably a good one. However, in a serious oversight, Spruance neglected to provide for air searches to obtain the information that he desired. Fortunately, Fletcher had sent out a scout mission before the *Yorktown* became disabled. One of these planes found the *Hiryu* at approximately 2:45 p.m.

Admiral Spruance now acted swiftly, sending up most of the airworthy attack planes left on the two operational U.S. carriers. The *Enterprise* contributed twenty-four dive bombers, ten that were members of her indigenous air wing and fourteen that were transplants from the stricken *Yorktown*. The *Hornet* sent fifteen of her Dauntlesses aloft a few minutes later. Neither bunch of attackers had any fighter escort as all remaining Wildcats were hoarded to protect the carriers. The composite group from the *Enterprise* was under the command of Lieutenant Earl Gallaher, pinch hitting for a wounded Wade McClusky. After sighting the Japanese ships, Gallaher divided his formation, leading his own contingent against the *Hiryu* while sending Lieutenant DeWitt Shumway's *Yorktown* refugees against the battleship *Haruna*. However, Shumway switched the bulk of his group to the enemy flattop on his own initiative after watching the bombs from Gallaher's first three planes miss their target. Together, the concentrated groups scored four hits on the *Hiryu's* flight deck and left her burning from end to end. Dauntlesses from the *Hornet* then arrived and went after the escorts but managed only a few near misses on the heavy cruiser *Tone*. The *Hiryu* burned well into the night before torpedoes from the destroyer *Makigumo* sent her to join her three sisters at the bottom of the Pacific. Admiral Yamaguchi refused to abandon ship and went down with her.

Spruance then made what was perhaps the most crucial decision of the battle. He ordered his task force to sail west, away from the enemy, despite the dictum that a defeated enemy must be pursued aggressively. Spruance recognized that the Japanese surface force was still overwhelming and the loss of its air cover meant that it could only be employed in a night engagement. By sailing east until midnight and then reversing course back toward Midway, Task Force 16 could avoid a night battle and still position itself to defend the island. A night battle was precisely what Yamamoto sought and Spruance's strategy had foiled him completely. He was forced to call retreat when this became apparent next morning. U.S. flyers continued to dish out punishment during the Japanese withdrawal, sinking one heavy cruiser and

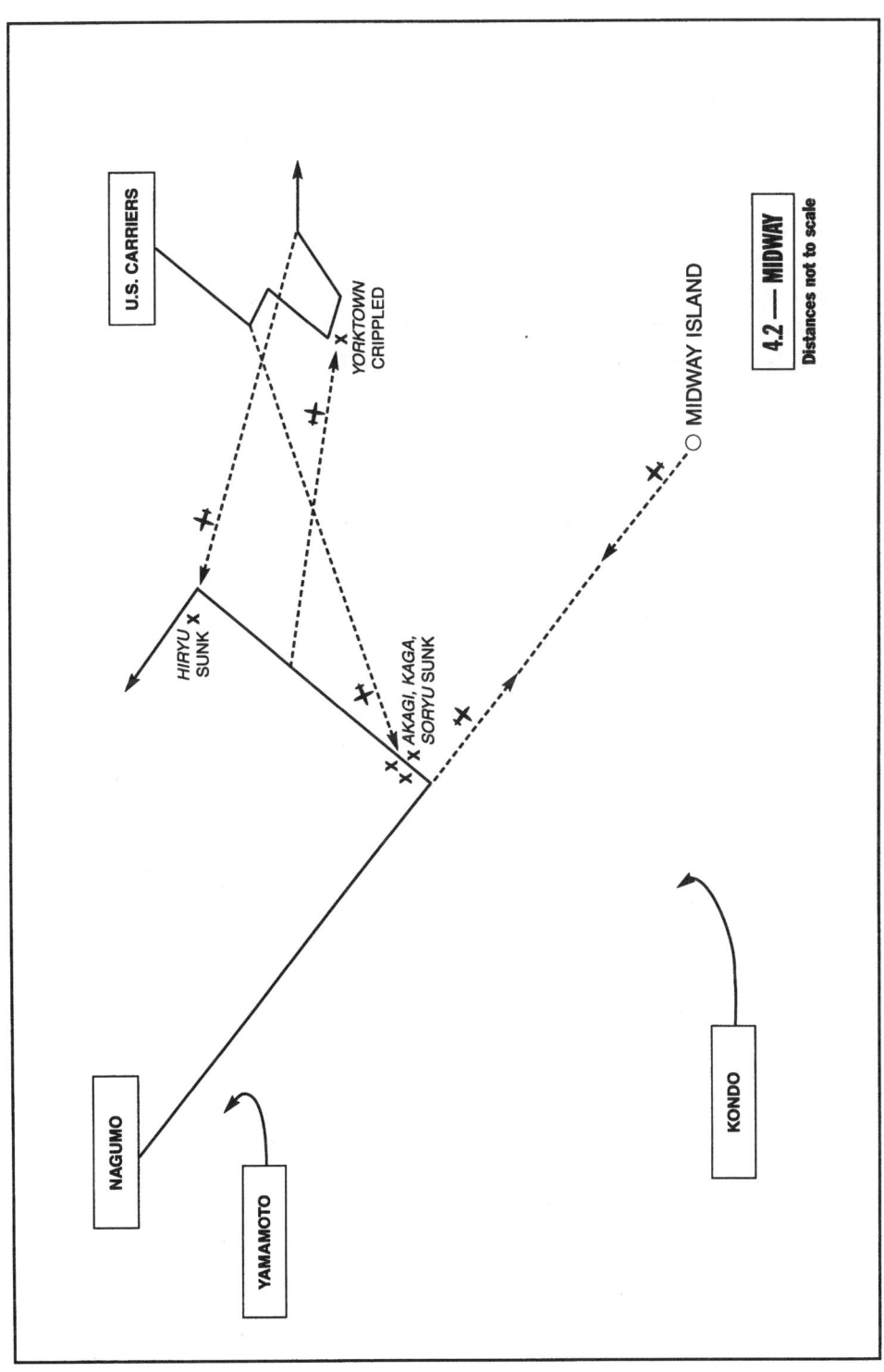

U.S. CARRIERS

YORKTOWN
CRIPPLED

HIRYU
SUNK

x *AKAGI, KAGA,*
x *SORYU* SUNK

NAGUMO

YAMAMOTO

○ MIDWAY ISLAND

KONDO

4.2 — MIDWAY

Distances not to scale

badly damaging another. Spruance finally ended the battle on the evening of June 6 when he realized that Japanese movements were bringing him dangerously close to Wake Island's land-based aircraft.

The Battle of Midway was a tremendous victory for the U.S. Navy, doubly sweet considering the disparity of the forces involved. Japan lost four fleet carriers, one heavy cruiser, 2,500 men, and more than three hundred planes at a cost to the United States of the *Yorktown*, a destroyer, 307 men, and 147 planes.[18] (The *Yorktown* survived the damage inflicted by the *Hiryu*'s aircraft and was being towed to Pearl Harbor when it was sunk by submarine I-168.) Strategically, the Japanese losses served to redress the balance of military power in the Pacific. Nimitz's command emerged from the battle well positioned to regain the initiative if the opportunity presented itself. Midway also provided the best evidence yet presented that the age of the battleship had passed. On June 5, Yamamoto's Main Body, Kondo's Invasion Force, and Nagumo's remnant possessed seven battleships. Stripped of their air cover, these ships ignominiously withdrew from the scene despite the fact that not a single U.S. counterpart opposed them. Clearly, the aircraft carriers had become the true "main body."

The Japanese navy committed a catalog of errors in the Midway operation. Yamamoto squandered his superiority by dispersing rather than concentrating his forces. He gave Nagumo the joint objectives of taking Midway and destroying the U.S. Fleet without making it clear which took precedence. Operationally, this was extremely problematic because the first mission required adherence to a rigid schedule, whereas the second depended on flexibility. Nagumo conducted sloppy search procedures and hesitated fatally once the U.S. carriers were discovered. The Japanese naval leadership had become infected with a complacency that was later described as "Victory Disease." [19] Their uninterrupted string of successes had spawned contempt for American fighting abilities and a belief that future successes were guaranteed. Indeed, when gaming the Midway operation, one scenario predicted a flank attack by U.S. carriers that would score nine hits, sinking two carriers and damaging another. But this did not fit the mood at Combined Fleet Headquarters, so the chief of staff, Admiral Matome Ugaki, reduced the damage to three hits and one lost carrier.[20] Apparently, Togo's heirs had forgotten to tighten their helmet straps in the hour of victory.

The U.S. victory was not merely a story of Japanese mistakes. It was a triumph of military intelligence and a showcase for the courage and initiative of the officers and men of the Pacific Fleet. Most of all, it was a tribute to the balanced and decisive leadership of Admiral Spruance. The "battleship admiral" used his carriers to perfection. When the enemy carriers were located, Spruance unhesitatingly used his entire force to deliver a knockout blow. He then showed great fortitude in waiting for definite information before sending his diminished force against the *Hiryu*. Finally, Spruance showed wise judgement and appreciation of the tactical situation by steaming east on the evening of June 4. Without Nagumo's carriers, Yamamoto could only withdraw or precipitate a surface battle at night. If he chose the former course, Midway was safe, four Japanese carriers had been sunk and the U.S. Fleet was still afloat. If Yamamoto chose the latter course, as is now known to be the case, it was imperative to stay out of range of the guns and torpedoes of his surface ships. Therefore, pursuit was the *worst* possible move the Americans could have made on June 4. It would not have enhanced their ability to defend Midway, but would have exposed them to possible disaster. Spruance's decision to sail in a box eliminated the danger to his own ships and positioned them to launch air strikes with impunity against any Japanese ships which had continued to advance throughout the night.

The logic of Spruance's tactics was lost on many staff officers who supposedly had a better understanding of naval aviation. The decision to sail east continued to be criticized as "overcautious" long after Spruance assumed his duties as Nimitz's chief of staff. When a report issued by the Naval War College also reflected this view, Spruance had had enough. He met with Captain Layton and requested information on Japanese movements during the night of June 4, 1942. After four days of searching, Layton came up with a captured track chart and radio message log. The documents clearly showed that if Spruance had sailed west on June 4, he would have collided with powerful Japanese surface forces.[21] Spruance sent the material to Admiral Nimitz and resumed his duties with a relieved state of mind.

VI

The war that Spruance was planning had been fought many times at the Naval War College in the 1920s and 1930s. It envisioned a drive across the Central Pacific focusing on the great Japanese naval base at Truk, in the Carolines. It would climax somewhere in a great naval battle on the order of Jutland. But the Japanese did not fall in line with American pre-war theories. They focused back on the South Pacific planning an assault on Port Moresby across New Guinea's Owen Stanley Mountains. General Douglas MacArthur's Americans and Australians would have to deal with this. The Japanese intended to support their advance by establishing airfields on Guadalcanal, in the Solomon Islands. When it became apparent that the first airfield was nearing completion, Admiral King ordered Nimitz to take Guadalcanal. The Solomons lay in the Southwest Pacific Theater and were therefore under MacArthur's jurisdiction. But because the U.S. Navy would be supplying the men and the ships, Nimitz felt the operation more properly belonged to Vice-Admiral Robert L. Ghormley's South Pacific Theater. After much haranguing between the parties, the boundary was shifted slightly to the west to accommodate the navy's wishes.

On August 7, 1942, the U.S. First Marine Division under Major General Alexander Archer Vandegrift seized Guadalcanal and its nearby islands. King had designated his offensive as "Operation Watchtower," but its participants preferred "Operation Shoestring" because of its hasty planning and shaky logistical foundation. The shoestring was frayed in the early morning hours of August 9, when a Japanese cruiser force inflicted a disastrous defeat on the Allied ships covering the landing. The Battle of Savo Island cost the Allies four heavy cruisers and forced the half-unloaded transports to leave the area. The U.S. Marines dug in and made do. They supplemented their rations with captured rice and finished the airfield with construction equipment that had been abandoned by the enemy. By August 20, Marine fighters and dive bombers were flying from the airfield, officially designated Henderson Field, but called Cactus by its inhabitants. These aircraft gave the Americans control of the approaches to Guadalcanal during the daylight hours. But the night belonged to Rear Admiral Razio Tanaka's "Tokyo Express," running from Rabaul to Guadalcanal through the passageway known as "the slot." Tanaka used destroyers to make express deliveries of men and supplies and then get out of range of air attack before sunrise. Heavier ships would also transit the same route to bombard Henderson Field and its defenders. The initial attempt by the Japanese army to evict the Marines employed frontal assaults in inadequate strength and failed miserably. It seemed that Japanese generals also suffered from a strain of Victory Disease.

Admiral Fletcher extracted a slice of revenge for Savo Island on August 24 in the Battle of the Eastern Solomons where his carrier planes sank the light carrier *Ryujo*. This was offset a week later, however, when a Japanese submarine put a torpedo into the *Saratoga* and sent her to the repair yards for three months. Fletcher was slightly wounded in the attack, so he accompanied his flagship to Pearl Harbor and then went stateside for recuperative leave and a meeting with Admiral King. The chief of naval operations was not sure if Fletcher was unlucky or inept, but he was sure that two carriers sunk and another damaged was enough for any admiral at this stage of the war. Fletcher was reassigned to shore duty and never again held a command at sea.

Meanwhile, neither the planes at Henderson Field nor the tactical victory in the Eastern Solomons had stopped the flow of Japanese reinforcements through "the slot." During two nights of hell on September 12 and 13, the Imperial Army's second thrust against the Marines' enclave was repelled in what became known as the Battle of Bloody Ridge. Although their assault was an abject failure, the piles of corpses littering Henderson Field's perimeter at least opened the eyes of the Japanese high command who now realized that their drive in the Solomons needed more power. Accordingly, the army suspended its offensive against Port Moresby and began transferring two entire divisions to Guadalcanal.

U.S. reinforcements and supplies also came to the island, sometimes at a heavy cost. The carrier *Wasp* was torpedoed and sunk by a Japanese submarine while convoying the 7th Marine Regiment in mid-September. U.S. surface combatants achieved more satisfactory results while covering the next convoy. On the night of October 11–12, 1942, Rear Admiral Norman Scott's cruisers and destroyers gave the Imperial Japanese navy its first ever surface defeat in the Battle of Cape Esperance. Scott's success was a minor tactical victory, costing the Japanese one heavy cruiser and one destroyer in exchange for one destroyer of his own. Strategically, it was no more than a draw. Although the Battle of Cape Esperance protected the ships carrying the U.S. Army's 164th Regiment, it had no effect whatsoever on the Tokyo Express. By mid-October, it was apparent to Nimitz that the Japanese were winning the battle of the build up and a major offensive was imminent. Low Allied morale was the most troubling aspect of the whole situation. Admiral Ghormley was a competent but uninspiring leader who gave off a strong air of defeatism from his headquarters at Noumea, New Caledonia. Both Nimitz and King agreed that the South Pacific needed a more aggressive commander. They also agreed that Bill Halsey was just the tonic to cure the Malaise.

Halsey was already en route to the South Pacific when the decision was made. He thought he was going to command Ghormely's carriers. On his arrival in New Caledonia, Halsey received sealed orders that placed him in charge of the entire theater of operations. After reading them, he proclaimed, "Jesus Christ and General Jackson! This is the hottest potato they've ever handed me!"[22] This strong reaction was not merely a reflection on the magnitude of the task ahead. Ghormley was an old friend and to Halsey friendship was sacrosanct. Before assuming his new duties, Halsey consoled his old comrade and solicited his advice.

Halsey's first decision as theater commander was characteristically decisive and aggressive. He canceled the construction of an airfield on the island of Ndeni, some 400 miles southeast of Guadalcanal, and ordered that the troops earmarked as its garrison be sent instead to bolster Vandegrift. The Joint Chiefs of Staff in Washington had envisioned Ndeni's airfield as a platform for reconnaissance flights and a guardian of their South Pacific supply lines. Halsey felt that the main business was on the front lines and had no qualms about exercising his authority as the commander on the scene to alter the plans of a higher authority.

The change of command was well received by the rank and file throughout the South Pacific, especially on Guadalcanal itself. One survivor later wrote of the reaction:

One minute we were too limp with malaria to crawl out of our foxholes; the next, we were running around whooping like kids. I remember two Marines working up to a brawl. One of them was saying that getting the Old man was like getting two battleships and two carriers and the other was swearing he was worth two battleships and three carriers. If morale had been enough, we'd have won the war right there.[23]

The upswing in morale came just in time as Yamamoto unleashed his onslaught in late October. But although the Japanese army came on in greater numbers it did not change its tactics. Bayonette charges against the marines and newly arrived army units yielded the same disastrous results. At sea, the opposing fleets fought to a draw in the Battle of Santa Cruz Island, which saw the end of the *Hornet*. Japanese carrier planes also hit the *Enterprise* and probably would have sunk her too if not for anti-aircraft fire from the new battleship *South Dakota*. The *Enterprise* was now the only U.S. aircraft carrier in the entire Pacific and she needed repairs before she could fight again. No Japanese ships were sunk at Santa Cruz, but damage to the *Shokaku* and the loss of one hundred planes forced Yamamoto to remove his carriers from the Solomons' chessboard.

October's fighting decided nothing except that more fighting would come in November. Halsey made a quick trip to Guadalcanal to assess the situation and attempt some direct morale building. At an impromptu press conference, he summarized his war strategy as "kill Japs, kill Japs, and keep on killing Japs."[24] Halsey took great pains to disparage and verbally abuse the Japanese throughout the Pacific War. His comments and correspondence was riddled with references to "yellow bastards" and "monkeymen," giving them more than a slight tinge of racism. But Halsey's attitude had less to do with the hue of his opponent's skin than with his own black-and-white perception of the war's underlying issues. He genuinely hated the Japanese for what he saw as their brutal militarism, treacherous diplomacy, and dishonorable way of making war. Halsey was a true believer whose "everyman" morality led him to dehumanize the enemy he had to kill. However, he was also a skilled leader and at least some of his lambasting of Japanese fighting abilities was undoubtedly calculated to boost the spirit of his own men as well as that of the general public back in the states.

Halsey's presence on Guadalcanal was reassuring to its reluctant residents but morale alone can only do so much. The Tokyo Express was making deliveries at a feverish pace in early November. Halsey countered by sending a package of his own: six thousand troops plus liberal amounts of food, fuel, and ammunition. He also mobilized every available combat ship for the coming showdown. Even the *Enterprise*, with her forward elevation still inoperable, would be sent into the fray. The climax to four months of struggle came in a three-day battle beginning on November 13. Tanaka's herculean efforts had brought the total of Japanese ground forces on Guadalcanal to 30,000.[25] But the destroyer's limitations as cargo ships did not allow for an adequate build up of supplies to support this mass. Therefore, Tanaka was ordered to go to Guadalcanal with a convoy of twelve conventional transports, carrying an additional 13,000 soldiers and enough supplies to fuel the offensive that would finally dislodge the marines. Because the transports could not make the trip in one night, the Japanese also planned to send strong surface forces down the slot to neutralize Henderson Field and two new strips called Fighter-1 and Fighter-2.

The first attempt to force the slot was made by the battleships *Hiei* and *Kirishima*, screened by a light cruiser and eleven destroyers. They were opposed by a surface action group under Rear Admiral Daniel Callaghan and the convoy escort group under Rear Admiral Scott, the latter freed up for battle after the delivery of its precious cargo on November 12. Because Callaghan was the senior officer, he led the combined force, which numbered two heavy cruisers, one light cruiser, two anti-aircraft cruisers, and eight destroyers.[26] Each side had the same lucky total of thirteen warships, but the sixteen 14-inch guns on the *Hiei* and *Kirishima* literally dwarfed the American's heaviest armament of eighteen 8-inch guns on the cruisers *San Francisco* and *Portland*. A few of the U.S. ships had radar but the new device had not yet been integrated with the U.S. Navy's surface tactics and would be a negligible factor in the coming battle.

In the early morning hours of November 13, 1942, these two groups of ships collided in what can only be described as a bare knuckles brawl. When the smoke cleared, Admirals Callaghan and Scott, along with most members of their staffs, were dead. The cruiser *Atlanta* and four U.S. destroyers were sunk, while three other cruisers and two more destroyers were badly damaged. (The heavily damaged cruiser *Juneau* would later be sunk by a Japanese submarine with the loss of nearly her entire seven hundred man crew, including all five of the Sullivan brothers.) Two Japanese destroyers were sunk and the *Hiei* was battered into a drifting wreck. More importantly, the remaining Japanese vessels retreated without laying a glove on Guadalcanal's airstrips. When daylight returned, the marine pilots displayed their undiminished potency by combining with planes from the *Enterprise* to finish off the *Hiei*.

The failure of the bombardment group forced Tanaka to temporarily reverse course to keep out of range of Guadalcanal's aircraft. The next evening, the Japanese tactic of dispersing their forces finally paid some dividends. While the Americans focused their attention on the slot, a group of cruisers came in from the northeast and put hundreds of shells into the island's airfields. This was not sufficient to shut down the Cactus Air Force, however, and its flyers sank one of the assailing cruisers the next morning. They then went after Tanaka's transports, which had kept coming after receiving word of the previous night's bombardment. Joined by planes from the *Enterprise*, the marines sank seven transports, and forced another to retire to Rabaul.[27]

But the Japanese were still not finished. A force of fourteen ships, headed by the battleship *Kirishima*, sailed through the slot to take one more crack at Henderson Field. They were met by the fast battleships *Washington* and *South Dakota* and four destroyers under Rear Admiral Willis A. Lee.[28] The battleships had been too far south to help Scott and Callaghan on November 13, but their commitment to battle would not have been a foregone conclusion in any case. Existing naval doctrine emphatically frowned on sending battleships into narrow and restricted waters such as those surrounding Guadalcanal. Now, the big ships were Halsey's last pair of aces.

Lee's vessels were not a cohesive force. His dreadnoughts had never fought together and his four destroyers were all different types drawn from four different squadrons. Nevertheless, the scratch group of American "tin cans" performed well in the battle's early stages, damaging the light cruiser *Nagara* and putting the destroyer *Ayanami* in sinking condition. Although none of the Japanese ships had radar, their crews were still the masters of nocturnal combat. They now proved as much by dispatching each U.S. destroyer in rapid succession. The *Preston* was hit by two shells from the *Nagara* and then flattened by 8-inch rounds from a heavy cruiser. She capsized just thirty seconds after her skipper ordered the crew to abandon ship. The *Walke*, hit by a torpedo and peppered by 8-inch shells, stood straight up out of the water and went down bow first. The *Benham* was struck by a torpedo which blew off her bow and lifted her four feet out of the water. She limped away and sank the next day. The *Gwin* was hit by numerous 5-inch rounds but continued to engage two enemy destroyers until they disappeared into the shadows of nearby Savo Island. The wounded U.S. destroyer then ceased fire and moved off to safety.

Meanwhile, the U.S. battleships were blazing away in support of their destroyers but their targets were mostly phantoms. After suffering a brief power failure, the *South Dakota* renewed firing only to have a muzzle flash from her aft 16-inch battery ignite fuel vapors in her scout planes and start a multitude of small fires on her fantail. Although the fires were rapidly extinguished, they burned long enough to serve as a beacon for the *Kirishima* and the heavy cruisers *Atago* and *Takao*. Japan's heavy ships opened up on the *South Dakota* and scored hits of all calibers which damaged the American's superstructure and destroyed her radio antenna. At this point, Lee's *Washington* found its range and reduced the *Kirishima* to a blazing hulk with radar-directed salvoes from her 16-inch and 5-inch guns. The reprieved *South Dakota* then joined the *Washington* in dishing out severe punishment to the two hostile heavy cruisers.

The naked U.S. dreadnoughts soon left the scene, but so did the Japanese. Henderson Field passed its last night of danger unscathed. Next morning, its aircraft returned to ravage Tanaka's remaining transports. Tanaka beached his four ships in an effort to salvage the maximum amount of their cargo. About two thousand soldiers made it to shore and, most importantly, they took only 260 cases of ammunition and 1,500 bags of rice with them.[29] There would be no more Japanese offensives on Guadalcanal.

Although the crisis had passed, the campaign was far from over. Two more naval battles and miles of grim jungle fighting remained before the island was secured on February 9, 1943. The campaign for Guadalcanal was an agonizing battle of attrition that exhausted both adversaries. It was also the turning point of the Pacific War. U.S. forces emerged from their ordeal of victory with the initiative and would never again relinquish it. As overall commander, Halsey loomed even larger at Guadalcanal than Spruance did at Midway. His one indisputable contribution was morale, especially among the lower ranks. He spoke their language and made them feel valued and appreciated. But Halsey also had a substantial impact on the campaign's strategic direction. Ghormley's leadership had been timid and unfocused. He had diverted far too many resources to supply lines that were already secure and he hoarded his ships like a miser's gold. Halsey would never have accused his old friend of these transgressions, but he quickly reversed both polices. Rear-area garrisons were stripped of men and equipment in order to concentrate them on the frontline at Guadalcanal. The navy's ships were spared no risk in their efforts to supply the island and deny the Japanese the ability to do the same. On the night of November 12–13, Halsey turned back Japanese battleships with an outgunned force of cruisers and destroyers. Two nights later, he sealed the victory by sending his own battleships into the Solomon's narrow waters with a minimal destroyer screen, in a clear contradiction of the tactical principles taught at the War College.

At Guadalcanal, Halsey definitely remembered Nelson's dictum: "No captain can do wrong by placing his ship next to that of an enemy."[30] His efforts there earned him the four-star pins of a full admiral as well as a "Halsey Day" in hometown Elizabeth, New Jersey. Characteristically, he also remembered the men who expended themselves to bring him such acclamation. When word of his promotion was confirmed, Halsey removed his old three-star pins and handed them to an aid, saying, "Send one of these to Mrs. Scott and the other to Mrs. Callaghan. Tell them it was their husbands' bravery that got me my new ones."[31]

VII

By the summer of 1943, the Joint Chiefs in Washington had decided how the newly won initiative would be exploited. Relying mainly on land-based air cover, MacArthur would advance along the northern coast of New Guinea, while Halsey moved up the Solomons chain on his right flank. The navy's cherished Central Pacific Offensive, whose air support depended on aircraft carriers, would kick off later that year. U.S. strategists utilized Ulysses S. Grant's Civil War methodology of negating a foe's advantage of interior lines by engaging him simultaneously at multiple points. America's fully mobilized industrial base would provide the material largess necessary to put this theory into practice. The short-term focus of each advance was a Japanese stronghold: Rabaul in New Britain and Truk in the Carolines. The two drives would eventually converge somewhere in the "Luzon Bottleneck," the area between Formosa, China and the Philippines.

Operation Galvanic, the seizure of the Gilbert Islands, was scheduled for November and it was not a foregone conclusion that Spruance would lead it. In May, Nimitz had told Spruance, "There are going to be some changes in high command of the fleet. I would like to let you go, but unfortunately, I need you more here." Spruance replied with his customary stoicism, "Well, the war is the important thing. I personally would like another crack at the Japs, but if you need me here, this is where I should be." But the very next morning, Nimitz told his chief of staff, "I have been thinking this over during the night. Spruance, you are lucky. I decided that I am going to let you go after all."[32] Nimitz still did not inform Spruance that he intended him to command the Gilbert's invasion. This occurred only after Admiral King approved the appointment and promoted Spruance to vice admiral.

The man to whom Nimitz and King entrusted the navy's fortunes in the Central Pacific was a creature of habit and moderation. Spruance's routine included exercise and plenty of rest, sometimes at the expense of work. He often exasperated his staff by breaking up a meeting to take a brisk walk or to turn in for the night. Such practices, coupled with his penchant for delegating details, made Spruance appear lazy to some contemporaries, but he was actually following a deliberate and effective method of dealing with the rigors of high command. Spruance need not hate an enemy in order to destroy him. He was a great admirer of Admiral Togo and managed to retain his respect for Japanese culture and military prowess throughout the war. But his admiration for the enemy never caused him to pull any of the punches he threw at them. Spruance was an intellectual assassin who viewed the necessities of war with professional dispassion. He could decry the Japanese custom of fighting to the death as a tragic waste of life while at the same time noting that it spared him "the bother of guarding, feeding, and transporting a lot of POWs, most of whom would contribute little of value in the intelligence line."[33]

Any attempt to advance in the Central Pacific would be dependent on the carrier arm. During the spring of 1943, two new types of flattops began arriving at Pearl Harbor. The Essex-class fleet carrier (CV), displacing 27,000 tons, would be the main battery. It was supplemented by the Independence-class carrier (CVL), converted from cruiser hulls and displacing 11,000 tons. Four of the new fleet carriers were christened *Lexington*, *Yorktown*, *Wasp*, and *Hornet*, in deference to the flattops lost during the prior year's fighting. The carriers came with an alphabet soup of new technology, heavily dependent on radar. They were run from a CIC (Combat Information Center), maintained high speed formation with a Position Plan Indicator (PPI) and identified their in-coming aircraft with an Identification, Friend-or-Foe (IFF). Voice radio had already given carrier commanders a means of real time communications with both planes and ships. In 1943, the U.S. Navy began using a four-channel VHF radio that permitted a ship to carry on four separate conversations simultaneously, all of which were secure from enemy eavesdropping. The carriers would be protected by an integrated layered defense, beginning with the fighters of their combat air patrols, then the guns of an ever increasing escort screen, and finally their own ample allotment of anti-aircraft guns. Each *Essex* was given twelve 5-inchers, sixty-eight 40mms in quadruple mounts and more than fifty single-mounted 20mms. The light carriers had twenty-six 40mms, in both quad and double mounts, and about forty of the 20mm singles.[34]

The planes that the carriers sent into battle were also state of the art. Devastator torpedo planes had long since been replaced by Avengers and the venerable Dauntless was gradually being phased out by the Helldiver. But it was the new fighters that gave naval aviators their real trump card. The F4F Wildcat had held its own against the Japanese Zero once U.S. pilots learned to exploit the Japanese fighter's lack of armor and self-sealing fuel tanks.

But the Wildcat's performance was never sufficient to give the navy true air supremacy. This changed with the arrival of the F6F Hellcat. Although the Hellcat could not outmaneuver a Zero in a dogfight, it possessed superior speed, service ceiling, climbing ability, and firepower. These characteristics coupled with armor and self-sealing fuel tanks would allow the Hellcat to dominate Pacific skies for the war's duration. Each Essex-class carrier had thirty-six of them, along with thirty-six dive-bombers and eighteen torpedo planes. The CVLs carried twenty-four Hellcats and nine Avengers.[35]

Vice-Admiral Jack Towers was entrusted with the task of turning this growing aggregation of men and machines into a cohesive fighting force. As commander of naval air, Pacific (ComAirPac), Towers held an administrative, not tactical billet. One of his duties was the formulation of doctrine. Although multicarrier task forces had already supplanted dispersal as the preferred tactical organization, many questions remained as to the carriers' employment. Throughout his tenure, Towers advocated the placement of aviators in high staff positions and the use of carriers in mobile operations, independent of the amphibious operations that they supported. The latter position often put him at odds with Spruance who favored a closer association between the two missions. This might well be categorized as a clash between the archaic "battleship" point of view and the more progressive "carrier" thinking. Spruance did often see things through the bore of a battleship's 16-inch guns. But that is only part of the story. While the focus of the aviators was always on destroying Japanese ships and aircraft, the leaders of the amphibious assault were just as consistent in their focus on the land objective. Rear Admiral Richmond Kelly Turner made it quite clear that he wanted the carriers tied close to the invasion beaches in order to provide maximum protection for his transports and air support for his Marines.[36] As overall commander, Spruance had to weigh all opinions. While he did so, the new carriers refined their technique in raids throughout the Central Pacific.

Spruance's compromise was tilted against the airmen. He would permit air raids on nearby bases before the landings and possibly thereafter. But during the ground fighting, the carriers would be tied to defensive sectors. One group would cover the marines on Tarawa, while another would perform a similar function for the army on Makin. A third group would block air attacks from the Marshalls, and a fourth group would be held in reserve. Spruance also decided that Lee's five fast battleships would initially be parceled out among the carrier groups but would immediately concentrate if the Japanese Fleet sortieed to contest the invasion.

The conquest of the Gilberts provided a bloody baptism of fire for the navy's Central Pacific amphibious team. Although the lightly defended

Makin fell easily, the battle for Tarawa was a near-run thing despite an intense preinvasion bombardment that the planners hoped would obliterate most opposition. But the majority of the Japanese garrison safely rode out the barrage in their sand-covered bunkers and pillboxes of concrete or coconut logs. The first waves of attackers were decimated and the battle quickly turned into a small unit melee where groups of marines inched forward to clean out Japanese positions with satchel charges and flame-throwers. Tarawa was secured only after four days of combat against fanatical defenders that cost the Second Marine Division nearly one thousand dead and more than two thousand wounded.[37]

Operation Galvanic produced no naval battle due to prior events in the South Pacific. On November 1, the Third Marine Division came ashore at Empress Augusta Bay on Bougainville. Since Bougainville's airfields were within fighter range of Rabaul, the Japanese detached a force of seven heavy cruisers from Truk to eliminate the threat. They were accompanied by the planes of Carrier Division 1, the most experienced air group in the combined fleet. Halsey responded by sending his two carriers, *Saratoga* and *Princeton*, to raid Rabaul before the superior enemy surface strength moved against his beachhead. The spoiling attack was remarkably successful, heavily damaging four heavy and two light cruisers. Nimitz had previously decided to bolster Halsey by loaning him a carrier group from the Central Pacific. On their arrival, these ships combined with the two carriers on the scene to launch a second attack on Japan's southern stronghold. The men and machines of Carrier Division 1 were consumed by these raids as well as the unrelenting activity by Allied land-based squadrons. When landings in the Gilberts commenced on November 20, the Combined Fleet, its cruiser force crippled and its air group decimated, was unable to respond.

This interplay continued into the next year when the planes of Carrier Division 2 were diverted to Rabaul's defense. These were also rapidly chopped up by Halsey's meat grinder. Thus, the Combined Fleet remained impotent when Operation Flintlock hit the Marshalls in February. Rear Admiral Marc A. Mitscher's Task Force 58 included an unprecedented twelve flat-tops for the assault in the Marshalls. After the seizure of Kwajalein, some of them were allowed to slip the bonds of the beachhead. While one group covered the landings on Eniwetok, Spruance and Mitscher led the other three groups against no less a target than Truk itself. The raid was a huge success, destroying nearly three hundred Japanese planes, and sinking three light cruisers, four destroyers, and thirty merchant ships.[38] When no moving targets were left, U.S. planes proceeded to wreck a good portion of Truk's facilities. Spruance then sent Mitscher further west with two groups to raid the Marianas.

By the spring of 1944, Allied planners had good reason to be optimistic about the course of the Pacific War. The dual thrust strategy had kept the Japanese off balance and on the defensive. The achievement of tactical superiority was just as encouraging. Even when the Japanese were able to concentrate, they were soundly beaten. The raids on Rabaul had succeeded despite being launched in the face of superior numbers of enemy aircraft. It now became apparent that the original focal points of each axis, Rabaul and Truk, need not be assaulted. The Joint Chiefs had already expressed their preference that Rabaul be neutralized rather than captured. MacArthur and Halsey were in the process of accomplishing this by ringing Japan's southern bastion with airfields. The raid on Truk displayed that carrier task forces could facilitate the same strategy in the Central Pacific. Accordingly, Japan's "Gibraltar of the Pacific" would also be bypassed.

Admiral Nimitz was quick to grasp that the U.S. Navy need no longer fear its enemy. After the Rabaul raids, he confidently stated, "Henceforth, we propose to give the Jap no rest."[39] Nimitz decided to deal with the rigors of his accelerated campaign by employing a rotating, two-team command system. One fleet headquarters would fight while the other rested and planned. Because MacArthur's advance past Rabaul had turned the Solomons into a backwater, Halsey would soon be available for duty in the rotating command structure. Meanwhile, the next target would be the Marianas and it belonged to Admiral Spruance, now wearing the four-star pins he had received on his return from the Marshalls.

VIII

The Marianas were part of Japan's inner defense perimeter. The four islands of Guam, Saipan, Tinian, and Rota formed the center of a network of "unsinkable aircraft carriers" that stretched from the Volcanoes to the Western Carolines. Theoretically, Japan could shuttle planes from island to island and concentrate superior air power in any threatened sector. If the Marianas fell, the ring would be breached and its northern and southern portions isolated from each other. Even more ominous was the fact that the island's airfields would put Japan within range of the new B-29 bombers. The strategic importance of the Marianas left no doubt that the Japanese fleet must fight in their defense.

Operation Forager was slated to commence with the invasion of Saipan in mid-June. Landings on Guam and Tinian would follow. Rota was to be neutralized and bypassed. Spruance's Fifth Fleet was up to the challenge. Turner's amphibious forces had their own personal "bodyguard" in the form of Vice-Admiral Jesse B. Oldendorf's bombardment group, which included seven old battleships and seven escort carriers with some 170 planes.[40] The escort or "jeep" carrier was an expediency produced by putting a flight deck on the hull of a merchant ship. It was designed for convoy escort and was later adapted for ground support and logistical missions. The heart of the Fifth Fleet was Mitscher's Task Force 58. It now included the *Enterprise*, six Essex-class carriers, eight light carriers, and seven modern battleships, screened by ample numbers of cruisers and destroyers. Mitscher's carriers operated 900 aircraft, including about 480 Hellcats.[41] (The inflated total of fighters results from the fact that U.S. fleet carriers now included a small section of specially equipped night fighters in their air groups.) Task Force 58's operational stamina was boosted by its replenishment group, Service Squadron 10, which provided fuel from its tanker and replacement aircraft from its jeep carriers.

The Japanese faced the coming storm without their inspirational leader. Admiral Yamamoto had been killed in April 1943 when his plane was ambushed by U.S. Army P-38 fighter planes. His successor, Admiral Mineich Koga, died the following spring in an air crash. Admiral Soemu Toyoda now received the top naval command with clear instructions to seek a decisive battle with the U.S. Fleet. The resulting A-Go plan envisioned achieving victory through a coordinated effort by naval forces and land-based aircraft. Most of the ships at Toyoda's disposal were in Vice-Admiral Jisaburo Ozawa's Mobile Fleet.

The Mobile Fleet was based in the Dutch East Indies in close proximity to its source of fuel. U.S. submarines had enjoyed such success against Japanese tankers that deployment further east became untenable. Although it also contained strong surface forces, the core of the Mobile Fleet was its nine aircraft carriers. Carrier Division 1 included the Pearl Harbor veterans *Shokaku* and *Zuikaku* as well as the brand new *Taiho*, Ozawa's flagship. These three vessels were legitimate fleet carriers, roughly equivalent to the *Essex*. At 29,000 tons and with an armored flight deck, the *Taiho* was probably the most formidable carrier in the entire Pacific. Divisions 2 and 3 were not as impressive. Their members were all conversions ranging from fleet carriers *Junyo* and *Hiyo* to four light carriers of varying displacements. By June, Ozawa's airwings had been rebuilt to 450 aircraft, including new "Jill" and "Judy" attack planes and many improved Zeroes. However, the new planes were accompanied by new pilots whose inexperience was a matter of great concern. In the war's early days, the Japanese pitted their well-trained veterans against Allied novices. Now the situation was reversed. Ozawa's flyers averaged only 275 air hours experience as opposed to more than 525 hours for their American counterparts.[42]

Ozawa was an intelligent and well-informed commander who certainly knew that his naval forces did not stack up well against those of Spruance. However, he also knew that various other factors might even the odds. The Mobile Fleet would be supported by more than five hundred land-based planes whose mission was to whittle down U.S. naval strength before the fleet battle occurred. Also, due to their lack of "luxuries" such as armor and self-sealing fuel tanks, Ozawa's carrier planes had a greater attack range than those of his rival. This superior reach could be extended by the use of land bases for one-way shuttle attacks. The forces of nature provided even further enhancement of this advantage. Prevailing eastern trade winds would allow the Mobile Fleet to conduct flight operations while sailing toward its targets while Mitscher's carriers would have to turn away to launch and recover their aircraft. Finally, Ozawa's study of Spruance's prior campaigns convinced him that the U.S. carriers would remain close to the beachhead until the island was secured. The Japanese commander approached the coming showdown confident that he would locate the enemy fleet and strike a decisive blow against it before it could respond in kind.

Spruance opened the Marianas Campaign on June 11, 1944, by sending more than two hundred Hellcats to take on the planes of Vice-Admiral Kakujo Kakuta's "unsinkable aircraft carriers." These pre-emptive "fighter sweeps" had been conceived by Mitscher and employed with great success in the Marshalls and against Truk. By the end of the day, Mitscher's flyers had effectively eliminated local enemy air strength, proving once again that carrier mobility could defeat aircraft tied to stationary targets. The carrier planes then joined Lee's battleships in attempts to soften up Saipan for the invasion troops. The fast battleships proved ineffective in this role, but things improved with the arrival of Oldendorf's older dreadnoughts on June 14.

Both Spruance and Mitscher were aware of Japanese ability to reinforce the Marianas from their outlying bases. They agreed that this should be pre-empted by expanding the zone of battle to include Japanese staging areas. On June 14, the task groups of Rear Admirals J. J. Clark and William K. Harrill were sent to plug the northern pipeline by hitting airfields on Iwo Jima and Chichi Jima. Mitscher's other two carrier groups under Rear Admirals John Reeves and Alfred E. Montgomery remained to cover the landings with four CVs and four CVLs. (The southern approaches were less troublesome because MacArthur's invasion of Biak had consumed the bulk of enemy planes that might come from that direction.) That same evening, Spruance received his first notice that the Mobile Fleet had left its anchorage at Tawi-Tawi. Accordingly, he ordered Clark and Harrill to do their business in one day and return as soon as possible.

On the morning of June 15, assault troops from the 2nd and 4th Marine Divisions began landing on Saipan. From the start, it was apparent that this battle would be more akin to the bloodbath on Tarawa than the walkovers on Kwajalein and Eniwetok. Spruance followed the marines' progress from the cruiser *Indianapolis* while awaiting more information about the Japanese Fleet. He received it that evening when submarine *Flying Fish* reported its sighting of a large body of ships clearing San Bernardino Strait. Submarine *Seahorse* also reported a smaller group of ships moving northward from a position several hundred miles to the south.

Spruance now drew a picture of Japanese intentions that was logical but incorrect. Previous Japanese operations at Coral Sea, Midway, and Guadalcanal had invariably employed dispersed forces with specific tasks and objectives. Often, one force served as a diversion which sought to make the Americans reveal their position or uncover a vital objective. Spruance therefore assumed that his adversaries were coming on in two groups, one to engage his carriers and the other to destroy his beachhead. In fact, the Japanese were uncharacteristically concentrating their forces and their goal was a decisive fleet engagement. The southern group spotted by *Seahorse* was built around the super battleships *Yamato* and *Mushasi*. It had originally been positioned for action against MacArthur and was now moving to link up with Ozawa's main body. Spruance' subsequent decisions would be based on his misconceptions of June 15.

On the morning of June 16, Spruance met with Kelly Turner to discuss the situation and formulate a response. They came up with a comprehensive plan of action. Task Force 58 would be reinforced with ships from the fire support group, swelling its numbers to fifteen carriers, seven battleships, eight heavy cruisers, thirteen light cruisers, and sixty-six destroyers.[43] Once reunited with his northern strike force, Mitscher would take his entire task force west in search of the Japanese Fleet. Lee's battleships would be pulled from the carrier screen and formed into a separate task group before heading west. Oldendorf's seven old battleships, three light cruisers, and five destroyers would remain to protect the beachhead.[44] His escort carriers would continue to fly ground support missions, but could be diverted to support the battleships if necessary. Finally, Spruance convinced a reluctant Kelly Turner to withdraw most of the transports 200 miles east during the night of June 17. However, Turner warned his boss that the touch-and-go situation ashore would require some of the ships carrying essentials such as food and ammunition to return to the beachhead by the morning of June 19.

Task Force 58 left Saipan the following morning and headed for its rendezvous with Clark and Harrill. That afternoon, Spruance communicated his battle plan to Mitscher on the *Lexington*:

Our air will first knock out enemy carriers, then will attack enemy battleships and cruisers to slow or disable them. Battleline will destroy enemy fleet by fleet action if enemy elects to fight or by sinking slowed or crippled ships if enemy retreats. Action against the enemy must be pushed by all hands to ensure complete destruction of his fleet. Destroyers running short of fuel may be returned to Saipan if necessary for refueling.[45]

Spruance's orders were somewhat fanciful in that they contemplated a clash between the battle lines in broad daylight, an unlikely event in the age of naval airpower. However, it is not fair to say that this reference reflects on an outdated view that the battleship was still the arm of decision. Spruance was a thorough planner and his communiqué characteristically covered all contingencies. It stressed the role of carrier planes while allowing for the possibility of a surface engagement against either an intact enemy battle line (unlikely) or a bunch of cripples (more likely). His message also remained true to form by following a mild exhortation with the mundane matter of refueling the destroyers.

Although his guns were loaded, Spruance was still unsure in which direction to point them. Prior to the battle, naval intelligence had provided what proved to be a newly flawless appraisal of the Japanese order of battle. But as the moment of contact neared, the U.S. commander was woefully lacking data concerning the position and disposition of the enemy fleet. During the night of June 17–18, he received his next tidbit of information when submarine *Cavalla* reported fifteen ships 800 miles west–southwest of Saipan. The size and location of this force was very suspicious to Spruance. He concluded that the Japanese Fleet was still dispersed and was not coming on at full speed. Perhaps it was hovering beyond the range of air searches in order to draw Task Force 58 away from the beachhead. The situation was still cloudy the following dawn when Spruance communicated, "In my opinion, the main attack will come from the west but might be diverted to come from the southwest."[46]

Spruance's command style was to issue general directives and leave tactical details to his subordinates. During the morning of June 18, with a reunited Task Force 58 in hand, Mitscher calculated that his search planes could locate the enemy before sunset and pinpoint him for an attack by Lee's battleship at night. When he sought Lee's concurrence, Mitscher received an emphatic negative response, "Do not, repeat NOT believe we should seek night engagement. Possible advantages of radar more than offset by difficulties of communications and lack of training in fleet tactics at night."[47] The U.S. battleship commander retained a healthy respect for Japanese night fighting capabilities and had been unable to perfect his own due to the Fifth Fleet's pace of operations and its emphasis on carrier escort duties.

This turn of events left the Americans no choice but to reverse course at dusk to avoid blundering into a night battle. But Spruance's orders added that "Task Force 58 must cover Saipan and our forces engaged in that operation."[48] This cautious reminder stood out in stark contrast to the previous day's Nelsonian directive that talked about "pushing the action" for the "complete destruction" of the enemy fleet. It seems that Spruance had suddenly shifted his attention from the Japanese Fleet and focused it on the beachhead. In fact, his strategic gaze had never left Saipan. With no new information as to the whereabouts of the Japanese Fleet, Spruance concluded that the only prudent course was to fall back and cover the beachhead. The timing of the decision indicates that it was related to the discussion of the night engagement. It is hard to determine whether Spruance was more upset by Mitscher's proposing it or Lee's inability to fight it. An amateur psychiatrist might submit that Spruance lost his confidence when faced with the shortcomings of his dreadnought icons. More likely, it was the final bit of confusion that drove a logical mind to choose a safe but certain course of action.

At 10 p.m., Spruance received a report from a "Huff-Duff" (high-frequency direction finder) that pinpointed an enemy radio transmission 355 miles to the west. Mitscher became convinced that this was the Japanese main body and had his staff draw up a plan to go after it. They calculated that if Task Force 28 began steaming west at 1:30 a.m. it would be within 200 miles of the Japanese at daybreak. This would preclude any night battle while putting the carriers in optimum position to launch airstrikes. Meanwhile, Spruance had became aware of a "jammed" radio message from submarine *Stingray* some 175 miles east–southeast of the radio direction contact. In a leap of misguided intuition, Spruance decided that this garbled transmission was *Stingray's* attempt to report the position of the Japanese southern force. Thus, when Mitscher requested permission to implement his plan, Spruance replied that it was not "advisable," citing the danger of an "end run" to the beachhead.[49] This reply was not well received on board the *Lexington* as it was considered a guarantee that the Japanese would land the first punch. The most bitter irony of this whole affair was that a search plane positively identified Ozawa's entire force at 1:15 a.m. but was unable to report its find due to atmospheric conditions.

The Mobile Fleet was steaming in two groups but for a different reason than Spruance envisioned. Ozawa had placed the light carriers *Chitose*, *Chiydoa*, and *Zuiho*, of Carrier Division 3 in the van, some 100 miles ahead of his other six flattops. Japanese surface forces accompanying the spearhead included four battleships, four heavy cruisers, one light cruiser, and eight destroyers. Carrier Divisions 1 and 2 followed in two separate groups, sharing a combined escort of one battleship, four cruisers, and fifteen destroyers. Six tankers and an equal number of destroyers brought up the rear.[50] At Midway, Yamamoto placed his battleships behind Nagumo's carriers where they did no good whatsoever. Ozawa placed his in the van where they served as a shield for the carriers in any prospective night battle and might also draw attacking planes into the fire of their anti-aircraft batteries. (Mitscher had similar thoughts on the employment of Lee's ships.)

Midway had also taught the Japanese the importance of naval reconnaissance. Accordingly, Ozawa's air searches were massive and effective. On the afternoon of June 18, he learned that the U.S. Fleet was 350 miles away and steaming toward him. Because it was too late in the day for an attack, Ozawa decided to maneuver outside the range of U.S. search planes and attack in the morning. The commander of the Mobile Fleet took this course of action based on the premise that Spruance would not stray very far from Saipan. His reconnaissance planes proved him correct when they found Task Force 58 the next morning, about 300 miles east of the vanguard. This put the Americans within range of an airstrike but beyond the range of a response. At 8:30 a.m., Ozawa began launching the first of four attack waves that he hoped would reverse the course of the Pacific War.

Although Japanese aircraft carriers threw the first punch in the Battle of the Philippine Sea, U.S. submarines actually landed the first blow. As the second attack wave was clearing the flight decks, *Albacore* penetrated the thin destroyer screen and fired a full spread of six torpedoes at *Taiho*. Warrant Officer Sakio Komatsu spotted one of the "fish" while taking off from the flagship and unhesitatingly crash-dived into it. His sacrifice gave only momentary relief, however, for another torpedo struck the *Taiho* forward on its starboard side, rupturing fuel lines and oil tanks. The damage seemed minor and the large carrier continued to operate with undiminished effectiveness.

The U.S. Task Force received its wake-up call at about 10 a.m. when the battleship *Alabama* picked up an incoming flight that did not register on IFF. About eighty Hellcats were already aloft, many doing battle over Guam with Kakuta's meager leftovers. These were joined by some 140 more fighters, all of which were vectored toward the intruders. Mitscher then sent all of his attack planes to orbit east of Guam, leaving his carrier decks free to operate fighters. The attack planes would later expend their ordinance by cratering the runways of Guam's airfields.

Ozawa's first wave consisted of sixteen fighters, forty-five dive bombers, and eight torpedo bombers from his vanguard. Most fell to the Hellcats in the first of the day's many one-sided contests. Lieutenant Alexander Vraciu of the *Lexington* needed only 360 rounds to score six kills in less than ten minutes of combat. (Ensign Wilber B. Webb of the *Hornet* would match this score later in the day.) The bogeys that got through the fighters concentrated on the battle line. One landed a bomb on the *South Dakota*, killing twenty-seven men but having no effect on the ship's fighting ability. Another crashed into the side of the *Indiana*, merely scratching the dreadnought's armor. Altogether, this group lost forty-two aircraft to Mitscher's Hellcats and Lee's anti-aircraft batteries. None even laid eyes on the U.S. carriers.

The second wave included forty-eight Zeroes, fifty-three Judys, and twenty-seven Jills from Carrier Division 1. This bunch was mistakenly fired on as it passed over the ships of the vanguard, resulting in two planes destroyed and eight badly damaged. Eight additional aircraft were forced to turn back due to engine trouble. The remaining 109 planes found their targets and were annihilated for their efforts. In exchange for the loss of more than ninety aircraft, they managed to score near misses on the carriers *Wasp* and *Bunker Hill*.

Ozawa's third wave of forty-seven planes from Carrier Division 2 generally missed its targets and was only lightly engaged, losing seven of its number. His final strike force of eighty-two aircraft was drawn from Carrier Division 2 and the *Zuikaku*. It was directed toward empty ocean and had to improvise. One small group was able to find the U.S. carriers and suffered heavy losses in return for no hits. Another group, totaling forty-nine aircraft, headed for the supposed safety of Guam. All were destroyed, either shot down by Hellcats or crashed on the island's cratered runways. Only nine planes of the fourth wave made the return flight to their mother ships.

Meanwhile, the Mobile Fleet was having more trouble with U.S. submarines. At 12:20 p.m., the *Cavalla* put four torpedoes into the *Shokaku*, three of which exploded. The Pearl Harbor veteran became a blazing inferno and sank, bow first. She was soon joined by the *Taiho* whose damaged fuel lines and oil tanks had filled the ship with highly explosive vapors. A spark ignited these vapors just after 3:20 p.m., blowing Japan's mightiest carrier into oblivion. More than 2,900 Japanese sailors and twenty-two planes went down with the two large flattops.[51] Ozawa was not among them. He escaped injury and transferred his flag to the cruiser *Haguro*.

Japanese airmen were so ineffective on June 19, 1944, that the first phase of the Battle of the Philippine Sea became known as the "Marianas Turkey Shoot." Ozawa entered the fight with more than 400 carrier planes and awoke the next morning with only 102.[52] Of the 326 aircraft that comprised his four attack waves, more than 220 were shot down. Some of the survivors returned with damage that rendered them inoperable, whereas others landed in the Marianas and were never seen again. Operational losses, disproportionately high among the inexperienced Japanese pilots, and aircraft lost on scout missions added to the tally. About fifty land-based planes had also been destroyed. Japanese naval aviation would never recover from this slaughter. The cost to the U.S. Fifth Fleet was twenty-nine aircraft and twenty-seven pilots and aircrewmen.[53]

Spruance now wished to attack the enemy fleet but still did not know its location. Incredibly, Ozawa was not in retreat, but had merely drawn off to re-fuel and re-organize. An Avenger from the *Enterprise* finally found him at 3:40 p.m., June 20, 1944. The sighting placed the Mobile Fleet 275 miles away, easy for the Hellcats but extreme range for the dive bombers and tor-peckers. Mitscher had tactical control, so the call was his. He decided to launch two strikes despite the distance and regardless of the fact that return-ing aircraft would have to land at night. Only twelve carriers were present since Harrill's group had withdrawn to refuel. All of these except the CVL *Princeton* participated in the launching of eighty-five Hellcats, fifty-four Aven-gers, fifty-one Helldivers, and twenty-six Dauntlesses.[54] Soon after, Mitscher received a corrected report that placed the enemy fleet an additional 60 miles away, beyond the specified operational radius of his attack planes! He promptly canceled the second strike and ordered the task force to steam ahead at full speed in order to reduce the distance as much as possible.

The U.S. flyers attacked in a ragged manner, probably due to fatigue and preoccupation with the length of the return trip. Avengers from the *Belleau Wood* torpedoed and sank the carrier *Hiyo*, whose demise was confirmed from the water by two of the squadron's downed aircrewmen. Helldivers from the *Wasp* sent two tankers to the bottom and damaged a third. Pearl Harbor veteran *Zuikaku* caught the attention of planes from four U.S. carri-ers. She suffered multiple hits that started fires so severe that her departing assailants thought she was a goner. But the fires were brought under control and the well-traveled flattop lived to fight one more battle. Due to the linger-ing trauma caused by the slaughter of the Devastators at Midway, most of the Avengers at the Philippine Sea carried bombs rather than torpedoes.[55] Three squadrons so armed converged on the *Chiyoda*, wrecking her flight deck but leaving her afloat. An Avenger from the *Enterprise* dropped its payload on the carrier *Ryuho* and, although it reported seeing a high explo-sion, had actually inflicted only negligible damage. The *Junyo* received two hits that caused substantial damage to her bridge and flight deck, but she too would survive the engagement. The final U.S. tally also included another sixty-five Japanese planes destroyed.[56]

The attackers then endured a gut-wrenching return flight in the dark, cul-minated by frenetic landings in which pilots picked the first available flight deck. A dive bomber pilot from the new *Hornet* whose plane had been hit by anti-aircraft fire described the experience:

As we flew along, the voices of other returning pilots kept coming over the air to report they were out of fuel and landing in the water. Trying not to think about my steadily falling fuel gage needle, I concentrated on maintaining a direct course back to the *Hornet* at the most economical engine setting. I could no longer see my damaged wing and the slow flexing of the outer section in the darkness but could feel the movement in the controls and it was frightening. Continuing to hold the stick in a far left position to maintain level flight, I kept shifting it between left and right hands as each arm became tired from the strain. The wing might fail without warning, resulting in an uncontrolled crash into the water below, but as time passed I put this possibility out of my mind, and I lived each minute of continuing flight, sipping them like fine cognac. . . . We were with the first to arrive back over the task force. Radios came to life as anxious pilots began calling the various carriers for instructions to land. Soon the air was filled with frantic voices all trying to talk at once—each was an emergency due to a low fuel state. Using the air group frequency, I told my flight to pick a carrier and land.[57]

To aid his returning flyers, Mitscher decided to fully illuminate his carriers, using not only deck lights but searchlights and starshells. Spruance went along with the decision, despite some strident advice to the contrary from one of his intelligence officers. The expedient landing procedure caused considerable confusion regarding losses. Once sorted out, the tally showed twenty planes shot down and eighty more lost from ditching and crashes. All but sixteen pilots and thirty-three aircrewmen were eventually rescued.[58]

The Battle of the Philippine Sea was a decisive U.S. victory by any standard of measure. It not only ensured the conquest of Saipan, Guam, and Tinian, but also destroyed Japanese naval airpower for the duration of the war. But it was not an annihilating victory such as Trafalgar or Tsushima. This quite naturally raises questions concerning the quality of Spruance's leadership. When assessing Spruance's performance, one must remember that his mission was more complex than that of Jellicoe, Togo, or Nelson. His Fifth Fleet included both amphibious units and battle groups whose objective was the conquest of the Marianas. The destruction of the Japanese Fleet was a desirable event, but not his overriding concern. Of course, if the Mobile Fleet was destroyed, the main threat to the invasion would be removed and its success virtually guaranteed. The ships and planes of Task Force 58 were more than sufficient to accomplish this, if they knew where to find the enemy. Spruance was severely handicapped by lack of intelligence data concerning the location of his adversaries and he proved most lacking in the guessing game that resulted.

There is no question that Spruance formed an incorrect picture of enemy intentions and was never able to escape its influence. He judged the Japanese to be advancing in multiple formations, whose main objective was the landing beaches. In fact they were concentrated and seeking to destroy the U.S. battle fleet. In judging his conduct, however, the relevant question is not whether his conclusions were incorrect but whether they were reasonable at the time. Prior experience and the scanty intelligence data then available could reasonably support the conclusions that Spruance reached. To his credit, Spruance sought battle while he attempted to sort out the confusion. His battle orders on June 17 clearly contemplated a climatic confrontation with the Mobile Fleet. But the limits of this strategy had been reached by the evening of June 18. The Japanese were now near striking distance and the U.S. commander still did not know where they were or what they would strike. In the face of this uncertainty and Lee's admitted inability to fight a night battle, the U.S. commander had no option but to reverse course at the end of the day.

He did have the option to turn around again during the night and seek an engagement at dawn, as Mitscher proposed. Spruance rejected the advice of his carrier commander and chose to stay near his beachhead. He later wrote of his decision, "As a matter of tactics, I think that going out after the Japanese and knocking their carriers out would have been much better and more satisfactory than waiting for them to attack us; but we were at the start of a very important and large amphibious operation and we could not afford to gamble and place it in jeopardy."[59]

Spruance's explanation that he feared an "end run" is superficially unconvincing because his original dispositions contemplated just that eventuality. Most of the transports had withdrawn and Oldendorf's old battleships and baby flattops were waiting for any subsidiary force that might come from the south. But it becomes much more convincing if based on the assumptions that Ozawa's main force would come from the south and the transports would return to the beachhead on June 19 as scheduled. *Cavalla's* report on June 18 identified only a small enemy force that seemed to be hovering to the west. Spruance had already decided that his major concern was protection of the foothold on Saipan. If the Japanese commander sought to destroy the beachhead, it followed that he might use a diversionary force to draw Task Force 58 to the west while sending a more powerful force around its southern flank. Oldendorf's success against such a force was no sure thing. His battleships were best equipped for shore bombardment and his aircraft were armed and trained for ground support missions. With all of these variables and possibilities rattling around in his head, Spruance resolved the issue by taking the safe but sure course. His reliance on the flimsy evidence of the "jammed" submarine transmission merely shows that his decision had already become irrevocable by the evening of June 18.

The decision to cover Saipan's beachhead did not sit well with the navy's brotherhood of aviators whose members generally distrusted Spruance's understanding of the weapon they wielded. One carrier admiral bluntly concluded, "Spruance was still thinking in terms of a surface action. He did not grasp the tremendous power of our air weapons or their ability to strike in any direction to the limit of their fuel supply. There were no 'ends' in aerial warfare."[60] (This was said of the man who used his carriers to near perfection at Midway!) In truth, any Japanese vessels that reached Saipan from the south would probably have been cut off and eventually sunk by planes from Mitcher's carriers. But the guaranteed destruction of Ozawa's raiders did not preclude their ability to sink the U.S. transports that Spruance assumed would be unloading supplies on June 19. Ironically, an improved situation on shore allowed Turner to keep his ships away for an additional day. Unfortunately, Turner never communicated this fact to Spruance and Spruance was understandably too preoccupied to ask for an update.

Yet, even with the transports out of range, a Japanese naval force could still disrupt the land battle by shelling Marine positions, blowing up their supply dumps and perhaps destroying their source of tactical air support. Spruance's experience with the desperate fight on Tarawa had convinced him that the margin between success and failure in an amphibious attack against strongly defended positions was a narrow one. His doctrine for the prosecution of such operations was "violent, overwhelming force, swiftly applied."[61] The ferocity of Japanese resistance on Saipan seemed to conform his predisposition. The Marines had suffered heavy casualties and Turner's strategic reserve division had already been committed. Spruance would not risk the addition of any more weight to Japan's side of the scale. Although this view may evidence a cautious military philosophy, it is an appropriate perspective for a U.S. officer. There had been a huge public outcry in the United States following Tarawa, which was a victory, although a costly one. A disaster on Saipan would have had grave repercussions even if it was accompanied by the destruction of a large portion of the Japanese Fleet. In a nation whose war effort is subject to the whims of popular opinion and ambitious politicians, this is no small consideration.

IX

By the summer of 1944, the "live-and-let-live" policy that allowed Nimitz and MacArthur to pursue independent advances across the Pacific was about to expire. A decision had to be made as to where the two drives would converge to cork the Luzon bottleneck. Nimitz and MacArthur agreed that landings should take place in the southern and central Philippines but their opinions differed regarding subsequent objectives. MacArthur favored Luzon, whereas Nimitz, backed by King, looked toward Formosa and the China coast. This would eventually be resolved in Luzon's favor due to the political necessity of liberating a former possession and the greater numbers of ground troops required to take Formosa. Each drive had one more bolt to fire: Moratai for the army and the Palaus for the navy. They would then converge at Mindanao on November 15 and move up to Leyte on December 20.

Halsey assumed command of the navy's Central Pacific forces on August 26, 1944, placing his flag on the battleship *New Jersey*. Although the ships in his Third Fleet were essentially those that had sailed under Spruance, Third Fleet headquarters came complete with new commanders for the carriers and the amphibious units. Vice-Admiral Theodore S. Wilkinson was the designated commander of the Third Amphibious Force, whereas Vice-Admiral John Sidney "Slew" McCain was slated to lead the newly designated Task Force 38. Wilkinson took his charges in tow on schedule, but Mitscher was reluctant to rotate after only seven months at sea. He remained at the helm of Task Force 38, leaving McCain without a job. McCain soon found gainful employment as the temporary commander of one of the carrier groups and would continue in that capacity until replacing Mitscher at the end of October.

Halsey had not been at sea since leading Task Force 17's two carriers and tiny escort back to Pearl Harbor in May 1942. He was now in charge of an aggregation of naval power that could only be dreamed of two years before. Halsey had no intentions of keeping that power closely tied to the landings in the Palaus. Indeed, the commander of the Third Fleet took little interest in the assault, leaving those details to Wilkinson. Halsey had once summarized his strategic philosophy as, "Get to the other fellow with everything you have as fast as you can and dump it on him."[62] His method of "covering" an invasion was to let the carriers range far and wide in an effort to destroy every enemy ship or plane which might eventually oppose the landings. After plastering Peleliu and Angaur, Task Force 38 headed for the Philippines.

U.S. strategy for returning MacArthur to the Philippines was premised on the existence of strong enemy airforces in the islands. These would be chopped up during a proposed ten weeks of carrier raids. Mindanao's seizure would provide airfields to further support the advance up the chain to Leyte. On September 13, after two days of ravaging the Central Philippines with impunity, Halsey became convinced that Japanese defenses were an empty shell. His suspicions were further supported by Ensign Thomas C.

Tillar of the *Hornet*, who had been shot down over Leyte and rescued by natives. Tiller returned to the *Hornet* full of his benefactors' stories detailing enemy weaknesses in the area. After consulting with his staff, Halsey decided that the U.S. timetable could be greatly accelerated. His recommendation to Nimitz proposed that Mindanao be skipped altogether and that Leyte be invaded as soon as possible. This was forwarded to the Joint Chiefs who, in an incredible show of confidence in their Pacific Admirals, accepted it within ninety minutes. Halsey had also recommended that the Palaus operation be called off but Nimitz decided that it was too late for that. This proved most unfortunate as the conquest of Peleliu cost two thousand American lives and was perhaps the only truly unnecessary amphibious assault undertaken by the U.S. Navy in the Pacific War.

The invasion of Leyte was re-scheduled for October 20, 1944. It would be an army affair, involving the soldiers of General Walter Krueger's Sixth Army. Transport, support, and supply of these troops would be the responsibility of Admiral Thomas C. Kinkaid's Seventh Fleet. Kinkaid's previous work for MacArthur had been managed on the cheap, utilizing land-based air and small numbers of amphibious craft and surface ships. But Leyte was beyond the range of land-based planes and its capture imposed a logistical burden that exceeded the resources of the Seventh Fleet. Therefore, Kinkaid's command received strong reinforcements from the central Pacific. Oldendorf's bombardment group, eighteen escort carriers under Rear Admiral Thomas L. Sprague, and Wilkinson's Third Amphibious Force all became temporary property of the Seventh Fleet. Halsey was left with only Task Force 38, which, for all practical purposes, would be synonymous with the Third Fleet throughout the campaign.

Admiral Nimitz had been greatly disappointed by Spruance's failure to destroy the Japanese Fleet in the Battle of the Philippine Sea. His orders to Halsey clearly evidenced his determination that the Japanese would not escape again. After a series of numbered sentences directing the cover and support of the invasion, one unnumbered sentence stood out, "In case opportunity for destruction of major portion of the enemy fleet offered or can be created, such destruction becomes the primary task."[63] In a subsequent dispatch to Nimitz, Halsey clarified his interpretation of the orders:

I intend, if possible, to deny the enemy a chance to outrange me in an air duel and also to deny him an opportunity to employ an air shuttle against me. If I am to prevent his gaining that advantage, I must have early information and I must move smartly.

Inasmuch as the destruction of the enemy fleet is the principal task, every weapon must be brought into play and the general co-ordination of those weapons should be in the hands of the tactical commander responsible for the outcome of the battle.

My goal is the same as yours, to completely annihilate the Jap fleet if the opportunity offers.[64]

On October 6, Halsey took the Third Fleet from its newly acquired anchorage at Ulithi and began the preliminary bashing of Japanese airpower that had become the standard opening act of every amphibious operation. After hitting airfields on Okinawa and Luzon, Task Force 38 descended on Formosa. In the three-day air battle that began on October 12, Mitscher's flyers destroyed almost six hundred enemy planes as well as three dozen cargo ships and auxiliary craft.[65] Many of the Japanese aviators who fell before the guns of the Hellcats were newly trained carrier pilots, earmarked to replace the heavy losses sustained in the Marianas. Toyoda committed them to the defense of Formosa after receiving overly optimistic reports of the first day's fighting. When these offerings were consumed in Halsey's inferno, Ozawa's carriers were rendered toothless once more. Tokyo's official public position regarding the Formosa fighting was to proclaim it a Japanese victory which had cost the United States eleven aircraft carriers and two battleships sunk, plus eight carriers and two battleships badly damaged.[66] In fact, her fliers had only been able to torpedo two U.S. cruisers, which both left the action under tow. As Task Force 38 sailed toward the Philippines, Halsey answered Japan's exaggerated claims of damage to the U.S. Fleet by reporting to Nimitz, "The Third Fleet's sunken and damaged ships have been salvaged and we are retiring at high speed towards the enemy."[67]

Halsey "retired" to the Philippines for three days of preinvasion softening up. On October 20, the Seventh Fleet began landing four army divisions on Leyte's beaches. MacArthur's invasion troops seized all of their objectives on schedule and without heavy losses. With the beachhead secured, Halsey began to look for the Japanese Fleet. Unlike Spruance, he need not be distracted by the progress of the land battle or even by the protection of the invasion beaches. These were Kinkaid's concerns and he had sufficient forces to deal with them. Halsey's own force included nine fleet carriers, eight light carriers, six fast battleships, fifteen cruisers, and fifty-eight destroyers.[68] Fleet carriers now operated with fifty-four fighters, twenty-four dive bombers, and eighteen torpedo planes. Due to their experience at the battle of the Philippine Sea, Avengers would now truly reflect their official designation by carrying torpedoes into battle. Most of the light carriers retained their arrangement of twenty-four fighters and nine torpeckers. The light carrier *Independence*, which had recently been designated the Navy's first night carrier, operated twenty radar-equipped Hellcats and eight similarly equipped Avengers.[69] The total number of planes on Mitscher's flattops now well exceeded one thousand.

It might seem that entering battle with a clear division of labor between Halsey and Kinkaid was a positive development. However, there was one disturbing aspect to the arrangement. Neither MacArthur nor Nimitz would surrender overall command to the other. Further aggravating the situation was the failure to set up a direct line of communication between the Third and Seventh Fleets. Messages had to be routed through a radio station on Manus Island where they were decoded and retransmitted based on the local operator's best guess at priority. It was not surprising, therefore, that messages sometimes arrived at their destination late, garbled or out of sequence. This was a grave defect in planning that can rightfully be attributed to a U.S. strain of Victory Disease.

Toyoda's response to the Leyte invasion was a reversion to Japan's traditional practice of employing a complicated plan involving multiple formations. His Sho 1 operation focused on MacArthur's landing beaches rather than Halsey's battle fleet and involved no less than four separate groups of ships. Admiral Ozawa led a northern force that included four aircraft carriers, two converted carrier battleships, three light cruisers, and eight destroyers.[70] Because the fiasco over Formosa left him with only 116 planes, Ozawa served mainly as a decoy. Japanese strategists assumed that the prospect of destroying the carriers would lure the U.S. battle fleet north and expose the beachhead to the other Japanese forces converging on it.

Vice-Admiral Shogi Nishimura led the main Southern Force composed of the battleships *Fuso* and *Yamashiro* plus the heavy cruiser *Mogami* and four destroyers. He was supported by Vice-Admiral Kiyohide Shima's small force of three cruisers and four destroyers.[71] These two groups were instructed to sail separately in order to avoid detection, but then coordinate their attack through Surigao Strait. Shima, who was senior commander, decided to let Nishimura force his way into Leyte Gulf (see Fig. 4.3) and save his own ships for action against the U.S. transports.

Japan's main killer was to be Vice-Admiral Takeo Kurita's Central Force going through San Bernardino Strait. This sledgehammer of surface power contained five battleships, including 68,000-ton *Yamato* and *Musashi* with their 18-inch guns, plus ten heavy cruisers, two light cruisers, and fifteen destroyers.[72] Theoretically, these ships were to be covered by hundreds of land-based aircraft dispersed among airfields so numerous that many were sure to survive Mitscher's fighter sweeps. But those planes were flown by inexperienced army pilots who had no effective liaison to coordinate their efforts with those of Kurita's. The Japanese admirals sailed to the Philippines without the illusions of glorious victory that had accompanied them to the Marianas. They were aware that even if they succeeded in smashing the

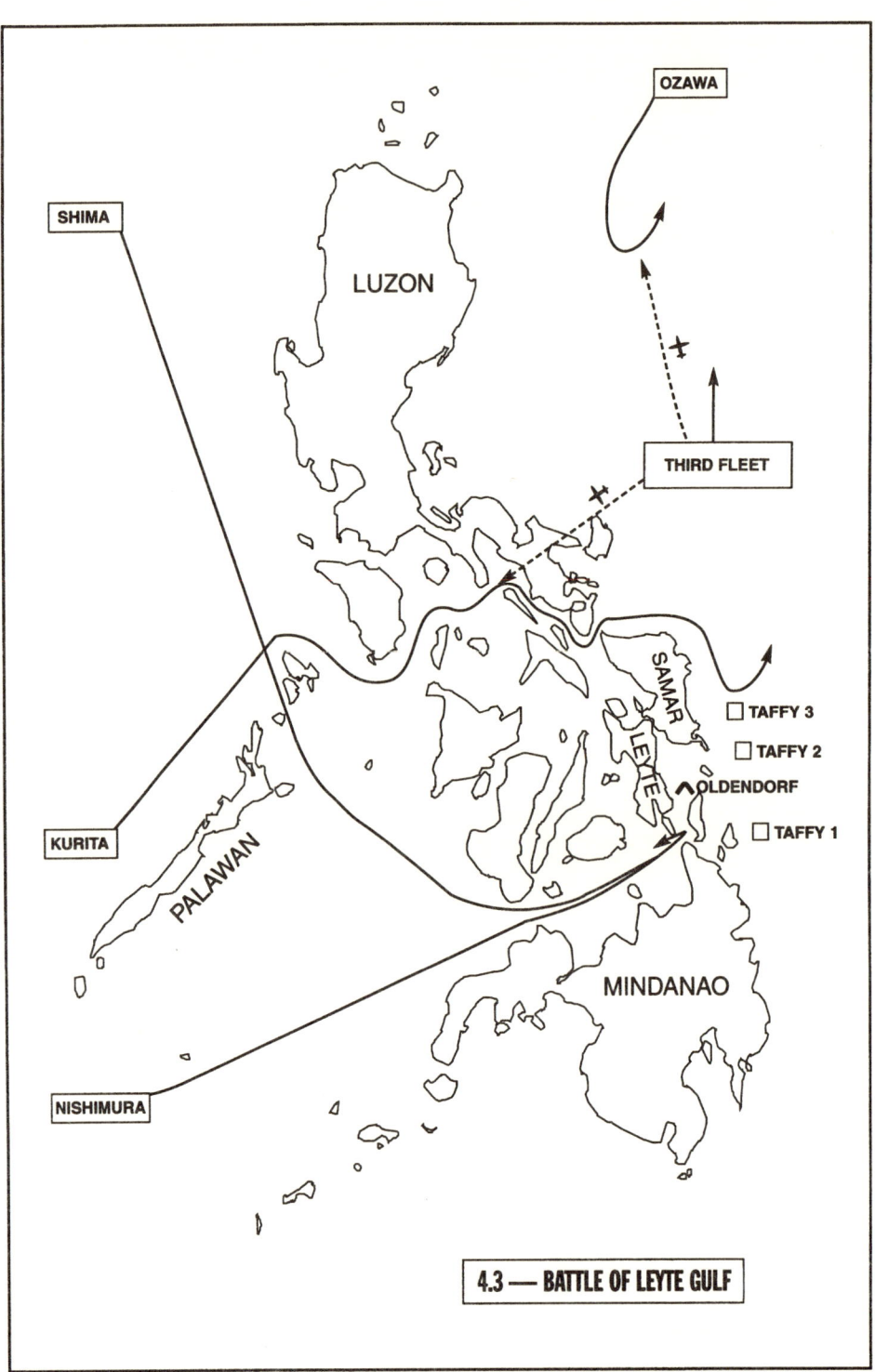

SHIMA

OZAWA

LUZON

THIRD FLEET

SAMAR

☐ TAFFY 3

☐ TAFFY 2

LEYTE

OLDENDORF

KURITA

PALAWAN

☐ TAFFY 1

MINDANAO

NISHIMURA

4.3 — BATTLE OF LEYTE GULF

invasion, U.S. superiority guaranteed that the coming battle would be a death ride for their precious ships.

On October 23, the now ubiquitous U.S. submarines sighted Kurita's force as it transited the Palawan Passage. The subs reported their find to headquarters and moved to attack. *Darter* put four torpedoes into Kurita's flagship, the heavy cruiser *Atago*, and sent her to the bottom. Kurita escaped unhurt and transferred his flag to the *Yamato*. Using his stern tubes, the *Darter's* captain then scored two hits on the *Takao*, which was forced to retire for repairs, accompanied by two destroyers. *Dace* joined the fight by launching four torpedoes at the *Maya*, which blew apart and sank. Kurita had not only been discovered before Ozawa's decoys, but had also lost three heavy cruisers in a matter of minutes. It was a small consolation that the *Darter* subsequently ran aground and had to be abandoned.

Halsey received word of the submarines' brilliant performance early next morning. He was temporarily down to eleven carriers as McCain's group was bound for replenishment at Ulithi and the *Bunker Hill* had already gone there to pick up additional fighterplanes. While his three available carrier groups launched air searches, Halsey recalled McCain and made arrangements for his group to be refueled at sea during its return trip. Air reconnaissance found both Kurita and Nishimara at approximately 8 a.m. Halsey quickly decided that the Central Force was his responsibility while the Southern Force belonged to Kinkaid. He, therefore, ordered his carrier groups to concentrate and direct their full power against Kurita's ships in the Sibuyan Sea. (It is interesting that Halsey never communicated this decision to Kinkaid, but merely assumed that the commander of the Seventh Fleet would reach a similar conclusion.)

After mounting an ineffective strike against Nishimura, Rear Admiral Ralph E. Davison's group headed north to join the groups of Rear Admirals Gerald F. Bogan and Frederick C. Sherman in their pummeling of Kurita. While launching its airstrikes, Task Force 38 was subjected to heavy attacks from land-based aircraft, one of which sank the light carrier *Princeton*. In return, Mitscher's airmen sank the *Musashi*, damaged a heavy cruiser sufficiently to put it out of the fight, and scored numerous hits on other vessels. At 2 p.m., the Japanese Central Force reversed course, in apparent retreat.

There now began a sequence of misunderstandings that almost led to disaster. Halsey anticipated that Kurita might reverse course again and attempt to force San Bernardino Strait at night. He informed his task force commanders that he would deal with any such occurrence by entrusting Lee with a newly formed Task Force 34, containing four battleships, five cruisers, and fourteen destroyers. In a second message, Halsey clarified that the plan was conditional, telling his subordinates, "If the enemy sorties, TF 34 will be formed when directed by me."[73] Although neither of these messages was intended for Kinkaid, his eavesdroppers overheard the first one, which led him to assume that Task Force 34 was already being assembled. This discovery came as a great relief for the commander of the Seventh Fleet. Kinkaid had reached the same initial conclusion as Halsey regarding their division of responsibilities and was making plans to cover Surigao Strait.

Meanwhile, Ozawa was steaming south, praying to the Gods of War for his discovery by the enemy. His numerous messages and simulated radio traffic went undetected due to faulty transmitters on the flagship *Zuikaku*. Ozawa launched an airstrike in the hope of attracting some attention, but the Americans assumed that his planes were just another batch sent out from bases in the Philippines. Finally, at approximately 4:40 p.m., Sherman's search planes made contact with Ozawa's ships some 180 miles east of Luzon's Cape Engano. Their report confirmed that the Japanese Northern Force included carriers. After consulting with his staff, Halsey decided to attack with his entire force. He sent the following to Kinkaid, "strike reports indicate enemy force Sibuyan Sea heavily damaged. Am proceeding north with three groups to attack enemy carrier force at dawn."[74] When air reconnaissance confirmed that Kurita had indeed turned around again, Halsey simply passed the information to Kinkaid and proceeded with his own plans. Kinkaid remained unconcerned, figuring that the "three groups" going north were the carriers, leaving Lee's "fourth group" behind to guard San Bernardino Strait.

As the ships of the Third Fleet gathered for their run north, some officers began to question the wisdom of the commander's decision. These doubts crystallized when a night search from the *Independence* revealed that Kurita had moved yet further east and that the navigation lights in San Bernardino Strait had been turned on. Admiral Lee concluded that the Northern Force was a decoy but his communications to the *New Jersey* drew no reply. Mitscher's chief of staff, Captain Arleigh Burke, felt likewise but failed to convince his boss to convey that opinion to Halsey. Admiral Bogan drafted a proposal to guard the strait with his carrier group and Lee's battleships, but decided not to relay it to the flagship.

Because he also had misgivings, Mitscher hoped to destroy the Japanese carriers as soon as possible and then return to cover the beachhead. Burke worked out a plan for a night engagement by the battleships followed by an air strike at dawn. Accordingly, Task Force 38 increased its speed from 16 to 25 knots. Halsey was more concerned with not letting the Japanese sneak by in the darkness. Waking from his first sleep in forty-eight hours, he noticed the increased speed and ordered it reduced back to 16 knots. Night air searchers then revealed the enemy ships to be less than 100 miles away.

Halsey had not followed Spruance's procedure of forming his battle lines before seeking combat. The enemy's proximity demanded that it be done now and Lee was given the order to form all six of his behemoths into a vanguard. But this was a tricky maneuver at night while in the company of nearly sixty other ships, so the U.S. task force was further slowed while the business was sorted out. As this was being done, Halsey radioed news of his contact with the enemy to Nimitz and Kinkaid, adding, "Own force in three groups concentrated."[75]

Meanwhile, things were heating up further south. Oldendorf deployed his ships in a layered defense throughout the length of Surigao Strait. On the frontline were thirty-nine PT boats, scattered about the western approaches in thirteen three-boat sections. Next came twenty destroyers, eager to prove how much they had learned about night fighting since the Solomons. These were backed up by eight cruisers divided into two groups. Finally, the battleships *Maryland, Pennsylvania, California, Tennessee, Mississippi,* and *West Virginia* and six additional destroyers lay across Surigao Strait's eastern exit.[76]

Nishimura's seven warships entered the passageway just after midnight. They dodged the PT boats but then sailed into a gauntlet of torpedoes fired by the U.S. destroyers. The first bunch of fish scored heavily on the *Fuso*, which broke in two and burned fiercely before sinking. Subsequent torpedo attacks mauled the destroyers, sinking the *Yamagumo* and *Michishio* and crippling the *Asagumo*. The *Yamashiro* also caught a few fish but continued to advance until it died in a rain of metal from the guns of Oldendorf's battle line. Nishimura died with his flagship. The *Mogami* and the destroyer *Shigure* retreated, leaving the *Asagumo* to be sunk by a "mop-up" force of cruisers. Shima advanced past the two survivors and began positioning his ships for an attack on the Americans. But when light cruiser *Abukuma* was struck by a torpedo, he too decided to exercise the better part of valor. However, his retreating ships would later be attacked repeatedly by U.S. planes that managed to dispatch both the *Mogami* and the *Abukuma*.

While Oldendorf's Pearl Harbor survivors were annihilating Nishimura, Kinkaid was holding a staff meeting to evaluate the security of the Leyte beachhead. The meeting adjourned at 4 a.m., with all participants in agreement that every contingency was covered. Immediately afterward, the Seventh Fleet's operations officer returned and said, "Admiral, I can think of only one thing. We have never directly asked Halsey if TF 34 is guarding San Bernardino Strait."[77] Kinkaid proceeded to do just that. As his message to Halsey took its long, circuitous course, Kinkaid continued to look south, sending Oldendorf into Surigao Strait to pursue stragglers. He finally got his answer from Kurita rather than Halsey. At approximately 7 a.m., the ships of Japan's Central Force emerged from the morning haze and began firing at Rear Admiral Clifton Sprague's "Taffy 3," the U.S. escort carrier group lying off Samar Island.

Halsey received Kinkaid's query at 6:24 a.m. and sent off a negative response which arrived long after Japanese shells began falling on Taffy 3. Although bewildered by Kinkaid's dispatch, Halsey saw no ominous implications in it. He remained preoccupied with the quest for the Japanese carriers. Mitscher had already launched his dawn search and then gambled by sending up his first attack wave. These planes circled some 50 miles ahead of the task force in anticipation of sighting the enemy. At 7:30 a.m., Hellcats from the *Essex* spotted Ozawa's ships and the airborne assault force immediately pounced. Its dive bombers sank the light carrier *Chitose* and blew up the destroyer *Akitsuki* for good measure. This group also managed to put a torpedo into the *Zuikaku* and two bombs onto the flight deck of the light carrier *Zuiho*. Mitscher's second strike torpedoed the light cruiser *Tama* and pummeled the light carrier *Chiyoda*, which burst into flames and went dead in the water.

As the aviators began their feeding frenzy, Halsey received his first notification that the escort carriers were under attack. This was closely followed by Kinkaid's plea, "Fast battleships are urgently needed immediately at Leyte Gulf."[78] Because the ships of Task Force 34 were more than 300 miles away from Leyte Gulf, Halsey saw no point in parting with them, especially as they could soon be employed against Ozawa's cripples. Oldendorf's old battlewagons were slower but much closer to the action. However, McCain's carrier group had a much longer reach than Lee's battleships. Halsey directed McCain to go to Kinkaid's assistance and ordered Lee to close on Ozawa.

Over the next hour, Halsey received a stream of frantic calls for assistance from Kinkaid. He ignored them and continued his efforts against the Northern Force in an atmosphere of ever increasing anxiety. Then, at 10 a.m., Halsey received a communiqué from Admiral Nimitz that read, "Where is repeat where is Task Force 34? The world wonders."[79] The second sentence was part of the usual meaningless padding that accompanied such dispatches and should have been eliminated by the decoder. A preliminary phrase, "turkey trots to water," was obviously nonsense and was removed during decoding. Unfortunately, the closing phrase made enough sense that it was left in. Nimitz's apparent sarcasm sent Halsey into a rage. He threw his cap to the floor and unleashed a stream of profanity that continued to flow until his chief of staff grabbed him and said, "What the hell's the matter with you? Pull yourself together!"[80] After stewing for nearly an hour, Halsey reluctantly took the battleships and Bogan's carrier group back to Leyte Gulf.

Mitscher remained with the rest of Task Force 38 and launched four additional air strikes against Ozawa's ships. Everyone's favorite target during the first of these attacks was the *Zuikaku*. The veteran fleet carrier was rocked by a multitude of bombs and torpedoes, lost control of her helm, and began to list. She slid beneath the waves at approximately 2:15 p.m. The next strike finished off the *Zuiho*, but the latter two inflicted only negligible damage on the hermaphrodite battleships *Ise* and *Hyuga*. Halsey's departure under duress robbed him of the opportunity to cap his victory by destroying the two Japanese dreadnoughts in a surface battle.

Meanwhile, a spectacular but unequal surface battle was occurring off Samar. Kurita had taken four battleships, six heavy cruisers, two light cruisers, and most of his destroyers through San Bernardino Strait.[81] He was opposed by the six jeep carriers, three destroyers, and four destroyer escorts of Taffy 3.[82] While the baby flattops struggled to get their planes aloft, their escorts made smoke and desperately charged the enemy ships. When Taffy 1 and Taffy 2 got word of what was happening, they sent their planes to join the donnybrook. The U.S. pilots were not used to attacking ships and their armament was heavily weighted toward light bombers and rockets rather than torpedoes. Nevertheless, with help from the destroyers, they managed to sink three heavy cruisers and send another limping off without a bow. American resistance was so fierce that many Japanese captains became convinced that they were up against the main strength of the Third Fleet! The defenders paid for their tenacity by losing the escort carrier *Gambier Bay*, two destroyers, and a destroyer escort. Every other jeep carrier in Taffy 3 was also hit. They stayed afloat only because most Japanese armor-piercing rounds passed right through their thin hulls without exploding. But with his enemy reeling and his objective almost within reach, Kurita lost his Bushido spirit. At 9:14 a.m., the Japanese commander broke off the engagement and ordered his scattered ships to reassemble. After three hours of maneuver and evaluation, Kurita decided to retire back through San Bernardino Strait.

But Sprague's little ships were not out of the woods just yet. On the heels of Kurita's departure came a flight of kamikazes, adversaries who fought with neither hope of survival nor intent of retreating. The suicide planes had made their combat debut a few hours earlier by crashing into the flight decks of Taffy 1's *Santee* and *Suwanne*. Now, the flying coffins hurled themselves down on the already battered jeeps of Taffy 3, sinking the *St. Lo* and further damaging three other escort carriers. It was a grim irony that the *St. Lo* had faced down Kurita's monsters only to fall victim to a smaller but more resolute opponent shortly thereafter. The kamikaze attacks were an ominous portent of the future of the Pacific War.

The Americans got some payback during the mop-up. Off Cape Engano, a cruiser-destroyer force dispatched the derelict *Chiyoda* and sank the destroyer *Hatsuzuki* while the submarine *Jallao* finished off the wounded cruiser *Tama*. As he expected, Halsey did not reach Leyte Gulf in time to be of any help to Kinkaid. When he did arrive, a night search from the *Independence* found only the destroyer *Nowaki*, lingering to pick up survivors for the sunken cruiser *Chikuma*. She was summarily demolished by the 6–inch guns of the cruiser *Biloxi*, *Vincennes*, and *Miami*. It is a commentary on night fighting that the U.S. Navy did not find out what it had obliterated until it gained access to Japanese records after the war. Contemporary reports from Halsey's ships identified a vessel ranging anywhere from a small destroyer to a *Fuso*-class battleship![83] Bogan's task group rendezvoused with McCain's later that night and the combined force sent up a 250-plane strike just before dawn. It found Kurita's fleeing ships and added to the final tally by sinking a destroyer and a light cruiser.

The Battle of Leyte Gulf cost Japan one fleet carrier, three light carriers, three battleships, six heavy cruisers, three light cruisers, and eight destroyers compared to losses of one light carrier, two escort carriers, two destroyers, and one destroyer escort for the United States.[84] (This tabulation reflects only the losses suffered by Japan's four main battle forces. Various accounts inflate the total by including ships sunk while on ancillary missions in Philippine waters.) The Japanese sacrifice was entirely in vain because the invasion of the Philippines proceeded without interruption. But Kurita came close to interrupting it, and his ability to do so put the quality of Halsey's leadership into question with some of his naval contemporaries as well as post-war historians. One critic summed up this attitude in a nutshell by writing that Halsey's judgments, "were not equal to his boldness, and boldness alone does not make a Nelson."[85] However, an examination of the conduct of the Third Fleet's commander must bear in mind that his primary mission, per his orders from Nimitz, was the destruction of the Japanese Fleet. By 1944, it was indisputable that "fleet" meant "carriers." Therefore, it was a foregone conclusion that Halsey would attack once enemy carriers revealed themselves. His orders combined with his aggressive personality precluded any possibility that he would stay put. Indeed, he had already explained to Nimitz how he intended to go after the flattops, with no dissent from his boss.

Admiral Nimitz received an unwelcome reminder of this fact on the evening of October 25. During dinner, he and his staff went over the day's unpleasant events, with the admiral repeatedly blaming Halsey for uncovering San Bernardino Strait and jeopardizing the landings. Also in attendance was Lt. Commander Chester Nimitz Jr., on leave from a long tour of submarine duty. The younger Nimitz asked to see Halsey's operational orders and after examining them concluded that the Third Fleet commander had been given carte blanc to abandon the beachhead and seek out the enemy fleet. With the candor that can only come from family, he told his father, "It's your fault." The admiral's retort, "That's your opinion," provided a less than convincing rebuttal.[86]

Halsey's true dilemma was whether to go north with his entire force or leave a portion behind to protect San Bernardino Strait. In his judgment, Lee's battleships alone would not suffice to cover the passageway. Without air cover, they would be vulnerable to the land-based airplanes that sank the *Princeton*. Admiral Lee undermined this argument somewhat when he stated afterward that he would have had no qualms about covering the strait without air cover.[87] But, considering the fate of ships such as the *Musashi* and the *Prince of Wales*, the wisdom of his position is questionable. A better alternative would have been to detach the four slowest battleships, *Washington*, *Alabama*, *Massachusetts*, and *South Dakota*, supported by one small carrier group. Halsey could then run north with the rest of his carriers and the 33-knot battlewagons, *Iowa* and *New Jersey*. However, this would have left Mitscher with only four CVs and three CVLs to confront an enemy force that was still an unknown quantity. In retrospect, this force would have been more than sufficient, because Ozawa had only twenty-nine operational aircraft on the morning of October 25, 1944.[88] But decisions made in retrospect carry little weight. Naval Academy doctrine stressed concentration of force and a ComAirPac analysis distributed one month prior to Leyte Gulf warned against the dangers of exposing a divided carrier force to air attack.[89] Therefore, Halsey would have been foolish to divide his ten available carriers while still unaware that Ozawa's carriers were relatively toothless. His decision to pursue his objective with his entire force not only conformed to the principle of concentration, but was correct in the surrounding circumstances. Halsey stuck to his guns after the war, writing, "My decision to strike the Northern Force was a hard one to make, but given the same circumstances and the same information as I had then, I would make it again."[90] However, he often hurt his cause by adamantly refusing to admit that he had followed a decoy, which in the context of Japanese strategic planning, Ozawa clearly was.

In making his choice, Halsey clearly underestimated the remaining strength of the Japanese Central Force. His dispatch to MacArthur after the battle is damning in this regard, stating, "I believed that the center force had been so heavily damaged in the Sibuyan Sea that it could no longer be

considered a serious menace to the Seventh Fleet."[91] Perhaps Halsey's years
away from carriers caused him to forget that a discount must be applied to
the after-action reports of pilots. However, he did correctly calculate that
Kurita's turn-away prevented him from coordinating his attack with those
of the Southern Force. This would give Kinkaid sufficient time to shift his
dreadnoughts to handle each threat. Halsey informed Seventh Fleet of his
intentions and also conveyed a timely warning that Kurita had reversed course
again. He justifiably expected that Kinkaid would respond accordingly.

Halsey could have made his plans clearer at the outset by signaling that
he was heading north with his entire force, rather than "three groups." Also,
his later communiqué reporting enemy contact off Cape Engano might have
been more illuminating if it included "am now forming Task Force 34"
rather than "own force concentrated." But Halsey is not accountable for
confusion over his prior dispatch about Task Force 34, because he was unaware that it had been overheard. Besides, the burden of resolving any
doubts about the security of the Leyte beachhead rested primarily with
Kinkaid, not Halsey. Yet, Kinkaid was extremely tardy in seeking to con-
firm the status of Task Force 34, despite details that should have raised some
eyebrows at his headquarters. For instance, Halsey's plan included his own
flagship, *New Jersey*, among the ships assigned to guard the Strait. It was
patently ridiculous to assume that Bull Halsey would stay behind while his
beloved carriers went to do battle with their Japanese counterparts. Also,
Halsey's parting message said, "Am proceeding north," a clear indication
that the *New Jersey* was sailing alongside Mitscher's flattops. Even when
some doubts were crystallized by his operations officer, Kinkaid made no
provision to shift his surface forces north and made only a half-hearted effort
to ensure that timely and adequate air searches were flown in that direction.[92]

Of course, if Oldendorf had been directed to cover San Bernardino Strait,
he too would have to operate without the umbrella provided by Mitscher's
carriers. But Sprague's escort carriers might have served as a reasonable
substitute with their five hundred planes, which included more than three
hundred fighters.[93] Theoretically, these same aircraft could have afforded
some protection to Lee's battleships if he had remained to cover the beachhead. But the awkward liaison channels between the Third and Seventh
Fleets would have made this a dicey proposition. It is reasonable to assume
that a smoother arrangement for air cover could have been worked out
among units entirely within the Seventh Fleet. In any case, ordinary prudence required Kinkaid to seek unequivocal confirmation that San Bernardino Strait was covered and to have Oldendorf ready to move north as a
contingency plan.

Clearly, Halsey's performance at Leyte Gulf was not without flaws. Witness his somewhat vague dispatches and underestimation of the Central Force's residual fighting capacity. Also, his run to the north slowed to a crawl due to his failure to arrange a prior formation of the battle line. Finally, Halsey was certainly culpable in losing his temper over Nimitz's message and then sending his battleships back toward the beachhead. This did nothing to help the Seventh Fleet and deprived the Third Fleet of an opportunity to sink Ozawa's battleships and screening forces in a surface action. But Kurita's threat to MacArthur's beachhead did not result from these errors. It sprang from a complacent attitude that allowed two independent campaigns to continue even after they had ostensibly been joined. This led to a flawed U.S. command structure that could not properly coordinate its available resources. A potential disaster was averted due to the men of Taffy 3 and Kurita's loss of nerve.

X

After its twin drubbings in June and October of 1944, Japan's navy would be incapable of offering any concerted opposition to U.S. amphibious landings. It was not even a true fleet-in-being, but merely a target that was destroyed piecemeal by planes and submarines. The kamikaze now became the U.S. Navy's major vexation in the Pacific. Halsey's men endured a torrent of the suicide planes while supporting MacArthur's subsequent conquests in the Philippines. Nature provided its own menace in the form of a typhoon that struck the Third Fleet on December 18, sinking 3 destroyers, destroying 146 planes, and drowning nearly 800 men. A court of inquiry blamed Halsey but its verdict was significantly softened by Admiral King.[94]

Spruance returned to action in late January 1945, with an itinerary that included amphibious operations against Iwo Jima in February and Okinawa in April. A few days before the landings on Iwo, Mitscher, who captained the *Hornet* during the Doolittle Raid, "returned" to Tokyo by sending his airwings on a massive sweep against the Japanese capital. The ferocity of the opposition from Japan's green but determined flyers reminded the men of the Fifth Fleet that the war was far from over. This was further driven home off Okinawa by kamikazes who subjected Spruance's ships to deprivations far greater than those experienced by the Third Fleet in the Philippines. During the onslaught, Spruance received welcomed reinforcements from four British carriers in Vice-Admiral Bernard Rawlings' Task Force 57. The biggest kamikaze was the *Yamato*. Japan's super-dreadnought sortieed in a suicide run but was sunk by Mitscher's planes far short of Okinawa's landing beaches.

On May 27, Halsey assumed command for the last time and soon made his own "return" to Japan by sending one of his carrier groups to bomb airfields on Kyushu. Immediately thereafter, he ran into another typhoon. No ships were sunk, but the flight decks of the *Hornet* and *Bennington* collapsed, the bow of the heavy cruiser *Pittsburgh* was wrenched off, seventy-six planes were destroyed and six men were killed. The court of inquiry again blamed Halsey and recommended that he and McCain be assigned to other duty.[95] This time, King wholeheartedly agreed with the findings of the tribunal. He decided to replace McCain with Jack Towers but still gave no serious consideration to relieving his popular fighting admiral. Japan itself was next on the agenda and Halsey would be needed there.

Okinawa was officially declared secure on June 22, 1945. The fees extracted by the three thousand kamikazes and conventional bombers that sortied in the island's defense totaled thirty-three ships sunk, more than 100 ships damaged, 790 aircraft, and 4,907 dead sailors.[96] The ordeal off Okinawa gave the U.S. Navy a brutal preview of what might lay ahead in the waters off Japan during an assault on the home islands. The ground fighting on Okinawa and the previous bloodbath on Iwo Jima had been just as instructive, costing the United States more than 65,000 dead and wounded soldiers and marines.[97]

Operation "Olympic," the invasion of Kyushu, was scheduled for November 1945, with MacArthur in charge of the ground forces and Nimitz in command at sea. Landings on Honshu were slated for the following March. The uninterrupted flow of ships and planes provided by U.S. industry finally allowed the Third and Fifth Fleets to operate simultaneously. Each of Nimitz's commanders received assignments befitting their talents. Spruance would oversee the landings and use his ten carriers to protect the beachhead and supplement the escort carriers in providing ground support. Halsey would be allowed to roam free with as many as twenty British and American flattops to create havoc up and down the Japanese coast. But then, two atomic bombs brought peace, leaving the story to the mythmakers and Monday morning quarterbacks.

5

The New Legacies

Nelson's twentieth-century heirs make up a diverse group of characters. Heihachiro Togo was a ruthless samurai who possessed an aggressive disposition and the iron discipline common to his warrior caste. John Jellicoe embodied the virtues of the idealized Victorian gentleman. He was scholarly, chivalrous, and pleasant of manner, but hard as flint at the core. Bill Halsey was a rowdy throwback who would have felt comfortable standing on a deck beside Francis Drake or John Paul Jones. He was a colorful personality who fought with emotion and genuinely despised his enemy. Ray Spruance was virtually colorless, but his immense intellectual ability and complete self-control made him the archetypal modern professional naval officer. He admired his adversaries yet destroyed them with dispassionate detachment. The only readily discernable common denominator among the four men is their wartime service as commander of a victorious nation's battle fleet. How then do their accomplishments in that capacity measure up to the Nelsonian standard that demands annihilating victories, decisive strategic consequences, and lasting moral impact?

Togo's performance in the role of his country's first fleet commander was outstanding. He destroyed two enemy fleets at a relatively low cost and his triumph at Tsushima was the twentieth century's only facsimile of Trafalgar. Togo did his work under adverse and restrictive strategic circumstances. Insular Japan needed to win at sea in order to win its war on the continent and the resources of the Combined Fleet would remain essentially finite for the duration of the struggle. Togo had to prosecute his operations against the Port Arthur Squadron while peering over his shoulder in anticipation of the

Baltic Fleet's arrival. When Rozhestvensky's ships finally appeared, Japan's material exhaustion mandated that they be disposed of by a quick knockout.

If we exclusively rely on the cherished American standard of measure known as the bottom line, the totality and economy of Togo's achievement might place him at the top of the hierarchical pyramid of twentieth-century admiralty. But in fairness to the men who came later, it must be remembered that Togo fought in an era of relative technical simplicity. Torpedoes were lethal only in night combat and there were no submarines or aircraft around to worry about. His task was further simplified by the small size of the forces involved. The opposing battle lines at Tsushima numbered only twelve ships apiece and were even smaller at the Yellow Sea. At Tsushima, Togo was the last naval commander who could visually control a major sea battle from his own bridge.

The biggest discount to Togo's achievement comes from the poor quality of his opponents. Russia's ships and crews were tactically deficient and for the most part her leadership was strategically inept. Other than Makarov, the Russians had no high-ranking admiral who was both competent and dynamic. But when analyzing the results of any contested struggle, military or otherwise, there is always the danger that by overemphasizing the loser's shortcomings we improperly reduce the winner to a mere bystander. History books are filled with the names of leaders who failed to exploit their enemy's weaknesses. In the final analysis, wars are won or lost on the battlefield not on the balance sheet and a commander bears the responsibility for planning and executing the final result.

Togo defeated the Russians by employing a flexible strategy that is worthy of envy. His victory was actually two distinctly different naval campaigns that employed distinctly different methodologies, each of which was ideally suited for its surrounding strategic environment. Tactically, Togo appeared schizophrenic. He declined the opportunity to close on a confused and demoralized enemy fleet at the Yellow Sea, yet he exposed his ships to the guns of a still cohesive fleet at Tsushima. But Togo's tactics merely followed his strategy and are perfectly logical when viewed in that light. Greater risks were not justified at the Yellow Sea because the eventual fall of Port Arthur was by then a foregone conclusion. The need for a swift victory at Tsushima necessitated a less chary course of action and Togo had already correctly surmised that the fatigued Russians would have little staying power.

The battle of Tsushima was the crowning glory in the war that signaled Japan's emergence as a world power. As such, it is generally ranked as Admiral Togo's most brilliant accomplishment. But his earlier campaign against Port Arthur, while less heroic in its recounting, was no less significant as a personal triumph. Although aggressive by nature, Togo was able to subordinate his inclinations and conform his conduct to the restrictive strategic environment. In doing so, he won a relatively economical victory of attrition and emerged with a finely honed instrument that then produced an annihilating victory when circumstances required one.

Togo was the beneficiary of good fortune during the naval war, most notably in Makarov's death and the last minute hits at the Yellow Sea. But in each case, luck was the residue of design or discipline. The mine that sank the *Petropavlovsk* was a deliberate countermeasure against Makarov's reckless tendencies, well known to Togo from his study of the Russian admiral's book and career. The two hits on the *Tsarevitch* that decided the battle of the Yellow Sea resulted from Togo's unshakable persistence in pursuing his strategy, despite the damage to his ships and injury to himself. Finally, luck held little sway at Tsushima where Togo calculated the risks, made his dangerous turn and came away with an epic victory. No matter what the quality of his opposition, Togo stands out as a timeless example of a great commander, possessing the insight to choose the correct strategic approach and the discipline to execute it resolutely.

Although Tsushima was a naval triumph on a par with Trafalgar, its impact was not as far reaching. Nelson's victory was the capstone on an edifice of British naval tradition that had been under construction for more than two hundred years. Togo's success was the foundation for the traditions of a fledgling service that had been in existence for less than forty years. Therefore, Tsushima did not elevate the Japanese Navy to the exalted position that the Royal Navy maintained for more than a century after the defeat of Napoleon. Indeed, many in the West devalued the Japanese achievement as a sideshow against a second-rate opponent and continued to doubt the ability of a "backward" nation to compete with the better navies of Europe and the United States. This was the same parochialism that caused Europe to ignore the lessons of the U.S. Civil War forty years before, some of which might have given an indication of the slaughter that would take place on the Western Front from 1914 to 1918. But one thing was certain: Tsushima made the Japanese believe they could compete with the West and that unshakable confidence would be a major factor when they proved themselves correct in the early months of World War II.

Some have accused Togo of leaving his service a legacy of perfidy because of his surprise attack on Port Arthur. (Admiral Halsey was a vocal proponent of this view even before Pearl Harbor.)[1] But surprise attacks pre-date Togo in Japanese military tradition, tracing back to the legendary samurai Tsukahara Bokuden, who defeated his opponents with a devastating sword-stroke delivered straight from the scabbard. Admiral Yamamoto, an honorable man by any other standard, used the same method at Pearl Harbor. Furthermore, the ploy was not just culturally endemic to Japan. It was also favored by certain elements in the nation that provided Togo with his training and inspiration. The British admiralty had no qualms about pre-emptively destroying the Danish Fleet in 1807, and Jack Fisher reportedly advised the King on several occasions to "Copenhagen" the German fleet before it matured into a lethal threat.[2]

Admiral Togo provided Japan with the ideal role model for its vibrant but still immature navy. He was a stern father figure whose legacy of skill and success gave future generations of Japanese naval officers very lofty goals to aspire to. His parting advice to "tighten your helmet straps in the hour of victory" is a lasting testament for all naval officers as well as all participants in any serious competition.

John Jellicoe never had to follow Togo's advice because he never won a clear-cut victory at sea. His only naval battle was a tactical draw and though his strategy brought ultimate victory, he was no longer in command when it finally came to fruition. But Jellicoe labored under circumstances more adverse than those surrounding the other members of our naval tetrarchy. He faced a very capable foe under a cloud of potential evil far darker than that which hung over Togo. A defeat of the Combined Fleet would have cost Japan victory in a war of limited objectives on the geo-political periphery of a sterile adversary. The defeat of the Grand Fleet in the uncompromising struggle against virile Germany could have cost England her empire and her way of life. Furthermore, Jellicoe fought in a technological shadowland lying between Togo's era of relative simplicity and the more complex but better understood era of Spruance and Halsey. His fleet was a lumbering monster which faced new terrors whose potency had yet to be measured in combat. Unfortunately, Jellicoe's major flaw as a naval leader, his pathological inability to delegate, aggravated the difficulties in resolving the myriad of questions presented by this fluid and ambiguous environment. His tendency to concern himself with the details of even minor issues undoubtedly contributed greatly to his eventual physical and psychological exhaustion. But perhaps even more debilitating was the unrealistically high level of public expectation that daily anticipated news of a naval triumph that matched the glories of Nelson.

From the war's outset, Jellicoe surmised the German intention of offering battle only as a ruse to whittle down the Grand Fleet piecemeal. His strategy of fighting exclusively on his own terms was mundane but indisputably correct. The combination of Germany's refusal to fight a straight-up battle and England's refusal to be ambushed created a strategic stalemate that worked to the latter's advantage in the long run. Jellicoe's tactics of engaging at long range in single line ahead under central control admittedly served to protect his own fleet more than to destroy his enemy's. However, as in the case of Togo's schizophrenia, the British commander's caution was a logical offshoot of his strategy. In retrospect, it seems that Jellicoe's assessment of the underwater threat to his ships was highly inflated. At no time during the war were the Germans able to coordinate the operations of their U-boats with those of their battle fleet and they never even attempted to lay mines in the British path of advance during a surface engagement. But wars are not fought in retrospect and our present conclusions would not have been warranted prior to Jutland.

In his one tangible opportunity for decisive victory, Jellicoe failed to annihilate his enemy despite holding the reins of the most powerful armada which a British admiral ever led into battle. That fact has understandably generated accusations that Jellicoe squandered the legacy left to his country by Nelson. The kaiser implied as much when he proclaimed after the battle, "The spell of Trafalgar is broken!"[3] Of course, the German monarch had ulterior motives for issuing such a statement and his subsequent conduct showed that it was the equivalent of whistling in the dark. The spell remained strong enough to keep his "victorious" battle fleet quiescent for the duration of the war. An American naval officer was more sincere when he wrote some twenty years later: "The British lost that imponderable and invaluable moral ascendancy at Jutland. . . . Never again would American or Japanese sailors be overawed by the powerful, even overwhelming, force of British naval tradition."[4]

Jellicoe did behave cautiously at Jutland but his caution was not excessive nor did it cost him victory. His mode of deployment into line of battle was superb and he chose it without hesitation despite a near vacuum of tactical intelligence. His turnaway from torpedoes was justified in light of the information then available and it probably saved at least a half-dozen British battleships from underwater damage. The maneuver was also used at various stages of the battle by ships under the command of Beatty, Hipper, and Hood without tagging any of those three men as being overcautious. Finally, the turnaway was probably no more responsible for the escape of the High Seas Fleet than was Scheer's disinclination to fight and skill at escaping. Jellicoe was culpable for being a poor soothsayer concerning Scheer's line of retreat, but his bad guess almost certainly would not have been made if the admiralty had been more forthcoming with its information or his own ships less reticent in their reporting.

Britannia's trident was tarnished by its failure to strike a death blow at Jutland mainly because the world still expected Trafalgars from a navy that could no longer produce them. In the Great War of 1914–1918, the Royal

Navy was still the most powerful on earth but it had nothing resembling the margin of superiority which it held during the Napoleonic era. Part of its trouble was in its materiel, a direct corollary to the relative decline of England's economy and industrial base vis-à-vis those of Germany. The Grand Fleet's disadvantages in shells, armor protection and optical equipment that surfaced at Jutland can in large part be traced to the nation's general economic slide. Additionally, the many years of unchallenged supremacy at sea had bred complacency and mental ossification among the Royal Navy's officer corps. Fisher tried hard to sweep away the cobwebs, but no large institution can reform itself overnight. The lack of initiative displayed by British ship captains at Jutland and the Dogger Bank proved that much of the rot remained. After Jutland, a despondent Beatty hit the nail on the head when he told a confidant: "There is something wrong with our ships; and something wrong with our system."[5]

How much of the system's shortcomings can be attributed to Jellicoe's battle orders that emphasized central control over individual initiative? Leveson's refusal to seek his own Trafalgar in the gathering darkness at Jutland might be explained as simply obeying the "ruling principle" of keeping the fleet together. But the problems with British naval leadership went far beyond written memoranda. For instance, Jellicoe's orders anticipated an absence of discernable signals in battle and instructed his ships' captains to deal with such situations by conforming their movements to those of the flagship.[6] Yet, at Jutland, Evan-Thomas twice continued steaming in the wrong direction until he received specific orders to the contrary from Beatty. He did so despite the easily perceived risk of losing contact with the battlecruisers in the first instance, and the prospect of grave peril to his own ships in the second. At Dogger Bank, four British battlecruisers chose to follow a literal interpretation of a questionable signal that led them to concentrate unnecessarily on a cripple and thus forfeit any hope of pursuing the enemy's main force. This occurred despite the fact that both the letter and spirit of Beatty's battle orders placed great emphasis on individual initiative.[7]

The deficiencies that plagued the British navy at Jutland were structural flaws that reflected the material and spiritual decline of its mother country. However, if fairness requires a conclusion that Jellicoe did not create the defective system at issue, accuracy also compels a finding that he made no major effort to fix it. For although he was Fisher's protégé, Jellicoe cannot in any sense be categorized as a dynamic force for change. Yet, this observation is of limited relevance in an assessment of him as a battle fleet commander. Even if he had been so inclined, Jellicoe could not have solved all the problems of his service from the bridge of the *Iron Duke*. His charge was to win the war, and when viewed in that context, his battle orders can be regarded as the proper marriage of tactics to strategy.

Circumstance placed Jellicoe in command of a powerful but flawed instrument that was essential to the survival of a fading empire in a desperate struggle against a formidable adversary. Denied victory in battle by the skill and strategic disposition of his opponent, he had the clarity of vision and strength of character to follow a winning strategy rather than pander to the irrationalities of popular opinion. Jellicoe's claim to greatness comes from the moral courage he displayed by maintaining his course despite personal frustration and public censure. His legacy to the British nation was victory and the freedom to control its own destiny. In the age of total war, perhaps that was glory enough.

During World War II, Japan put in a strong bid for England's naval scepter, but it was the United States that emerged from the conflict with the baton firmly in its grasp. The U.S. Navy won its laurels in the Pacific against a tough, aggressive, and skillful adversary who conceded nothing by default. Its mission of a carrier-supported amphibious advance was the most complex and logistically burdensome task in the history of naval warfare. In some respects, however, the higher degree of complexity was actually less vexing to Spruance and Halsey than the "simpler" level that troubled Jellicoe. Advances in communications made it feasible to directly control vast numbers of ships while greater specialization and an evolving progressive mind set made navies more readily adaptable to rapid changes in technology. The logistical hurdles could be vaulted because the U.S. war effort was underwritten by the world's most powerful industrial economy. This also made America's long-term strategic situation in the Pacific generally favorable, even in the dark days immediately following Pearl Harbor. Japan never had the wherewithal to "dictate peace in the White House" and the disaster at Midway eliminated her dubious prospects for "negotiating" a limited victory from Hawaii. Once fully mobilized, America's huge industrial base and reservoir of management skill would produce state-of-the-art equipment and top-notch personnel in unprecedented abundance.

The immensity of the U.S. industrial colossus is best illustrated by pointing out that it fueled a two-pronged drive across the Pacific while simultaneously devoting an even greater portion of its productive capacity to the defeat of Nazi Germany. In addition to supplying the needs of its own armed forces in a two-front war, the U.S. economy was able to provide substantial material support to the military forces of Great Britain and Soviet Russia. Of course, America's industrial mobilization did not occur in the blink of an eye. As the nation metamorphosed from sleeping giant to super power, many battles were waged in Washington over the allocation of resources for the bifurcated war. The European proponents usually won those battles because a concert of Allied authorities viewed Germany as the greater threat. However, because the U.S. Navy's role against Hitler would be mainly one of convoy escort, it could concentrate most of its large surface units in the Pacific and supplement them with new arrivals as soon as they became available.

But to paraphrase a Spartan proverb, skill and materiel which cannot fight is useless. The U.S. Navy could not beat the Japanese merely by showing up in great numbers. Embryonic principles of amphibious assault and carrier warfare had to be refined and melded into a unified doctrine that could only be proven in combat. Leadership was a crucial variable in the victory equation of a service that, despite a rich heroic tradition, had never in its history fought a full-fledged fleet battle.

Admirals Spruance and Halsey were instrumental in solving that equation, even before they received the full benefits of their country's material largess. At Midway, Spruance was outnumbered and on the defensive but won a victory that forever robbed Japan of her momentum. In the South Pacific, Halsey went on the offensive with only material parity but turned strategic equilibrium into an irreversible U.S. initiative. Later as fleet commanders, each man prevailed in a major sea battle, neither of which was a true victory of annihilation. But by then, Trafalgars only existed as quaint notions of an era long past, gone the route of the grand Napoleonic battle on land. War in the industrial age was a long haul and, taken in its entirety, the U.S. Navy's Pacific campaign was an annihilation quite worthy of Nelson. After Leyte Gulf, submarines and carrier strikes in Japan's home waters finished the job begun at Midway. When the emperor's plenipotentiaries signed the document of formal surrender on board the battleship *Missouri* on September 2, 1945, their country's navy had been virtually erased from the face of the earth. At war's end, the major Japanese warships still afloat totaled one battleship, two fleet carriers, two light carriers, five cruisers, and eighteen destroyers, most of which were battered hulks helplessly awaiting their fate.[8]

The methods of combat favored by Halsey and Spruance were more similar than their personalities or historical reputations might indicate. Neither man was a defensive fighter. Halsey, of course, knew only one way to fight: Go for the jugular. He never strayed from his dictum, "get to the other fellow with everything you have as fast as you can and dump it on him." (This statement is both profound and revealing but not necessarily original. Any Civil War buff worth his salt undoubtedly hears its echo of Confederate General Nathan Bedford Forrest's eloquent, "Get there firstest with the mostest!") Spruance also preferred the quick kill, evidenced by his dictum of "violent, overwhelming force, swiftly applied." However, he was more inclined to stalk his opponent before attempting to dispatch him. At Midway and the Philippine Sea, once Spruance pinpointed the enemy fleet, he hit it with everything he had. Halsey was a carrier admiral who believed wholeheartedly in the primacy of naval air power. Spruance was a battleship admiral whose heart may have remained with the dreadnoughts but whose head brought him to the same conclusion as his colleague. The Fifth Fleet's battle orders prior to the Philippine Sea proved nothing to the contrary about its commander's thinking. Spruance's reference to his battle line merely covered the contingency of a surface battle, most likely against cripples that had been severely wounded by carrier planes. Interestingly enough, the Third Fleet's carrier proponent foresaw the same contingency prior to the fight off Cape Engano. Halsey fully intended to finish Ozawa's ships off in a surface battle and afterward loudly bemoaned the missed opportunity.[9]

In practicing their craft, the two men often acted dissimilarly because of their variant personalities and perspectives. Spruance was a deliberative commander with a clear focus on his strategic objective, whether it be the defense of Midway or the conquest of the enemy's island bastions. Halsey was an intuitive hunch player whose focus was always on the enemy fleet. The contrast worked in favor of the United States at Midway. It is hard to believe that Halsey would have backpedaled as Spruance did on the night of June 4, 1942. In his reflections on the battle, Nimitz reached the same conclusion and said, with no slur intended, "It was a great day for the Navy when Bill Halsey had to enter the hospital."[10] Yet, the flip side of that contrast also worked in America's favor during the early stages of the Philippine Campaign when Halsey's intuitive assessment of Japanese weakness led to an acceleration of the invasion timetable. Faced with the same evidence, Spruance may not have taken such a quantum leap.

In the two great sea battles of 1944, the contrast worked against the U.S. Navy, albeit without serious consequences. Spruance declined to close on a concentrated enemy fleet because he feared a decoy. Halsey pursued a decoy because it included the aircraft carriers that he regarded as the top prize of naval warfare. But the actions of each commander were rational within the context of their respective missions. Spruance's conduct at the Battle of the Philippine Sea was judged timid by carrier officers who conveniently ignored the fact that he was not functioning as a carrier commander but rather as a mission commander whose strategic objective was the seizure of the Mariana Islands. At Leyte Gulf, Halsey was operating under orders that made the destruction of the enemy fleet his main priority and gave him the latitude to leave the beachhead if such an opportunity presented itself. Although Halsey's method of carrying out those orders is open to criticism, his judgment was essentially sound.

An affirmation of these divergent command decisions might seem contradictory because in each case, the task of protecting the landing beaches would have fallen to Oldendorf's old battleships. How can Halsey be exonerated from charges of negligence at Leyte for trusting in the same ships that Spruance was justified in doubting at Saipan? The answer lies in the mundane details of each situation. In the Marianas, the composition of Japan's phantom menace was unknown and might have included carriers whose planes could have made mincemeat of Oldendorf's dreadnoughts. Conversely, Kurita's force, while stronger than Halsey concluded, had been bloodied in the Sibuyan Sea and was known to include no carriers in its order of battle. Furthermore, the bombardment group's supporting cruisers and destroyers were far more numerous in the Philippines than at Saipan. Finally, and most decisively, the seven jeep carriers in the Marianas carried about 170 planes, while the three escort carrier groups at Leyte Gulf operated more than 500 aircraft. U.S. resources in the Philippines were more than sufficient to pursue dual objectives simultaneously. The Leyte beachhead was placed in jeopardy because a flawed command arrangement allowed both Halsey and Kinkaid to proceed on their own assumptions of each other's intentions rather than coordinate their actions under one higher authority.

A favorite "what-if" scenario for armchair admirals has Spruance and Halsey switch places for their two battles. If each stays true to form, the results are not difficult to visualize. Halsey goes straight for the Japanese Fleet in the Philippine Sea and massacres its carriers with no adverse consequences to a beachhead that was never threatened. Spruance covers San Bernardino Strait and not only protects an endangered beachhead but also gets to witness his cherished *Iowa* class battleships square off against the *Yamato*. Of course, this flight of theoretical fancy is doubly speculative because Nimitz could not base his command arrangements on battles that had not yet occurred and the projected change in the results of the first encounter would obviously force Japan to alter its plans for the second.

In any case, the variant character traits of the duo were clearly determining factors in the missions assigned each man once the rotating command system was put into place. It was no coincidence that the Fifth Fleet mounted the vast majority of amphibious assaults in the Central Pacific. Both Nimitz and King considered Spruance's patience and balanced judgement to be ideal for combined arms operations while they viewed Halsey's audacity and impetuousness better suited for pure carrier warfare.[11] Additionally, Admiral Spruance's command techniques were more appropriate for the intricacies of modern amphibious warfare than those employed by his cohort. Each man delegated extensively, but although Spruance maintained a tight administration over what he delegated, Halsey's management discipline was indifferent at best. Furthermore, his fierce personal loyalty could blind Halsey to the deficiencies of his staff. Spruance was appalled at the sloppy message files and general administrative chaos he found on the *Enterprise* prior to Midway. The fault lay with Miles Browning, who was anything but the ideal chief of staff. Yet, Halsey never took steps to rectify the situation and staunchly championed Browning's career both before and after the battle. Indeed, Browning may not have had a career without Halsey's patronage because the irascible officer alienated just about everyone else he ever came in contact with.

A crucial difference in the methods of the two men was summed up by Admiral Arthur Radford, who led carrier task groups under each of them. "When Admiral Spruance was in command, you knew precisely what he was going to do." The orders were written clearly and delivered promptly, and except for tactical changes, they stood as written. "But when Admiral Halsey was in command, you never knew what he was going to do." Every night the changes would come. And often, the changes were so complicated, and referred to so many different messages that the staffs of the task groups spent hours puzzling over the message board, hoping they know at the end what Halsey intended to do and what action they were supposed to take.[12] Clearly, the immense size of the U.S. Fleet and the growing complexity of its mission demanded Spruance's orderly and systematic approach to command rather than Halsey's "seat of the pants" style of leadership.

However, Halsey did totally eclipse Spruance in one aspect of modern warfare: public relations. This is not meant in the derogatory sense that implies style over substance. Halsey had plenty of substance, but he was also good copy for the audience provided by a democracy that had been infused with New Deal egalitarianism. His blunt style of expression and unassuming manner satisfied the public's need for a hero in which they could see a bit of themselves. A classic example of Halsey's impact on national morale came after he made an off-handed statement that he intended to ride Emperor Hirohito's white horse once Japan had been defeated. His headquarters soon became swamped by a deluge of equestrian paraphernalia from individuals and groups back in the states.[13] Conversely, Spruance shunned publicity, treated war correspondents with disdain, and issued battle orders that were less than stirring. His "exhortation" prior to Midway was, "The successful conclusion of the operation now commencing will be of great value to our country."[14] That kind of style, plus an outwardly dour personality, doomed Spruance to labor in virtual anonymity. He remains one of the least known high-ranking U.S. commanders of World War II.

Although some controversy lingers over their decisions in the fleet battles of 1944, the most salient point remains that Raymond Spruance and

William Halsey shared the operational command of the most remarkable naval achievement in history. Their individual contributions to that achievement abound in irony. Spruance, the battleship specialist, perfected amphibious warfare and won both the largest and most decisive carrier battles of all time. Halsey, carrier pioneer and sea dog, did his best work in the South Pacific with his headquarters on shore while relying primarily on land-based air power. Each man also made his own unique personal contribution to the legacy of his service. Halsey, the "sailor's admiral," was drawn directly from the navy's heroic past and epitomized its fighting spirit. Spruance, the "admiral's admiral," pointed to the future by providing the role model of consummate professionalism that the navy would need in an age of increasing technical and geo-political complexity. Taken together, their best traits would form an unbeatable combination in any age.

No major fleet battle has been fought on the world's oceans since Leyte Gulf. The U.S. Navy, which sailed home from the surrender ceremony in Tokyo Bay, soon adapted to its new role as a strategic deterrent and buttress for world stability. It gave a stellar performance in both roles throughout the century's third and longest period of conflict, the Cold War. During the latest round of the struggle between freedom and totalitarianism, the navy of the Soviet Union passed that of the United States in number of ships, but only the most blindly optimistic Russian would have contended that his service was superior. The prevailing U.S. attitude is well illustrated by a story that made the rounds concerning a "confrontation" between destroyers in the Mediterranean. When the Soviet blinked the greeting, "How does it feel to belong to the world's second largest navy?", the American instantaneously answered, "How does it feel to belong to the world's second best?"

The meltdown of the Soviet Union virtually guarantees that the United States will carry its naval predominance well into the new century. It is even conceivable that Americans can match the reign held by the English in the years between Trafalgar and Jutland. But there are no final words in history and complacency will always be the most fatal nemesis of success. The heirs of Spruance and Halsey should remember the parting words of Togo, lest they suffer the fate of Jellicoe.

Notes

CHAPTER 1

1. James Henderson, *The Frigates* (New York: Dodd, Mead and Co., 1971), p. 5.

2. Geoffrey Bennett, *Nelson the Commander* (New York: Charles Scribner's Sons, 1972), p. 78.

3. Ibid., pp. 130, 269–270 and G. J. Marcus, *The Age of Nelson* (New York: Viking Press, 1971), pp. 137, 286.

4. Marcus, *Age of Nelson*, p. 21.

5. Ibid., p. 229.

6. David Howarth, *Trafalgar: The Nelson Touch* (New York: Atheneum, 1969), p. 150.

7. Bennett, *Nelson the Commander*, p. 89.

8. Ibid., p. 104.

9. Ibid., pp. 260–261.

10. E.H.H. Archibald, *The Wooden Fighting Ship in the Royal Navy* (London: Blanford Press, 1968), pp. 75, 155.

11. Peter Padfield, *The Battleship Era* (New York: David McKay Co., 1972), pp. 23–24.

12. Ibid., pp. 44–46.

13. Ibid., p. 57.

CHAPTER 2

1. Armin Rappaport, *Sources in American Diplomacy* (New York: The Macmillan Co., 1966), pp. 75–76.

2. Chitoshi Yanaga, *Japan Since Perry* (New York: McGraw-Hill, 1949), pp. 243–247.

3. Rappaport, *Sources in American Diplomacy*, pp. 139–142.

4. Yanaga, *Japan Since Perry*, pp. 302–303.

5. Noel F. Busch, *The Emperor's Sword* (New York: Funk and Wagnalls, 1969), p. 25.

6. Ibid., and Georges Blond, *Admiral Togo* (New York: The Macmillan Co., 1960), p. 23.

7. Denis Warner and Peggy Warner, *The Tide at Sunrise* (New York: Charterhouse, 1974), p. 43.

8. Blond, *Admiral Togo*, p. 24.

9. Ibid., p. 75.

10. Busch, *Emperor's Sword*, p. 45.

11. Ibid., p. 50–51 and Blond, *Admiral Togo*, pp. 105–106.

12. Blond, *Admiral Togo*, p. 155.

13. Donald W. Mitchell, *A History of Russian and Soviet Sea Power* (New York: The Macmillan Co., 1974), pp. 206–209, and The Military Correspondent of the Times, *The War in the Far East* (New York: E. P. Dutton and Co., 1905), p. 17.

14. Ibid.

15. Blond, *Admiral Togo*, p. 153 and Mitchell, *Russian Sea Power*, p. 225.

16. Blond, *Admiral Togo*, p. 152.

17. Warner and Warner, *Tide at Sunrise*, pp. 10, 164–165.

18. Peter Padfield, *The Battleship Era* (New York: David McKay Co., 1972), pp. 8, 106, 136.

19. Warner and Warner, *Tide at Sunrise*, pp. 19–20.

20. Arthur J. Marder, *From the Dreadnought to Scapa Flow: Vol. I, The Road to War* (London: Oxford University Press, 1961), p. 329.

21. Warner and Warner, *Tide at Sunrise*, p. 202.

22. Ibid., p. 224.

23. Mitchell, *Russian Sea Power*, p. 225 and E. B. Potter, ed., *Sea Power: A Naval History* (Englewood Cliffs, NJ: Prentice-Hall, 1960), p. 355.

24. Warner and Warner, *Tide at Sunrise*, p. 325.

25. Mitchell, *Russian Sea Power*, pp. 225–227 and Padfield, *Battleship Era*, p. 169.

26. Mitchell, *Russian Sea Power*, pp. 207–209, 225.

27. Warner and Warner, *Tide at Sunrise*, p. 235.

28. Ibid., p. 330.

29. Ibid., pp. 332–333 and Potter, *Sea Power*, p. 356.

30. Richard Hough, *The Fleet That Had to Die* (New York: Viking Press, 1958), p. 20.

31. Ibid., pp. 22–23, Busch, *Emperor's Sword*, pp. 83–84 and Mitchell, *Russian Sea Power*, pp. 251–252.

32. Busch, *Emperor's Sword*, pp. 83–84, Hough, *Fleet That Had to Die*, p. 21 and Padfield, *Battleship Era*, p. 172.

33. Blond, *Admiral Togo*, p. 214.

34. Mitchell, *Russian Sea Power*, pp. 250–252.

35. Ibid., pp. 252, 256, Blond, *Admiral Togo*, p. 213 and Padfield, *Battleship Era*, p. 175, 181.

36. Busch, *Emperor's Sword*, p. 134.

37. Blond, *Admiral Togo*, p. 220.

38. Busch, *Emperor's Sword*, p. 146.

39. Hough, *Fleet That Had to Die*, p. 166.

40. Busch, *Emperor's Sword*, pp. 148–149.

41. Warner and Warner, *Tide at Sunrise*, p. 506.

42. Busch, *Emperor's Sword*, p. 154.

43. Warner and Warner, *Tide at Sunrise*, p. 496.

44. Busch, *Emperor's Sword*, p. 156.

45. Mitchell, *Russian Sea Power*, p. 262.

46. Ibid., p. 263.

47. Busch, *Emperor's Sword*, pp. 185–186.

48. Ibid., p. 186.

49. Hough, *Fleet That Had to Die*, p. 203.

50. Mitchell, *Russian Sea Power*, p. 265, Busch, *Emperor's Sword*, pp. 195–196, 203.

51. Eugene P. Trani, *The Treaty of Portsmouth* (Lexington, KY: University of Kentucky Press, 1969), pp. 162–166.

52. Blond, *Admiral Togo*, p. 243 and Busch, *Emperor's Sword*, p. 212.

CHAPTER 3

1. Paul M. Kennedy, *The Rise and Fall of British Naval Mastery* (London: Penguin Books Ltd., 1976), pp. 189–190.

2. Robert K. Massie, *Dreadnought* (New York: Random House, 1991), pp. 134–135.

3. Ibid.

4. Ibid., p. 172.

5. Ibid., p. 181.

6. Arthur J. Marder, *From the Dreadnought to Scapa Flow, Vol. I: The Road to War* (London: Oxford University Press, 1961), pp. 34–35.

7. Richard Hough, *Dreadnought: A History of the Modern Battleship* (New York: The Macmillan Co., 1964), p. 7.

8. Ibid., pp. 15–16.

9. Andrew Gordon, *The Rules of the Game* (Annapolis, MD: Naval Institute Press, 1996), p. 347.

10. Ibid.

11. Massie, *Dreadnought*, p. 461.

12. A. Temple Patterson, *Jellicoe* (New York: St. Martin's Press, 1969), p. 58.

13. Ibid., p. 17.

14. Gordon, *Rules of the Game*, p. 247.

15. Ibid., p. 274.

16. Ibid., p. 273.

17. Ibid., p. 281.

18. Patterson, *Jellicoe*, p. 28.

19. Ibid., p. 29.

20. Ibid., pp. 32–33.

21. Goeffrey Bennett, *Nelson the Commander* (New York: Charles Scribner's Sons, 1972), p. 295.

22. Patterson, *Jellicoe*, p. 46.

23. Kennedy, *British Naval Mastery*, p. 200.

24. Marder, *Dreadnought to Scapa Flow, Vol. I*, pp. 334–335.

25. Ibid., p. 439–442, Patterson, *Jellicoe*, pp. 255–256 and Admiral Sir John Jellicoe, *The Grand Fleet, 1914–1916* (New York: George H. Doran Co., 1919), pp. 7–8.

26. Jellicoe, *Grand Fleet*, p. 13.

27. Ibid. pp. 49–51 and Patterson, *Jellicoe*, pp. 66–67.

28. Geoffrey Bennett, *Naval Battles of the First World War* (New York: Charles Scribner's Sons, 1968), p. 142.

29. Jellicoe, *Grand Fleet*, p. 100.

30. Arthur J. Marder, *From the Dreadnought to Scapa Flow, Vol. II: The War Years to the Eve of Jutland* (London: Oxford University Press, 1965), p. 43.

31. Patterson, *Jellicoe*, pp. 70–71.

32. Bennett, *Naval Battles*, p. 153.

33. Marder, *Dreadnought to Scapa Flow, Vol. II*, p. 156 and Patterson, *Jellicoe*, p. 255.

34. John Costello and Terry Hughes, *Jutland 1916* (New York: Holt, Rinehart and Winston, 1976), p. 92.

35. Patterson, *Jellicoe*, p. 16.

36. Marder, *Dreadnought to Scapa Flow, Vol. II*, p. 420.

37. Costello and Hughes, *Jutland*, p. 93.

38. Marder, *Dreadnought to Scapa Flow, Vol II*, p. 420.

39. Patterson, *Jellicoe*, pp. 100–101.

40. Marder, *Dreadnought to Scapa Flow, Vol II*, pp. 423–424.

41. Bennett, *Naval Battles*, pp. 220–222 and Holloway H. Frost, *The Battle of Jutland* (Annapolis, MD: Naval Institute Press, 1936), pp. 536–538.

42. Bennett, *Naval Battles*, pp. 214–219 and Frost, *Battle of Jutland*, pp. 533–536.

43. Frost, *Battle of Jutland*, pp. 539–540.

44. Gordon, *Rules of the Game*, p. 8.

45. Marder, *Dreadnought to Scapa Flow, Vol. II*, p. 438.

46. Bennett, *Naval Battles*, p. 177 and Frost, *Battle of Jutland*, p. 539–540.

47. Bennett, *Naval Battles*, pp. 177, 214–222.

48. Frost, *Battle of Jutland*, p. 204.

49. Arthur J. Marder, *From the Dreadnought to Scapa Flow, Vol. III: Jutland and After* (London: Oxford University Press, 1966), p. 60.

50. Gordon, *Rules of the Game*, p. 120.

51. Marder, *Dreadnought to Scapa Flow, Vol. III*, p. 62.

52. Jellicoe, *Grand Fleet*, p. 342.

53. Bennett, *Naval Battles*, p. 204.

54. Marder, *Dreadnought to Scapa Flow, Vol. III*, p. 100.

55. Ibid., p. 112 and Gordon, *Rules of the Game*, p. 459.

56. Patterson, *Jellicoe*, p. 125.

57. Gordon, *Rules of the Game*, p. 471.

58. Costello and Hughes, *Jutland*, p. 204.

59. Ibid., p. 224 and Patterson, *Jellicoe*, p. 132.

60. Bennett, *Naval Battles*, p. 243.

61. Marder, *Dreadnought to Scapa Flow, Vol. III*, p. 188.

62. Winston Spencer Churchill, *The World Crisis, Vol. III* (New York: Charles Scribner's Sons, 1927), pp. 145-146.

63. Marder, *Dreadnought to Scapa Flow, Vol. III*, pp. 118–119.

64. Ibid., p. 125.

65. Ibid., p. 21.

66. Jellicoe, *Grand Fleet*, pp. 397–398.

67. Vice-Admiral Sir Peter Gretton, *Winston Churchill and the Royal Navy* (New York: Coward McCann, Inc., 1968), p. 228.

68. Churchill, *World Crisis, Vol. III*, p. 106.

69. Jellicoe, *Grand Fleet*, p. 70.

70. Patterson, *Jellicoe*, p. 148.

71. Ibid., p. 206.

72. Ibid.

CHAPTER 4

1. E. B. Potter, *Bull Halsey* (Annapolis, MD: Naval Institute Press, 1985), p. 13.

2. Thomas B. Buell, *The Quiet Warrior* (Boston and Toronto: Little, Brown and Co., 1974), pp. 97–98.

3. Gordon W. Prange, *At Dawn We Slept* (New York: Viking Penguin, 1981), p. 11.

4. Gordon W. Prange, *Miracle at Midway* (New York: McGraw-Hill, 1982) p. 6.

5. Ibid., p. 7.

6. Admiral William F. Halsey and J. Bryan, III, *Admiral Halsey's Story* (New York: McGraw-Hill, 1947), p. 2.

7. Ibid., p. 13.

8. Potter, *Bull Halsey*, p. 108

9. Edwin P. Hoyt, *How They Won the War in the Pacific: Nimitz and His Admirals* (New York: Weybright and Talley, 1970), p. 165.

10. E. B. Potter, *Nimitz* (Annapolis, MD: Naval Institute Press, 1976), p. 83 and John Prados, *Combined Fleet Decoded* (New York: Random House, 1995), p. 320.

11. Buell, *Quiet Warrior*, p. 42.

12. Ibid., p. 48.

13. Mitsuo Fuchida and Masatake Okumiya, *Midway: The Battle That Doomed Japan* (Annapolis, MD: Naval Institute Press, 1955), pp. 251–256.

14. Prange, *Miracle at Midway*, pp. 434–435.

15. Ibid., pp. 99–100 and Potter, *Nimitz*, p. 87.

16. Buell, *Quiet Warrior*, pp. 121–124.

17. Norman Polmar, *Aircraft Carriers* (Garden City, NY: Doubleday and Co., 1969), pp. 218–219.

18. Prange, *Miracle at Midway*, p. 396.

19. Fuchida and Okumiya, *Midway*, p. 245–247.

20. Prados, *Combined Fleet Decoded*, p. 313.

21. Buell, *Quiet Warrior*, p. 158.

22. Potter, *Bull Halsey*, p. 160.

23. Halsey and Bryan, *Admiral Halsey's Story*, p. 116.

24. Potter, *Bull Halsey*, p. 169.

25. Eric Hammel, *Guadalcanal, Decision at Sea* (New York: Crown Publishers, Inc., 1988), p. 50.

26. Ibid., p. 454.

27. Ibid., p. 367–382.

28. Ibid., p. 455.

29. Samuel B. Griffith, *The Battle for Guadalcanal* (Philadelphia and New York: J. B. Lippincott Co., 1963), p. 205.

30. Halsey and Bryan, *Admiral Halsey's Story*, p. 128.

31. Ibid., p. 132 and Potter, *Bull Halsey*, p. 175.

32. Buell, *Quiet Warrior*, p. 165 and Potter, *Nimitz*, p. 239.

33. Buell, *Quiet Warrior*, p. 293.

34. Polmar, *Aircraft Carriers*, p. 733.

35. Clark G. Reynolds, *The Fast Carriers* (New York: McGraw-Hill, 1968), p. 56.

36. Ibid., p. 89, Buell *Quiet Warrior*, p. 184 and Hoyt, *Nimitz and His Admirals*, p. 290.

37. Richard Wheeler, *A Special Valor* (New York: Harper and Row, 1983), p. 206.

38. Paul S. Dull, *The Imperial Japanese Navy* (Annapolis, MD: Naval Institute Press, 1978), p. 313.

39. Reynolds, *Fast Carriers*, p. 101.

40. Polmar, *Aircraft Carriers*, p. 347.

41. Ibid., pp. 351–352.

42. Ibid., p. 350 and Reynolds, *Fast Carriers*, p. 173.

43. Polmar, *Aircraft Carriers*, p. 351.

44. Reynolds, *Fast Carriers*, pp. 186, 191.

45. Buell, *Quiet Warrior*, p. 164.

46. Reynolds, *Fast Carriers*, p. 182.

47. Edwin P. Hoyt, *To the Marianas* (NY: Van Nostrand Reinhold Co., 1980), p. 132 and Samuel Eliot Morison, *History of United States Naval Operations in World War II, Vol. VIII: New Guinea and the Marianas* (Boston: Little, Brown and Co., 1953), p. 244.

48. Reynolds, *Fast Carriers*, p. 185.

49. Ibid., pp. 188–189.

50. James H. Belote and William M. Belote, *Titans of the Seas* (New York: Harper and Row, 1975), p. 255 and Polmar, *Aircraft Carriers*, p. 349.

51. Polmar, *Aircraft Carriers*, p. 360.

52. Dull, *Imperial Japanese Navy*, p. 321.

53. Polmar, *Aircraft Carriers*, p. 359.

54. Ibid., p. 362 and Reynolds, *Fast Carriers*, p. 198.

55. Morison, *U.S. Naval Operations, Vol. VIII*, p. 299.

56. Ibid., p. 300 and Belote and Belote, *Titans of the Seas*, p. 203.

57. Harold L. Buell, *Dauntless Helldivers* (New York: Orion Books, 1991), pp. 258–259.

58. Polmar, *Aircraft Carriers*, p. 365 and Reynolds, p. 203.

59. Buell, *Quiet Warrior*, p. 280.

60. Reynolds, *Fast Carriers*, pp. 205–206.

61. Buell, *Quiet Warrior*, pp. 214–215.

62. Potter, *Bull Halsey*, p. 37.

63. Ibid., p. 279.

64. Hoyt, *Nimitz and His Admirals*, pp. 424–425.

65. Polmar, *Aircraft Carriers*, p. 381.

66. Samuel Eliot Morison, *History of United States Naval Operations in World War II, Vol. XII: Leyte* (Boston: Little, Brown and Co., 1958), p. 194.

67. Halsey and Bryan, *Admiral Halsey's Story*, pp. 207–208.

68. Potter, *Bull Halsey*, p. 288, Polmar, *Aircraft Carriers*, p. 377 and Reynolds, *Fast Carriers*, p. 259.

69. Polmar, *Aircraft Carriers*, p. 373.

70. Edwin P. Hoyt, *The Battle of Leyte Gulf* (New York: Weybright and Talley, 1972), p. 86.

71. Ibid., p. 85.

72. Ibid., p. 4.

73. Potter, *Bull Halsey*, p. 293.

74. Ibid., p. 296.

75. Ibid., p. 300.

76. Thomas J. Cutler, *The Battle of Leyte Gulf* (New York: HarperCollins, 1994), pp. 174–180.

77. Ibid., p. 216 and Reynolds, *Fast Carriers*, p. 272.

78. Hoyt, *Leyte Gulf*, p. 313.

79. Reynolds, *Fast Carriers*, p. 275.

80. Potter, *Bull Halsey*, p. 303.

81. Dull, *Imperial Japanese Navy*, p. 336.

82. Cutler, *Leyte Gulf*, p. 224.

83. Halsey and Bryan, *Admiral Halsey's Story*, p. 225.

84. Polmar, *Aircraft Carriers*, p. 403.

85. Reynolds, *Fast Carriers*, p. 281.

86. Hoyt, *Nimitz and His Admirals*, p. 451 and Potter, *Nimitz*, p. 342.

87. Morison, *U.S. Naval Operations, Vol. XII*, p. 194.

88. Ibid., p. 319.

89. Reynolds, *Fast Carriers*, p. 267.

90. Halsey and Bryan, *Admiral Halsey's Story*, p. 217.

91. Morison, *U.S. Naval Operations, Vol. XII*, p. 193.

92. Gerald E. Wheeler, *Kinkaid of the Seventh Fleet* (Washington, DC: Naval Historical Center, 1995), p. 405.

93. Dull, *Imperial Japanese Navy*, p. 349 and Polmar, *Aircraft Carriers*, pp. 383–384.

94. Hans Christian Adamson and George Francis Kosco, *Halsey's Typhoons* (New York: Crown Publishers, 1967), pp. 144–150.

95. Ibid., pp. 190–193.

96. John Costello, *The Pacific War* (New York: Rawson, Wade Publishers, Inc., 1981), p. 627 and Polmar, *Aircraft Carriers*, pp. 445–446.

97. Wheeler, *Special Valor*, pp. 405, 441.

CHAPTER 5

1. Admiral William F. Halsey and J. Bryan, *Admiral Halsey's Story* (New York: McGraw-Hill, 1947), p. 12.

2. Richard Hough, *Dreadnought: A History of the Modern Battleship* (New York: The Macmillan Co., 1964), p. 47 and Robert K. Massie, *Dreadnought* (New York: Random House, 1991), p. 406.

3. Arthur J. Marder, *From the Dreadnought to Scapa Flow, Vol. III: Jutland and After* (London: Oxford University Press, 1966), p. 189.

4. Holloway H. Frost, *The Battle of Jutland* (Annapolis, MD: Naval Institute Press, 1936), p. 514.

5. Geoffrey Bennett, *Naval Battles of the First World War* (New York: Charles Scribner's Sons, 1968), p. 253.

6. Andrew Gordon, *The Rules of the Game* (Annapolis, MD: Naval Institute Press, 1996), p. 89.

7. Ibid., pp. 55–56.

8. Paul S. Dull, *The Imperial Japanese Navy* (Annapolis, MD: Naval Institute Press, 1978), pp. 357–367.

9. Halsey and Bryan, *Admiral Halsey's Story*, pp. 218–226.

10. Gordon W. Prange, *Miracle at Midway* (New York: McGraw-Hill, 1982), p. 81.

11. Edwin P. Hoyt, *How They Won the War in the Pacific: Nimitz and His Admirals* (New York: Weybright and Talley, 1970), p. 429.

12. Ibid., p. 489.

13. E. B. Potter, *Bull Halsey* (Annapolis, MD: Naval Institute Press, 1985), pp. 329–330.

14. Samuel Eliot Morison, *History of United States Naval Operations in World War II, Vol. IV: Coral Sea, Midway and Submarine Actions* (Boston: Little, Brown and Co., 1949), p. 98.

Bibliography

Adamson, Hans Christian; and Kosco, George Francis. *Halsey's Typhoons*. New York: Crown Publishers, 1967.

Archibald, E.H.H. *The Wooden Fighting Ship in the Royal Navy*. London: Blandford Press, 1968.

Belote, James H.; and Belote, William M. *Titans of the Seas*. New York: Harper and Row, 1975.

Bennett, Geoffrey. *Naval Battles of the First World War*. New York: Charles Scribner's Sons, 1968.

————. *Nelson the Commander*. New York: Charles Scribner's Sons, 1972.

Blond, Georges. *Admiral Togo*. New York: The Macmillan Co., 1960.

Buell, Harold L. *Dauntless Helldivers*. New York: Orion Books, 1991.

Buell, Thomas B. *The Quiet Warrior*. Boston and Toronto: Little, Brown and Co., 1974.

Busch, Noel F. *The Emperor's Sword*. New York: Funk and Wagnalls, 1969.

Churchill, Winston Spencer. *The World Crisis, Vol. III*. New York: Charles Scribner's Sons, 1927.

Costello, John. *The Pacific War*. New York: Rawson, Wade Publishers, Inc., 1981.

————; and Hughes, Terry. *Jutland 1916*. New York: Holt, Rinehart and Winston, 1976.

Cutler, Thomas J. *The Battle of Leyte Gulf*. New York: HarperCollins, 1994.

Dull, Paul S. *The Imperial Japanese Navy*. Annapolis, MD: Naval Institute Press, 1978.

Frost, Holloway H. *The Battle of Jutland*. Annapolis, MD: Naval Institute Press, 1936.

Fuchida, Mitsuo; and Okumiya, Masatake. *Midway: The Battle That Doomed Japan*. Annapolis, MD: Naval Institute Press, 1955.

Gordon, Andrew. *The Rules of the Game*. Annapolis, MD: Naval Institute Press, 1996.

Gretton, Vice-Admiral Sir Peter. *Winston Churchill and the Royal Navy*. New York: Coward McCann, Inc., 1968.

Griffith, Samuel B. *The Battle for Guadalcanal*. Philadelphia and New York: J. B. Lippincott Co., 1963.

Halsey, Admiral William F.; and Bryan, J. III. *Admiral Halsey's Story*. New York: McGraw-Hill, 1947.

Hammel, Eric. *Guadalcanal, Decision at Sea*. New York: Crown Publishers, Inc., 1988.

Hart, B. H. Liddell. *History of the Second World War*. New York: G. P. Putnam's Sons, 1970.

Henderson, James. *The Frigates*. New York: Dodd, Mead and Co., 1971.

Hough, Richard. *Dreadnought: A History of the Modern Battleship*. New York: The Macmillan Co., 1964.

———. *The Fleet That Had to Die*. New York: Viking Press, 1958.

Howarth, David. *Famous Sea Battles*. Boston and Toronto: Little, Brown and Co., 1981.

———. *Trafalgar: The Nelson Touch*. New York: Atheneum, 1969.

Hoyt, Edwin P. *How They Won the War in the Pacific: Nimitz and His Admirals*. New York: Weybright and Talley, 1970.

———. *The Battle of Leyte Gulf*. New York: Weybright and Talley, 1972.

———. *To the Marianas*. New York: Van Nostrand Reinhold Co., 1980.

Jellicoe, Admiral Sir John. *The Grand Fleet, 1914–1916*. New York: George H. Doran Co., 1919.

Kennedy, Paul M. *The Rise and Fall of British Naval Mastery*. London: Penguin Books Ltd., 1976.

Marcus, G. J. *The Age of Nelson*. New York: Viking Press, 1971.

Marder, Arthur J. *From the Dreadnought to Scapa Flow, Vol. I: The Road to War*. London: Oxford University Press, 1961.

———. *From the Dreadnought to Scapa Flow, Vol. II: The War Years to the Eve of Jutland*. London: Oxford University Press, 1965.

———. *From the Dreadnought to Scapa Flow, Vol. III: Justland and After*. London: Oxford University Press, 1966.

Massie, Robert K. *Dreadnought*. New York: Random House, 1991.

The Military Correspondent of the Times. *The War in the Far East*. New York: E. P. Dutton and Co., 1905.

Mitchell, Donald W. *A History of Russian and Soviet Sea Power*. New York: The Macmillan Co., 1974.

Morison, Samuel Eliot. *History of United States Naval Operations in World War II, Vol. IV: Coral Sea, Midway and Submarine Actions*. Boston: Little, Brown and Co., 1949.

———. *History of United States Naval Operations in World War II, Vol. VIII: New Guinea and the Marianas*. Boston: Little, Brown and Co., 1953.

————. *History of United States Naval Operations in World War II, Vol. XII: Leyte*. Boston: Little, Brown and Co., 1958.

Padfield, Peter. *The Battleship Era*. New York: David McKay Co., 1972.

Patterson, A. Temple. *Jellicoe*. New York: St. Martin's Press, 1969.

Polmar, Norman. *Aircraft Carriers*. Garden City, New York: Doubleday and Co., 1969.

Potter, E. B. *Bull Halsey*. Annapolis, MD: Naval Institute Press, 1985.

————. *Nimitz*. Annapolis, MD: Naval Institute Press, 1976.

————, ed. *Sea Power: A Naval History*. Englewood Cliffs, NJ: Prentice-Hall, 1960.

Potter, John Deane. *Yamamoto*. New York: Viking Press, 1965.

Prados, John. *Combined Fleet Decoded*. New York: Random House, 1995.

Prange, Gordon W. *At Dawn We Slept*. New York: Viking Penguin, 1981.

————. *Miracle at Midway*. New York: McGraw-Hill, 1982.

Rappaport, Armin. *Sources in American Diplomacy*. New York: The Macmillan Co., 1966.

Reynolds, Clark G. *The Fast Carriers*. New York: McGraw-Hill, 1968.

Scheer, Admiral Reinhard. *Germany's High Seas Fleet in the World War*. London: Cassell and Co., 1920.

Trani, Eugene P. *The Treaty of Portsmouth*. Lexington, KY: University of Kentucky Press, 1969.

Tuchman, Barbara W. *The Guns of August*. New York: The Macmillan Co., 1962.

Warner, Denis; and Warner, Peggy. *The Tide at Sunrise*. New York: Charterhouse, 1974.

Wheeler, Gerald E. *Kinkaid of the Seventh Fleet*. Washington, DC: Naval Historical Center, 1995.

Wheeler, Richard. *A Special Valor*. New York: Harper and Row, 1983.

Yanaga, Chitoshi. *Japan Since Perry*. New York: McGraw-Hill, 1949.

Index

Individual ships are listed by country under "Ships." Events within battles are listed in chronological order in each specific battle entry.

About the Author

RONALD ANDIDORA is an independent researcher whose publishing history includes articles for *Military History Magazine*, *World War II Magazine*, *Parameters*, and the *Naval War College Review*. He worked for more than 20 years in the Pennsylvania Senate.

ISBN 0-313-31266-4

90000>

EAN

9 780313 312663

HARDCOVER BAR CODE